Journey through Womanhood

D1602733

Journey through Womanhood

Meditations from Our Collective Soul

Tian Dayton, Ph.D.

HAZELDEN®

Hazelden
Center City, Minnesota 55012-0176

1-800-328-0094
1-651-213-4590 (Fax)
www.hazelden.org

Library of Congress Cataloging-in-Publication Data

Dayton, Tian
   Journey through womanhood : meditations from our
collective soul / Tian Dayton.
     p. cm.
   Includes bibliographical references and index.
   ISBN 1-56838-882-9 softcover
   1. Women—Conduct of life. 2. Meditations. I. Title.

  BJ1610 .D39 2002
  155.3'33—dc21

                           2002068644

Editor's note
The following pages contain material that has been reprinted with permission: pages 1–2: © 1971 Veronica A. Shoffstall; page 251: © Dorothy Law Nolte, from the book *Children Learn What They Live: Parenting to Inspire Values,* Workman Publishing Company; pages 351–52: Copyright © 1993 Portia Nelson, from the book *There's a Hole in My Sidewalk,* Beyond Words Publishing, Inc., Hillsboro, Oregon, U.S.A.

06 05 04 03 02   6 5 4 3 2 1

Cover design by David Spohn
Interior design by Rachel Holscher
Typesetting by Stanton Publication Services, Inc.

To my sisters
Kutzi, Eve, Lucy, Annie, and Lynne
with love

Contents

Acknowledgments

FIRST AND FOREMOST, I would like to acknowledge you, the reader. I think being a woman is one of the most demanding and challenging roles we can play in today's world. So many experiences fall within the parameters of womanhood. Today, we're able to experience more variety, more than at any other time in history. We're cocreating our roles together and defining as we go.

Next, I want to acknowledge the women in my life. My daughter, Marina; my mother, Elaine Walker, and grandmothers, Anna Legeros and Marina Barbatsis; my mothers-in-law, Gwen MacPhail and Ruth Stricker Dayton; my stepmother, Alice; my sisters, Kutzi and Eve; my sisters-in-law, Lucy, Anne, and Lynne, and my ex-sisters-in-law, Alida and Gretchen; my aunts, Connie, Dorla, Patty, Mary Lee, Judy, Lucy, Mary, and Wendy; and all of my wonderful nieces and cousins. Family is important to me, and I have been blessed by coming from one wonderful family and marrying into another.

Next, I would like to acknowledge my women friends who also feel like extended family to me and with whom I have shaped who I am today. You know who you are. I would like to express my gratitude to my female mentors, Beatrice, Sharon, and Zerka, for lighting a path personally and professionally. Lastly, in this intimate category, I want to acknowledge my students, trainees, and clients; being a part of your journeys is a very important part of mine. We are all woven into the fabric of each other's lives, and I am grateful.

I have also been lucky to work with a wonderful staff at Hazelden. Karen Chernyaev has been a kind, ever-intelligent, and supportive editor to work with; Connie Carlson is enthusiastic and genuine in bringing this book to the marketplace; Judy Peacock, whose copyediting was just right and perfectly orchestrated; and Peter Bell who heads up the publishing division at Hazelden and forwards its mission to help people in meaningful ways and to help fight the disease of addiction through conscientious and careful action. I want to thank you all. You have made working on this book a complete pleasure.

I also want to thank Trish Roccuzzo who prepared this manuscript with her usual competence and creativity, which was no easy task.

To the best of my knowledge, all of the quotes in this book are from women (even the ones under men's pennames). I ask the reader's indulgence only occasionally when quoting a man's research was too irresistible to leave out. Other than those few exceptions, this book represents a symphony of feminine voices. Many beautiful quotes are from the incredible collections of Rosalie Maggiot who has done a masterful job on her collections of the wise words of women.

Thank you to each and every one of you. You are all a very important part of these pages. It's great to be alive with all of you.

Introduction

WOMEN ARE MANY THINGS to many people. The roles we play are of such fundamental importance that we, as a whole, can make or break society by how we play them. Women are relational beings, wired by evolution and destiny to nurture and sustain life. We carry those we love around in our lockets and in our hearts. So, when asked how we are, if we include in our answer a report on the state of our primary relationships and what those we're connected to are up to, it doesn't necessarily mean we're nuts, pathological, or in need of treatment. We most likely are just being women operating how we operate.

Women are the keepers of a constant flame, keepers of the hearth; and if that flame blows out, society blows out. This is the secret that none of us are saying, the truth well-hidden right under our noses, where no one would think to look.

The real challenge for women is to maintain a sense of self while in connection with others. How do we do this?

In the 1950s we thought we had to give up a self in order to have others in our lives. In the 1960s and 1970s we thought we had to give up others to have a self. In the 1980s we thought we needed the trappings first—cars, houses, careers—and somehow a self would emerge. In the 1990s some of us began to realize that having it all isn't necessarily having it all. . . .

Who are we, now that more doors are open to us? If we add

new roles, does it have to mean we forsake others? Do we have to become like men to succeed in a man's world, or do we just stretch our hearts, hands, and days to include more? If we increase our life spans by thirty or so years due to advanced technology, can we now afford the luxury of having it all—as long as we don' t have to have it all in the same decade?

Research over the past three decades, spearheaded by the Stone Center of Boston, has revealed that women develop and self-define not according to the John-Wayne-lone-star model of tough autonomy, but in a relational, connected way. We women have our own special way of operating, our unique take on the world, our own *modus operandi*. We value relationships highly, not necessarily at the expense of self but in recognition that sustaining and nurturing relationships become part of our inner and outer lives.

When asked the question, How are you? our mothers may well have answered by telling how everyone close to them was BUT themselves. Today, we'll tell you about those close to us AND ourselves. This is a subtle but huge movement. We have shifted from living on the periphery toward living at the center of our own lives. Periphery living doesn't work. We envy those closer to the center. We develop resentments.

As women we have our own kind of strength. We draw wisdom from day-to-day experiences of the most ordinary kind. Our sense of place, meaning, and the worth of life is found not only from within but also in a context, tied to our biological role of holding and nurturing. Nature has charged us with a most awesome responsibility. If we stop drawing identity, wisdom, and a sense of purpose through being profoundly connected to self and others, we're in trouble and so is our world.

With a predicted average of three extra decades added to our life span in the past century, we can work, wife, mother, grandmother, mentor, and still have time to spare. We can do what we're so brilliant at: multitasking. We can adjust and be ingenious, flexible, and creative in our approach to living multiple roles.

In writing this book, I did a lot of reflecting on my own journey. Raised in the 1950s to the dream of wifehood and motherhood (a virgin if ever there were one), I suddenly found myself in the throes of the feminine revolution during the 1960s, a decade of new cultural markers. For the first time, we saw women out of the home and men in it (sometimes), women marching toward the workplace, bra-burning as a symbol of release from bonding, and women dressing for success in the workplace.

As women, we were redefining ourselves and challenging the roles we had played for centuries. The threat of pregnancy was removed by birth control and along with it the horror of being "knocked up" and left pregnant and alone. The workplace was no longer only a province of men. We could dream of being self-sustaining and having meaningful professions.

Then I found out that taking care of small children gives new meaning to the word *work*. Nothing could be harder. Or better. Or more rewarding, taxing, unnerving, and glorious. Then the real meaning of wifehood began to reveal itself, carving out an intimacy that is alive and terrifyingly close, creating with my husband a third entity called a relationship and sharing responsibilities for everything from a toothbrush to a life. And the need for a continued life passion became evident, sustaining a work that actualized my own talents, needs, and dreams and that allowed me to declare my space in the world and make a meaningful contribution to society.

So much role definition and redefinition stretches across these powerful decades, with such mythical meaning and importance, that women's roles can really only be captured by archetypes. And the archetypes form complicated, interwoven patterns. The Virgin has to become the Huntress and go after her life in the world. The Warrior is also the Mother who fights for her right to care for her children in a society that grossly undervalues the critical importance of motherhood.

We are the Huntress as we seed our children a bit at a time into society at large, the Martyr when we sacrifice our needs for theirs, and the Wise Woman in the way that we live our lives, raise our children, conduct our marriages, and shape our careers. The archetypes emerge in other ways too. As physician and author Christiane Northrup suggests, these qualities of womanhood are "stamped into our biology." Many women who may never have children still mother in their workplaces, families, and communities every day, or, like Hestia, the goddess of wifehood, they faithfully keep the community hearth. The goddesses are, as Jean Shinoda Bolen, M.D., says, in every woman.

Some roles wax or wane over time, some overlap, some co-exist nicely while others conflict. Some lie dormant, others become dominant, but each stage has its own developmental task. The Virgin's task is to develop a sense of selfhood so that the Huntress, in touch with her gifts, strengths, and weaknesses can find her feet in the world, her life's passion, and her own ground. The Warrior summons the strength and courage to meet the challenges and fight the battles that are a part of any woman's life. She confronts her own dark side and gains power and wisdom from self-mastery. The Lover exposes her heart, her need for partnership, and calls out to the infinite to provide her with her soul mate. The Wife tends the hearth, creates a home, builds a safe and secure nest as an anchor and respite in this changing world. The Mother brings forth life, nourishing each little one in her charge until that little person can become self-sufficient and stand on her own two feet. Then the Martyr releases this life into the world and returns to her empty nest to shed her tears and to find new ways to fill her soul.

Here is where the Wise Woman must take over because the tasks at this age are spiritual ones. She must find a deeper source of meaning by going within and by transcending the temporal life that surrounds her. "I have a body, but I am not only that body; I have a mind, but I am not only that mind. I am something infinite and beyond. I will shed the body one day, for it is only a container. I am not the bulb but the light that shines through it, and that light will never go out because it is spiritual in nature, as I am."

The Wise Woman's task is to dis-identify with the body and to identify with the deeper aspects of life. To find and create positive meaning and to pass that on to the generations that she will leave behind. To mentor, love, and teach by example. To reassure. According to Christiane Northrup, M.D., our brains and bodies are being rewired at this stage of life to encourage self-reflection and spiritual growth. The hormones that once wired us for nuturing and connection are rewiring us for attaining wisdom (see p. 354 in "Wise Woman"). Hormones that fostered caretaking behaviors are shifting or being rerouted to parts of the brain associated with resolving early painful memories and unfinished business while at the same time stimulating the pituitary gland, the "God spot" of the brain, the seat of wisdom, or the "third eye" as it is sometimes called. This means that a task at this age seems to be to resolve our pasts and become more spiritual.

Each well-completed stage becomes the roundation for all that follow. The stages intersect and interweave. They are ever present.

Ancient Greek women were very limited in the society in which they lived. They could not vote, own property, or engage in business in most places. One of their few rights was to freely worship the goddesses. This was the arena in which they could expand into a greater sense of self, try on new roles, and move beyond convention. The rebirth of interest in goddess imagery may be allowing us, as modern women, to do the same. Understanding the archetypal meaning and significance of the roles we play allows us, too, to grow into more of who we are and explore who we can be.

Our journey through womanhood requires strength and courage. Living from our own center gives us a place from which to operate that makes sense, that allows us to be who we are so that we can allow those close to us to be who they are too. There is room for all when our souls aren't being crowded out, when we can breathe and have our own source of oxygen.

The kind of selflessness, self-examination, love, and forbearance that is required by the roles that Mother Nature has asked us to play can also be a path toward spiritual renewal and ultimately our own freedom. We are woven into the web of life and we know it in our bones. This path ultimately can and often does lead to a kind of self-realization that women understand. It's a quiet, private thing that we carry in our hearts.

The archetypes in this book represent roles along this journey. They also symbolize the interaction, growth, and comfort that can be had when the generations take care of each other throughout life. When the young give their freshness and vitality to the old and the old share their wisdom, care, and support with the young. We all need each other. This is "the village." Our world may be expanding, but our basic needs have remained remarkably constant. It is our humanness that we honor and nourish when we play our roles well.

Stages of the Journey

Modern society is pressing us to evolve. Our roles are transforming us as we move from one way of being toward another. It helps to understand this if we divide the process of transformation into three stages. According to Robert Johnson in his book *Transformation,* in the *first* stage, all is clear and simple; our roles are defined and happiness and satisfaction can be derived from playing them well. In the *second* stage, after the questioning has begun, all is in flux, examined, re-evaluated, and torn apart. We feel insecure as if the center isn't holding. This is a vulnerable time . . . nothing is as it was, but where we're going isn't clear either. It can be exciting, challenging, scary, or all of the above. If we can get through this period of uncertainty, all can become simple again. Finally, in the *third* stage, we find ourselves reintegrating into what feels whole again, with aspects of our previous selves integrated into our newfound sense of who we are. We come to realize that happiness and satisfaction are found not only in playing our roles well but also in understanding their deeper meaning to our lives.

Once the questioning begins as it did in the 1960s, there is really no going back. Going back would be to adopt a somewhat superficial version of a role, repressing all that does not fit in. While before we were simply not conscious of what other possibilities there were, now we are aware of them, and the only path is to explore and experiment, to expand and reintegrate the whole of our vision, or to suffer the shadow, the hidden or suppressed part of us, asserting itself, creating pressure from within.

These past decades have surely been a time of expansion and experimentation. We have now had a generation to accomplish all of this complicated transition. The fruits of these labors are our own renewed selves, a new whole, and another way of being in the world. We're doing our lives in some ways very differently from our mothers and in some ways much the same. Other fruits are marriages infused with the vitality of equality and respect and a new way of operating that we can thrive in and pass on to our children. Today our daughters take for granted opportunities and challenges that we had to fight for. A new generation of balanced, responsible, brilliant young women with an emotional intelligence that seems to come naturally to them has emerged. We have a lot to be proud of.

Intergenerational Living

This book celebrates our multilayered lives. Imagine a family or a group of women occupying all the roles represented in these pages relaxing together around a kitchen table. What an enriching scene for all concerned. The energy and innocence of one generation interacting with the maturity and wisdom of the others, feeding each other, nourishing each other, the women interrelating to create a richer, better whole. And then envision all of the roles represented here being naturally internalized within each person present. This is not a vision of an ideal world. This experience is available here and now. All we have to do is look for it, recognize it, and work toward it.

The generations need each other. Countries where the old and young are cared for and venerated tend to be countries where we are of daily, practical use to each other. Grandparents play a strong role in the care and feeding of the young. The young provide security and a purpose for living for the aging generation, and those in the middle face the world and child rearing with significant support and an inbuilt sense of the "big picture." In our affluent culture, where many of us can "survive" on our own, we have forgotten that our hearts and souls need nourishment as much as or more than our bodies.

It has been my thought that "dysfunctional" families, in part, are families that have not understood how to stay connected in a world that has been pulling us apart through technological and monetary advancement. Some of us have turned our pain at disconnection into alienation and defended against feeling our sense of loss by pathologizing distance. It has taken us a couple of generations to understand that airplanes go in both directions and to actively create ways of staying connected that work. Happiness does not begin "after the kids leave and the dog dies," as the saying goes. That mentality reflects a cool detachment that misunderstands the need for connection throughout life.

Intergenerational living is nature's design to provide for the needs of all the generations. Sequestering ourselves into what I call "peer ghettos" provides no role relief or cross-fertilization. People, like crops or flowers, need to cross over into each other's worlds to stay healthy and strong season after season. Otherwise, we become nutrient poor.

I have written most of this book in the first person because it gives me an intimate connection with you, the reader, heart to heart. It also allows me to take psychological concepts and distill them into thoughts for the day that can be easily metabolized both psychologically and emotionally. Some of the experiences are mine and some are inspired by women I have worked with over the years. Complicated psychological concepts that are deeply personal and intimate by nature can be lost, I find, in language that feels too distant from the real self.

I recommend using this book in whatever way works best for you—go from back to front, start in the middle, leapfrog, open to any page, or journal in the margins. I see it as a bedside reader—personal and easy to pick up. It should work for any age. For young women it can provide support and inspiration and help them put their struggle to find their identity into words; for women in the middle of their life tasks it can be a daily source of self-nuturing and thought alignment; and for older readers it can help them to consolidate, to feel more whole, and to move into the further inner challenges life holds. For every reader it should feel like an inner voice, I hope, a sort of heart friend. The idea is to create a positive sense of meaning and purpose. Because all life is really a journey of deepening our spiritual understanding and daily life is our vehicle, it seems fitting that this book is a daily reader. It has long been my experience that my clients who have a spiritual belief system—whether it be church, synagogue, mosque, temple, or Twelve Step work— heal better than those who do not have a way of both seeing spirit in the world and making deeper meaning out of the seemingly random events of our lives.

May your journey be rich and challenging and ultimately lead to greater expression of self, deeper appreciation of relationships, and the peace and harmony that passes all understanding.

The Virgin

Development of Self

After a while you learn
the subtle difference between
holding a hand and chaining a soul
and you learn
that love doesn't mean leaning
and company doesn't always mean security
And you begin to learn
that kisses aren't contracts
and presents aren't promises
and you begin to accept your defeats
with your head up and your eyes ahead
with the grace of a woman, not the grief of a child
and you learn
to build all your roads on today
because tomorrow's ground is
too uncertain for plans
and futures have a way of falling down
in mid-flight.
After a while you learn
that even sunshine burns
if you get too much
so you plant your own garden
and decorate your own soul
instead of waiting for someone
to bring you flowers.

And you learn that you really can endure
you really are strong
you really do have worth
and you learn
and you learn
with every goodbye, you learn . . .

—Veronica A. Shoffstall
"After a While"

The Virgin

I AM THE GIRL, the Virgin; the beauty within me is waiting to be born. I contain the seeds of womanhood waiting to burst into full and feminine expression. I am the Virgin whose innocence and beauty bring the tender blossoms of spring into this world. I am the bud on its way into full and glorious bloom. I sense within me the seeds of life itself. My heart is filled with longing and my mind rushes with the yet-to-be-fulfilled dreams of someday. I am preparing myself to bring forth life from my own body. I contain within my heart the promise of my lover yet to come and life yet to be born. We will carry forth the generations. I am a gift to this world.

I am a part of the universe's life-giving force.

"See there within the flesh
  Like a bright wick, englazed
  The soul God's finger lit
  To give her liberty
  And joy and power and love."

—MECHTILD VON MEGDEBURG
"Love Flows from God"

Inner Search

TODAY I RECOGNIZE that my life is lived through no one but me. I am the source of sustenance and strength that I am looking for. Within me lies all the beauty, strength, and wisdom it will take to create a self. I am my own best friend and my beacon in the storm. My light lives within, and I am the keeper of my own flame. I do not need to wait to be granted a self from some outside source. I will be the grantor. Accumulating accolades from outside in an attempt to establish an inner identity will not accomplish what I am hoping for. Ultimately, I will need to locate myself from within; the soul that I search for, I already have.

I am on a journey toward my soul.

"A soul is partly given, partly wrought."

—ERICA JONG
Fanny (1981)

Redefining Selfishness

TAKING CARE OF MYSELF doesn't have to mean that I am selfish. Taking care of myself is like putting the oxygen mask on myself first so I can breathe. Once I can breathe, I am able to cope with another person or situation effectively—without having to run, without gasping for air. Taking care of myself is a recognition that I am no good to anyone without a self. If I let my own sense of self disappear, I will inevitably try to replace it with another person's or a substance or a false sense of self. I will cultivate the self that I care for. I need to go quietly into the interior of my own inner world. Self is there—waiting to be uncovered. It is when I lack a sense of self that I run away from those I love, physically or emotionally in search of something. Or I try to incorporate them into me to fill the emptiness. When I take care of my own self, I recognize the self of others and I allow them to take care of themselves with my blessing.

I look within for my true self.

"Selfishness is not living as one wishes to live; it is asking others to live as one wishes to live."

—RUTH RENDELL
A Judgment in Stone (1977)

Self-Acceptance

I ACCEPT MYSELF as I am; this is no easy task. Constantly I find myself in internal bouts of self-criticism and self-doubt. I second-guess myself and doubt my ability to be up to the challenges of my life. Life can seem much more complicated than it did when I was a child. What does it mean to accept myself as I am? Does it mean that I stop growing and trying to be better or that I am arrogant and don't feel I need to learn more in life? Or does it mean that I am enough for today, that life isn't a race and that it is better for me and everyone around me if I can learn to take it a day at a time, to relax and enjoy the ride. Being hard on myself wounds the person I am closest to, me, and leads me to be hard on those around me. I teach others how to treat me by how I treat myself. Today I will begin to be fair and nice to myself and others.

I accept myself each day as I am.

"The world is terribly apt to take people at their own valuation."

—AMELIA B. EDWARDS
Half a Million of Money (1866)

Self

WHAT IS SELF and where do I find it? We all search for "self" because we sense that self is where we operate from, where we return to, and what sustains us. But what is it? Paradoxically we develop self both in relationships and in resting within. Our sense of self is highly impacted by those who raise us in both the nuclear and extended family and by the relational world of community and school that surrounds us. This is where we learn through the reflected appraisals of others how we're seen. This is where we model and where we learn about relationships. We internalize all of this information and these impressions to form a working model of the world and of self. Secondly, we go within. We meditate. We contact that part of us that is unchanging and eternal. The steady reservoir of life itself as it dwells within us and we dwell within it.

I go within for integration of my inner and outer selves.

"The self is what we experience inwardly when we feel a relationship to oneness that connects us to everything outside us. At this spiritual level, 'connecting' and 'detachment' are, paradoxically, the same."

—JEAN SHINODA BOLEN
Goddesses in Everywoman (1984)

Shaping Myself

How DO I SHAPE myself today? Who am I—what will I become? In the turmoil of creating me, I sometimes get lost—lost to myself. Lost to others. When I tune in on my own voice, I cannot always hear the difference between my voice and the voices of others. I can feel confused, like I have too many messages in my head. Be this—don't be that—so many messages it can be hard to mobilize my own energy and strike out on my own. I feel torn between missing where I came from and not knowing where I am going. At times I want to return to the safety of being a child and at other times I want to plunge into an adult life. I don't always understand what is happening to me—it feels like there are so many MEs inside of me. Who will I be when I grow up? Will I ever know?

I will be quiet enough to hear my own inner voice.

"We make ourselves up as we go."

—KATE GREEN
If the World Is Running Out (1983)

Self-Talk

How DO I TALK to myself? What do I say to myself when I make a mistake or fall short of expectations? Or how about when I'm looking for love or standing in front of a mirror? Am I my own worst enemy or my own best friend? *Self-talk is what we say to ourselves on the inside.* We need to pay attention to our own *self-talk* as we go through our day. Am I encouraging and compassionate with myself or critical and discouraging? If we don't like what we hear, *we can change it.* Let's try talking to ourselves the way we wish a wonderful friend or relative would talk to us. This may feel fake, but it's as real as the negative talk we might be doing now—we just need to get used to it—to let ourselves hear what we really want to hear. People who are kind to themselves tend to be kind to others. Often, we treat those close to us the way we treat ourselves. Let's treat ourselves well today. Let's talk to ourselves with kindness.

I talk to myself in a supportive, encouraging voice.

"Beneath the surface of our daily life, in the personal history of many of us, there runs a continuous controversy between an Ego that affirms and an Ego that denies."

—BEATRICE WEBB
My Apprenticeship (1926)

Developing Inner Wisdom

INNER WISDOM is exactly what it sounds like—wisdom that comes from within. Creating quiet time when we can be calm and "go within" is critical to developing inner wisdom. It's really less cognitive than it sounds. Rather it springs from "being still and knowing." If we are serious about developing inner wisdom, here are a few things we can do. Buy books that will lead us in that direction. Create downtime in our day when we can become calm and be with ourselves in an unhurried manner. Learn to meditate. What we don't do is as important as what we do. It's not good to run ourselves ragged or to overvalue what is outside of us and ignore our inner world. Do enjoy the journey!

I create quiet in my day to be with me.

"The perfection of wisdom and the end of true philosophy, is to proportion our wants to our possessions, our ambitions to our capacities."

—FRANCES WRIGHT
A Few Days in Athens (1822)

Staying Connected to Myself

WE LIVE IN A CULTURE of media images. We place high value on
how things look on the outside. We have the power through
media and print technologies to barrage ourselves with the pictures of cultural icons who set our standards of beauty, speed,
grace, and cool. We are drowning in ideals of what we are supposed to be *before* we can be what we are, before we can relax and
embrace the strength and power of being ourselves. We are in-
undated with "shoulds." The "I-gotta-be-me" or the "me" generation sprang up in the 1980s perhaps to counter this feeling that
being who we are is somehow not good enough. But it missed
one important point: We are all connected. We need each other,
and we depend upon each other for everything from directions
to lifelong love. The challenge is *how do we stay connected to ourselves while in relationship to others,* whether those others are
partners, siblings, friends, or coworkers (to say nothing of our
garage mechanic, the waitress who takes our order, or the local
dry cleaner)? How do we balance being "me" with letting others
be "them"? How do we compromise—neither giving too much
away nor hoarding the self-space of another? How do we stay
connected to our self in a world that is constantly trying to pull
us off center?

I retain a sense of self in the presence of another.

"You can live a lifetime and, at the end of it, know more
about other people than you know about yourself."

—BERYL MARKHAM
West with the Night (1942)

Development of Self

WE NEED A RELATIONSHIP with self in order to have a relationship with another, and part of how we learn about the self and develop the self is through interaction with other people. Development of self is dynamic. Nature and nurture are constantly interacting. As children, we interact with our primary caregivers, adding to who we are and helping to shape self. We then interact with our newly developed self. This elicits a new set of responses that add to our self. Then we interact with this newly developed self and elicit new responses. Nature *and* nurture interact constantly to develop and define who we are. Relationships become part of our incorporated sense of self. Each tiny interaction affects how our sense of self gets built. We see ourselves through our own eyes and through the eyes that gaze upon us.

I am the sum total of all my experiences and my basic self.

"You need only claim the events of your life to make yourself yours. When you truly possess all you have been and done, which may take some time, you are fierce with reality."

—FLORIDA SCOTT-MAXWELL
The Measure of My Days (1968)

Identifying My Own Needs

THE IDEA OF IDENTIFYING my own needs is to know myself better. This is a deep and painstaking process. Understanding at some basic level what my needs are and being willing to know and feel them is very liberating. It forces me to see what I am like. Filling them is much easier than knowing them. When I focus on filling them rather than on knowing them, I run the risk of replacing self with stuff or substances or emotionally blackmailing people close to me. Every time I think I have a need, rather than tolerating the experience of sitting with it and feeling it, I ask someone or something else to fill me up. Knowing my needs does not mean that other people have to fill them. It just gives me choices. Sometimes I can ask someone to fill them, sometimes I need to figure out ways of filling them in the world, and still other times I need to postpone gratification. Knowing them is information for me.

Everyone has needs and so do I.

"A child should be allowed to take as long as she needs for knowing everything about herself, which is the same as learning to be herself. Even twenty-five years, if necessary, or even forever. And it wouldn't matter if doing things got delayed, because nothing is really important but being oneself."

—LAURA RIDING
Four Unposted Letters to Catherine (1993)

Putting Myself First

I REALIZE THAT TO LET MYSELF be first in my life is actually the way of the spirit. Each of us is connected to God through our higher selves. Only from the place of my self can I truly be with another person. When my focus is constantly on another, rather than "be" with them I "become" them, and we enter into a competition for one life, one self. My self is the place from which I operate. There is nothing holy about relinquishing it. The way to be generous is to expand or extend my self—not to give my self away. When I center in the moment and in self, I see things differently. I take care of myself by living from a centered place where I am in touch with my own spirituality and inner wisdom. I am in a position to care for and about others. I take responsibility for keeping my well filled. I give from a full, rather than an empty, container. It is not so much about what I do but where I am within my own being.

I am in touch with a higher self.

"The strongest, surest way to the soul is through the flesh."

—MABEL DODGE LUHAN
Lerenzoin Taos (1932)

Being on My Own

I LOVE THE FEELING of being on my own—strong and self-sufficient. I have the energy and the drive to conquer the challenges of my life—to move forward, to fight to win. I feel power welling up inside of me—power that I can use to get to where I want to go. I am ready—ready for life—my life. I have the ability to define goals, then apply myself daily toward achieving them. Many small actions add up and eventually I find I have built a solid structure a brick at a time. There is so much to do—so many worlds to explore—so much still waiting to happen for me.

I embrace my life.

"Of my own spirit let me be in sole and feeble mastery."

—SARA TEASDALE
"Mastery"
Love Songs (1917)

The Inner and the Outer Worlds

As CHILDREN, most of us were not afraid to let our inner selves show. But, as awareness of the outside world increased, we learned to edit our insides to fit into our ideas of what was expected and accepted on the outside. Though this is a natural process, it can lead us to edit our own self-discovery. Children often use transitional objects—teddy bears, pacifiers, blankets, even their parents—to keep their connection with their inner world alive as they reach toward the outside world. This enables them to stay connected to their inner world while reaching out to others. If we give ourselves space and permission to be alive on the inside while living in the world, our inner and outer worlds feel in more comfortable balance. When we learn how to be comfortable with what is inside of us and to allow more of that person to shine through into day-to-day living, we become more relaxed and available for life.

I allow myself to be seen.

"For every five well-adjusted and smoothly functioning Americans, there are two who never had the chance to discover themselves. It may well be because they have never been alone with themselves. The great omission in American life is solitude."

—MARYA MANNES
"To Save the Life of 'I'"
in *Vogue* (1964)

Self-Enjoyment

I WILL TAKE PLEASURE in myself, in the pleasant occupations of my day, in being with me. This is where it all begins. This is what gives my life that something special. If I cannot enjoy me, who can? Enjoying myself is a spiritual activity. God means me to do this. I have been given this body, mind, and spirit with all my senses in order to experience my own life. I am the vehicle through which spirit is made manifest; and one very important part of that manifestation is to quietly enjoy my own companionship, the pleasantness of my activities, and my connection with my Higher Power. This is how it is meant to be. Who will be diminished if I take quiet pleasure in my life? No one. I will simply be a better companion to myself and others and a better companion to God.

God wishes me to enjoy this beautiful, created world.

"Like any art, the creation of self is both natural and seemingly impossible. It requires training as well as magic."

—HOLLY NEAR, with Derk Richardson,
Fire in the Rain . . . Singer in the Storm (1990)

"I'm the kind of woman that likes to enjoy herself in peace."

—ALICE WALKER
The Temple of My Familiar (1989)

Sharing

I HAVE A NEED to share my innermost self. In the wanderings and meanderings of my mind and heart, I come upon my own sometimes strange, sometimes wonderful meaning. I am a delicate balance—a constellation of all the varied influences that have pressed their way into my being combined with the seeds of my own internal coding opening toward the light a bit each day. I am a story being written a page at a time with no last chapter; a work in progress. Who am I today, and who will I be tomorrow? How does my past live inside of me? Or not? Sometimes I simply need a stage on which I can sing my song and hear the echo of my own thoughts unraveled.

I have a need to be heard.

"Oh the comfort—the inexpressible comfort of feeling *safe* with a person—having neither to weigh thoughts nor measure words, but pouring them all right out, just as they are, chaff and grain together; certain that a faithful hand will take and sift them, keep what is worth keeping, and then with the breath of kindness, blow the rest away."

—DINAH MARIA MULOCK CRAIK
A Life for a Life (1866)

Connection

WOMEN NEED AUTHENTIC and mutual connection. We've all had traumas of one kind or another. Times when the events of our lives felt overwhelming and we felt powerless to improve or change them. Or ruptures in meaningful relationships that created deep wounds inside of us. Living with trauma tends to breed emotional and psychological disconnection both within the self and with others. In the absence of a true connection with self, we grab onto people, places, and things, creating an unhealthy connection with them. For example, we may attempt to connect to others in a way that does not allow us to be us and them to be them; we may alternate between fusion and disconnection, all or nothing. In our past, connection may have come to mean pain, rejection, and dashed hopes. We need to examine what connection has come to mean for us, understand it, and process all the feelings and meanings surrounding it. When we understand the anxiety and problematic expectations that keep us from being at peace in relationships, we can begin to work through them toward more comfortable connections.

I will look within at what connection means for me.

"Having someone wonder where you are when you don't come home at night is a very old human need."

—MARGARET MEAD, speech (1975)
Woman Talk, Vol. 1 (1984)

Seeing My Goals

I WILL SET ASIDE TIME EACH DAY to visualize my life's goals as being already achieved. I will picture myself functioning in the situation I wish to see manifest in my world. I'll operate in it "as if" it were really happening: smelling it, tasting it; moving, talking, interacting, and being in it "as if" it were real. I am not afraid to harness the power of my own mind in actualizing my dreams. I am also willing to do the work that it will take to get where I want to go. I'll be consistent. Picturing one thing one day and another the next, or picturing in a scattered, half-hearted way then feeling disappointed when things don't go my way, is not good and I know it. I'll stay with it on every level. I'll do the visualizing and the efforting so that circumstances can come together in a positive way.

I see my dreams fulfilled.

"What we truly and earnestly aspire *to be,* that in some sense we *are.* The mere aspiration, by changing the frame of the mind, for the moment realizes itself."

—ANNA JAMESON
A Commonplace Book (1855)

Me

I KNOW MYSELF from the inside out. I stare out at the world through my eyes, innocent and wide. My mind is my vantage point from where I look into the world. Part of what I see is what's actually out there; the other, and sometimes more important part, is how I see what's out there. I have a right to see myself as I choose to whether or not others always agree. I need to have a certain confidence in my opinion of me. I am as worthwhile as anyone else.

I cultivate my own philosophy of life.

"If what I am watching evaporated before my eyes, I would remain."

—ANNE TRUITT
Daybook (1982)

"I think I'm just as good as anyone. That's the way I was brought up. I'll tell you a secret: I think I'm better! Ha! I remember being aware that colored people were supposed to feel inferior. I knew I was a smart little thing, a personality, an individual—a human being! I couldn't understand how people could look at me and not see that, because it sure was obvious to me."

—BESSIE DELANY, in Sarah and A. Elizabeth Delany
with Amy Hill Hearth,
Having Our Say (1993)

My Home

I AM THE CHILD of the home I grew up in. I will always feel nostalgic for the home I had or the fantasy of what I wished it would have been. My home is wrapped up with each moment of my early development. It is where I learned to think, hope, and dream. It is the mirror in which I caught my first reflection of self. The people I grew up with live a little bit inside of me. So many of my meanderings into the world are shadowed by their presence. What I got for better and for worse has become a part of me. It is important, then, that I honestly confront both the strengths and weaknesses that I got from my past; the gifts and strengths that I can build upon or habits and thought patterns that might need changing. Perhaps equally or more important is that I love and respect my roots because my roots are in me, part of me. I need to connect with that strength and build upon it whether the strength was a positive attitude or my willingness to stand up as straight and as tall as I could when I was young.

I honor and come to terms with where I came from.

"Home can never be transferred; never repeated in the experience of an individual. The place consecrated by parental love, by the innocence and sports of childhood, by the first acquaintances with nature, by the linking of the heart to the visible creation, is the only home."

—C. M. SEDGWICK
Hope Leslie (1827)

Contentment

TODAY I WILL SEARCH MYSELF and find the contentment I am looking for. I will not assume that contentment is a mood or a feeling that suddenly comes upon me. I understand that I need to learn to build contentment within myself. I cannot meet the pressing and demanding pressures of my life if my inner world is in turmoil. Contentment and serenity allow me to do battle in the world effectively and judiciously. Contentment is my source of nourishment throughout the day. It doesn't drop from the sky. I have to work throughout my day to maintain the balance of emotions and thoughts that will allow my contentment to remain intact.

I take responsibility for my own contentment.

"Let nothing disturb thee;
Let nothing dismay thee:
All things pass;
God never changes."

—ST. TERESA OF AVILA (c. 1550)

Seeing Perfection in What Is

I WILL LEARN TO SEE PERFECTION in things as they are. Beauty always surrounds me if I can let go of my preconceptions of what it should look like. When I try to micromanage all that lies outside of me, it dissipates the fullness of the moment and disallows spontaneity and life. The presence of higher consciousness is in every moment if I can relax and allow it to be there. As I move along in my life, I learn that it is not so much what continues to accumulate around me, but my ability to appreciate what I already have that nourishes my spirit. It takes a healthy body to navigate the world, but it takes a healthy spirit to appreciate and enjoy it. It is the union between what I bring as the observer and that which I observe that creates beauty. I see beauty through the eye of the beholder (me).

I recognize the beauty of this world that surrounds me.

"The greatest possession is self-possession."

—ETHEL WATTS MUMFORD, in Oliver Herford,
Ethel Watts Mumford, and Addison Mizner,
The Complete Cynic (1902)

"I'm committed to the idea that one of the few things human beings have to offer is the richness of unconscious and conscious emotional responses to being alive. . . . The kind of esteem that's given to brightness/smartness obliterates average people or slow learners from participating fully in human life, particularly technical and intellectual life. But you cannot exclude any human being from emotional participation."

—NTOZAKE SHANGE, in Claudia Tate, ed.,
Black Women Writers at Work (1983)

Self-Forgiveness

I WILL TRY TO FORGIVE MYSELF today for my transgressions. When I do something that I feel bad about, I alternate between feeling defensive, trying to justify my actions, and feeling awful about myself. It seems I have little middle ground, little ability to step back and allow myself to make mistakes. I condemn them; I am much too hard on myself, and this leads me into hardened, defensive positions, where, in essence, I project that hardness onto someone else. Then together we descend farther and farther down into an abyss of rancor, losing our collective ability to step back, take a breath, and let go. The farther down I go into defensiveness, the harder it is to forgive myself for my behavior, and the harder it is to let go.

Just for today, I will go easy on myself.

"The idea of a finished human product not only appears presumptuous but even, in my opinion, lacks any strong appeal. Life is struggle and striving, development and growth—and analysis is one of the means that can help in this process. Certainly its positive accomplishments are important, but also the striving itself is of intrinsic value."

—KAREN HORNEY
Self-Analysis (1943)

Forgiving and Moving On

WHEN I FORGIVE I do so not to let someone off the hook but to let myself off the hook. Holding resentment is just that—holding it—in my own heart and mind. It hurts me and I never really get satisfaction from the other person; they still have power over me. They still live in my mind rent-free. The only thing I really have control over is how not to keep hurting myself. My revenge fantasies are natural, but I can't get back at anyone by hurting myself. Forgiveness is my ultimate way out of my own pain. It is a recognition not that another person is right but that my peace of mind and serenity are worth more to me in the long run than settling a score.

I forgive to preserve my own peace of mind.

"Forgiveness is the economy of the heart. . . . Forgiveness saves expense of anger, the cost of hatred, the waste of spirits."

—HANNAH MORE
Christianity, A Practical Principle (1811)

The Process of Forgiveness

FORGIVENESS IS A PROCESS, not an event. I still carry hurt and anger. I feel if I forgive, I am saying what the other person did was okay—I feel I am condoning what was, for me, wrong behavior. I feel blocked by this. But today I can use the tools available to me to work this out. I can reach out and talk through my hurt and anger. I can work through my painful feelings rather than try to move them aside and make myself forgive. I cannot force forgiveness. I can, however, put myself on a road that leads toward forgiveness. Each step I take on that road brings me closer to myself. When I get close to myself, I want to take care of me. Forgiveness, ultimately, is taking care of me because it allows me to move on in my own life toward my greater good.

I work through the steps of forgiveness.

"Forgiveness is the act of admitting we are like other people."
—CHRISTINA BALDWIN
Life's Companion (1990)

A Letter to God

CLOSE YOUR EYES and think about a situation in your life that is bothering you. Then imagine how you would like that situation to change. Allow yourself to really see, feel, taste, and mentally participate in this situation as you would like to experience it in your life. Divide a piece of paper into three horizontal sections. In the bottom section, jot down a few phrases or sentences describing the situation as it is today. In the top section, jot down a few phrases or sentences describing the situation as you would like it to be. Use what you saw during your reflection. Leave the middle section empty so that the divine hand of spirit, or a Higher Power, has space to work.

For every one step I take toward God, God will take four toward me.

"How can God direct our steps if we're not taking any?"

—SARAH LEAH GRAFSTEIN
The Feminine Face of God (1991)

The Friend

I AM THE FRIEND, steadfast and feminine. I listen and am attentive to what I hear with my ears and read with my eyes. I can be counted on as a safe harbor in times of need, a challenging voice when the truth must be spoken, and a wild, enlivening presence that transforms an ordinary cup of tea into a riot of giggles and laughter. I am available, here by choice not obligation, a companion to sweeten any and all of life's activities and a rock to lean on when life's inevitable troubles occur. I choose and am chosen according to mutual regard and preference. I hold my pettiness and fickleness in check and am generous with positive regard. I am one of life's treasures, someone with whom to share the mystery.

I am your friend.

"She is a friend of mind. She gather me, man. The pieces
I am, she gather them and give them back to me in all the
right order."

—TONI MORRISON
Beloved (1987)

Selflessness

IN OUR PERSONAL GROWTH over the last two decades, we have at times misunderstood selflessness. Because as women we have sometimes been sequestered into roles that ensnare our spirits, we may have generalized our fear of entrapment into a fear of selflessness. We confused genuine selflessness or our ability to temporarily put aside our own needs on behalf of other people with losing our identity and, in a sense, fusing or losing ourselves in them. Codependency is living in someone else's head *instead* of our own, identifying another person's needs and drives *as* our own. Like the joke we used to tell, "You know you're codependent if, when you're drowning, someone else's life flashes across your mind." The other good one was, "If codependents were offered a choice between entering two doors, one marked *Heaven* and the other *Lecture on Heaven,* they would go to the lecture on heaven." All of this implies a distance from the core self, which is how many of us have always defined codependency—a loss of connection with the self.

I will return to the spirit that lives within me.

"The divorce of our so-called spiritual life from our daily activities is a fatal dualism."

—M. P. FOLLETT
Creative Experience (1924)

"It was on that road and at that hour that I first became aware of my own self, experienced an inexpressible state of grace, and felt one with the first breath of air that stirred, the first bird, and the sun so newly born that it still looked not quite round."

—COLETTE
Sido (1930)

Friendship

"I suppose there is one friend in the life of each of us who seems not a separate person, however dear and beloved, but an expansion, an interpretation of one's self, the very meaning of one's soul."

—EDITH WHARTON
A Backward Glance (1934)

"There are people whom one loves immediately and forever. Even to know they are alive in the world with one is quite enough."

—NANCY SPAIN
Why I'm Not a Millionaire (1956)

"In meeting again after a separation, acquaintances ask after our outward life, friends after our inner life."

—MARIE VON EBNER-ESCHENBACH
Aphorisms (1893)

"The hearts that never leans must fall."

—EMILY DICKINSON (1881)

"I felt it shelter to speak to you."

—EMILY DICKINSON (1878)

The Daughter to Her Mother

I AM THE DAUGHTER; it is a strange alchemy that exists between us, molded from the same clay. Such a need to stay close and such a need to separate. I am of you but not you. I have your eyes but not your heart. I am built for a world beyond you, yearning for a life of my own. In your house I find myself again and again. Yet I must leave your house to have me. The future belongs to me and I must move toward it. I love you with all my heart and still my life is tinged with hate for needing you, for your needing me to feel whole—it makes it so hard to pull myself out of you—away from this suction, from this pool that both holds and drowns me, hate at the vulnerability of my position. I am not you and you are not me. I fear that these feelings of mine could destroy our closeness, which I cherish—is it okay to want to move beyond you?—I do not wish you to define the borders of my soul.

I want to be me with your blessing and support.

"Our mythology tells us so much about fathers and sons. . . . What do we know about mothers and daughters? . . . Our power is so oblique, so hidden, so ethereal a matter, that we rarely struggle with our daughters over actual kingdoms or corporate shares. On the other hand, our attractiveness dries as theirs blooms, our journey shortens just as theirs begins. We too must be afraid and awed and amazed that we cannot live forever and that our replacements are eager for their turn, indifferent to our wishes, ready to leave us behind."

—ANNE ROIPHE
Lovingkindness (1987)

Over-Functioning

I WILL LET GO NOW. I have seen enough of life to understand that expectations, preconceptions, and unnecessarily rigid standards do not bring happiness, peace of mind, or enjoyment. I can wait until life beats this lesson into my head a thousand times, or I can allow myself to learn the lesson through quiet observation of myself and others. What I can let be generally can let me be. When I get overly attached to and enmeshed in situations, they have too much impact on me. There is no reason for me to take each little thing so seriously that I lose my serenity. I don't have to be like an idling car, constantly revved up for action. If I am, by the time I need to act, I will be exhausted and ineffective. I will learn when to put my foot on the gas and when to rest in neutral.

I can be with things as they are.

"We are well advised to keep on nodding terms with the people we used to be, whether we find them attractive company or not. Otherwise, they run up unannounced and surprise us, come hammering on the mind's door at 4 A.M. of a bad night and demand to know who deserted them, who betrayed them, who is going to make amends."

—JOAN DIDION
"On Keeping a Notebook"
Slouching Towards Bethlehem (1968)

Information about My Feelings

IF I WANT ANYONE TO RESPECT or hear my feelings, I need to find a tolerable way to express them. I will reverse roles in my mind with someone I am getting upset with and contemplate what it might be like to be standing in their shoes. If I wouldn't like to be treated the way I am treating them, I will find another approach, another way to talk about my feelings that they might be able to hear. I will behave in such a way that the circumstance can move forward rather than blow up. I will use my emotions to inform me of something I need to be aware of and talk them out rather than act them out. I will self-reflect and witness what's going on in my inner world so that I can operate authentically and in tune with myself and others.

My emotions give me information, not license.

"Every time you don't follow your inner guidance you feel a loss of energy, loss of power, a sense of spiritual deadness."

—SHAKTI GAWAIN
Living in the Light (1986)

Trust and Faith

PAINFUL RELATIONSHIPS or circumstances can rupture relationships and destroy trust and faith. Disappointment, disillusionment, and feelings of rejection can leave us feeling bereft. We enter a kind of "pain reasoning," an attempt to make sense out of a senseless situation. Our pain reasoning distorts; it may tell us that it's dumb to trust because trusting only leads to pain. It's true we may avoid a degree of pain by not trusting, but we will avoid pleasure and joy right along with it. Sooner or later we need to become willing to take a leap of faith and trust something.

I am willing to trust in life.

"The unfolding of my life is not an issue of competence or control; it is an issue of faith."

—ANNE WILSON-SHAEF

"We are not born all at once, but by bits. The body first, and the spirit later; and the birth and growth of the spirit, in those who are attentive to their own inner life, are slow and exceedingly painful. Our mothers are racked with the pains of our physical births; we ourselves suffer the longer pains of our spiritual growth."

—MARY ANTIN
The Promised Land (1912)

Feeling Out of Sorts

THERE CAN BE A LOT OF REASONS for getting grouchy or impatient. If we find we are extra irritable, maybe we should try taking a deeper look. Is there some anxiety or frustration that we are projecting onto someone else? Is our inner life or career life feeling frustrating and making us want to lash out a little? Let's first look for the deeper reason, tune in, and honestly ask ourselves what's going on that needs our attention. Our inner worlds can be like small children tugging at our pants leg if we ignore them for too long. If there is something going on, let's attend to it, talk it out with a friend, make use of our support resources, and if it's more serious, check around for support groups or professional help. Let's try giving ourselves more relaxation, adding more of what we like to our lives, and subtracting some of what we dislike. We can create downtime to reduce stress and enhance calm and see if that helps. Added stress exacerbates any problem, while peace of mind soothes and brings order.

I take meaningful actions to improve my life.

"What makes us so afraid is the thing we half see, or half hear, as in a wood at dusk, when a tree stump becomes an animal and a sound becomes a siren. And most of that fear is the fear of not knowing, of not actually seeing correctly."

—EDNA O'BRIEN
Under Bow Bells (1974)

Mental Clutter

SOMETIMES WE MAY FIND ourselves on overload. We may feel mentally stressed, crammed too tight with information, random thoughts, all sorts of emotions, and too many disconnected activities. We yearn for a new start. We imagine wiping the slate clean, or living another life as a solution to feeling overwhelmed. But oftentimes what we really need to do most is sit still, calm down, and reduce the internal clutter. We need to mentally reorganize and re-prioritize. When I put clothes away in my room or groceries in the kitchen, I sometimes feel that there's not enough closet or cupboard space. Then I want a bigger room, a new kitchen. That's when I need to take a closer look; I go over what I have to see if it's still current, if I'm still using it, or if it's just taking up space. I reorganize. I consolidate, toss, and give away to someone who can use what I don't need. Suddenly I have enough space. By working with what I have in new ways in a calm and focused manner, I free myself.

I reduce clutter by increasing calm.

"Creativity can be described as letting go of certainties."

—GAIL SHEEHY
Pathfinders (1981)

"Stress is an ignorant state. It believes everything is an emergency."

—NATALIE GOLDBERG
Wild Mind (1990)

*H*ome *S*weet *H*ome

EACH OF US HAS A RESTING PLACE within our own minds, within our own self. This is our center, our place to relax, our home base. When we are able to relax and come "home," we are able to nourish ourselves and to draw sustenance from an internal source. We can quench our thirst by drinking from an internal well. When we feel secure that we have this center for relaxation within ourselves that we can return to at any time, we don't have to constantly run away from ourselves or search the outside world for an identity. We can relax and come home. Living this way allows us to construct a self-identity that grows naturally from an internal source. We need to guard time each and every day to relax and just be with ourselves and in this way connect with a little piece of eternity.

I will relax and come home.

"Peace—that was the other name for home."

—KATHLEEN NORRIS
Belle-Mère (1931)

Making a Decision

WHEN MAKING A LIFE CHOICE, let's try this. Take four pieces of paper. At the top of the first paper, we'll write down the choices we're grappling with. On the second paper, we'll write down all of the options we have. On the third paper, titled "Blocks," we'll write down anything real or imagined, emotional or psychological that's blocking us from moving forward. Finally, on the fourth paper, titled "How To," let's write down the choice we're working with along with the practical steps we need to take to make our decision happen, to turn it into reality.

Remember that life choices don't have to be forever. Sometimes we think we'll have to live with one for the rest of our lives, but life is full of unfolding choices. We can make, unmake, and remake life choices. The key is to not get immobilized or run around mindlessly without direction. We need to find a balance. All we can really do is to make as good and clearheaded a choice as we can today using all of the information and wisdom that we can muster. We need to balance our own inner voices with the voices of others because it is WE who have to live with the reality of our choices.

I have a right to choose.

"How cool, how quiet is true courage."

—FANNY BURNEY
Evelina (1778)

*F*eeling *A*lone

I AM ULTIMATELY ALONE IN LIFE. When I can learn to tolerate, even embrace my feelings of aloneness, I am then able to be with someone else without substituting them for me. The void that I fear falling into is just more of me. I will grow stronger if I can learn to abide my feelings of aloneness. This is different from being alone. Feeling alone can happen in a crowd, in the market-place, or among my family or friends. When it happens, rather than ask another to fill me up, I will sit with it, experience it, and make friends with it, knowing that it is only when I can be alone that I can be myself with another.

I am willing to sit with myself.

"What others regard as retreat from them or rejection of them is not those things at all but instead a breeding ground for greater friendship, a culture for deeper involve-ment, eventually, with them."

—DORIS GRUMBACH
Fifty Days of Solitude (1994)

Grabbing Something Good

CHOOSE A TIME IN YOUR LIFE when you felt particularly proud or good about yourself. It may be a period in your life or a single event. In your inner vision, allow yourself to emerge onto the stage of your mind. How did you look at the time you have chosen? Try to imagine and picture yourself. What are you wearing? How do you stand? What is the expression on your face and in your eyes? Now mentally reverse roles and become yourself at that time in your life. Write a monologue describing yourself and expressing all of who you are. For example, "I am eight years old, my name is Marina, and I think I am beautiful. Recently I was the lead in my school play. Everyone thought I did a wonderful job, and I felt that I was a star. Capable and talented." Continue to write in this fashion until you have said everything that you want to say, and then reverse roles again. Come back to your present-day self and read what you have written. How can you enjoy this part of yourself in your life today?

I draw strength and resilience from positive memories.

"Spirituality is basically our relationship with reality."

—CHANDRA PATEL, in Theresa King, ed.,
The Spiral Path (1992)

"If facts are the seeds that later produce knowledge and wisdom, then the emotions and the impressions of the senses are the fertile soil in which the seeds must grow. Once the emotions have been aroused—a sense of the beautiful, the excitement of the new and the unknown, a feeling of sympathy, pity, admiration or love—then we wish for knowledge about the object of our emotional response."

—RACHEL CARSON
The Sense of Wonder (1965)

On Loneliness versus Solitude

"Women especially are social beings, who are not content with just husband and family but must have a community, a group, an exchange with others. A child is not enough. A husband and children, no matter how busy one may be kept by them, are not enough. Young and old, even in the busiest years of our lives, we women especially are victims of the long loneliness."

—DOROTHY DAY
The Long Loneliness (1952)

"Loneliness is the poverty of self; solitude is the richness of self."

—MAY SARTON
Mrs. Stevens Hears the Mermaids Singing (1965)

"Solitude is that human situation in which I keep myself company. Loneliness comes about when I am alone without being able to split up into the two-in-one, without being able to keep myself company."

—HANNAH ARENDT
The Life of the Mind (1978)

Prayer

PRAYING IS DEEPLY PERSONAL. Prayer is our way of having a personal relationship with a God of our knowing. It reaches into unseen realms and connects us to a transforming power beyond and within us. If we have a problem in one of our relationships or a circumstance that we can't get past, we can try praying about it and asking for help from an unseen source. Our ability to ask, to communicate through prayer, has the power to open doors within us. According to research, prayer can even elevate the immune system. An open, sincere, and clean heart has a power all its own. We can pray on our own or with others. When we pray, we simultaneously marshal the power of prayer and surrender to what feels too overwhelming. We can get out of our own way. Prayer can help us to move through a stuck place inside ourselves toward inner calm and peace.

Prayer is one of my ways of connecting with God and my higher self.

"In saying my prayers, I discovered the voice of an innermost self, the raw nerve of my identity."

—GELSEY KIRKLAND
Dancing on My Grave (1986)

Prayer and Health

PRAYER, PART OF THE MYSTERY OF LIFE, has become a studied topic in some scientific circles. In a review of heart disease patients, Larry Dossey, M.D., discovered that prayer was more effective than anyone had imagined. In one study, half of the patients were prayed for, half were not. The prayed-for group was five times less likely to require antibiotics and three times less likely to develop fluid in the lungs. In another study, ten people from a prayer group focused their prayers on slowing the growth of a laboratory fungus while they were fifteen miles away from the cultures. Over 70 percent of the cultures showed retarded growth. The same results occurred sixteen times out of sixteen. The results of this study are phenomenal. What those who pray sincerely have known for centuries is today being scientifically proved. Prayer has the power to heal our hearts, minds, and bodies. When we pray, we contact and mobilize help from unseen sources. Though we may not "see" the power, we certainly can feel its effects.

I will trust the power of prayer.

"Prayer does not use up artificial energy, doesn't burn up any fossil fuel, doesn't pollute. Neither does song, neither does love, neither does dance."

—MARGARET MEAD, in Jane Howard,
Margaret Mead (1984)

Staying Connected While Retaining a Self

OFTENTIMES IN OUR RELATIONSHIPS, as author Harriet Lerner puts it, we confuse closeness with sameness. We operate as if there were one truth. Intimacy requires that we have a respect for difference. When we think we all have to be the same in order to be close or get along, we create strain. We ask everyone to hide the parts of themselves that might cause friction and to go along at the expense of inner comfort. Rather than intimacy providing a way to better understand the self, it becomes a false intimacy that takes us away from who we are. It stops us from feeling safe. We're making a big investment, but it's not based on the truth. We're prizing sameness over closeness because, on the surface, it looks easier to achieve. But in order to sustain sameness we have to give up big pieces of ourselves. Closeness that allows for individual differences is sustainable *and* allows the people involved to grow.

I will learn the difference between closeness and sameness.

"I don't want to get to the end of my life and find that I lived just the length of it. I want to have lived with the width of it as well."

—DIANE ACKERMAN
in *Newsweek* (1986)

Getting Out There

I CAN DO IT. If I am not my own cheerleader, no one will be—no one can be. This world is mine as much as it is anyone else's. Who am I hurting by having what I want in my life? If I don't believe in myself, how can I expect anyone else to? If I wait to have someone else grant me an identity, I will end up living someone else's vision of me. Wouldn't it be better if I created my own? I have time. Life is an experiment. I will use the trial-and-error method, trying on different roles to see how they feel. I'm not stuck. I can shift and adjust in a thousand little ways. Identity isn't fixed—it's fluid, porous, *and* solid. Multifaceted. Life is an adventure and I want to know that now, while I'm living it. I will set a goal today and meet it. It may be taking a walk, enjoying social time, or reading something I'm interested in. Or I will take one small step toward a larger goal such as looking for a job, training for a career, or developing a stronger relationship. I will believe that I can do it. I'll get help if I need to. And I will get to where I am going.

I can do anything I put my mind to.

"Self-trust, we know, is the first secret of success."

—JANE FRANCESCA, LADY WILDE
Miss Martineau's Notes on Men, Women and Books (1891)

The Child Within

I WILL TAKE THE CHILD that lives inside of me with me on my journey through adulthood. If I leave her behind, I feel sad and lonely, and yet I am not sure if she still belongs inside of me. Some days I want her to disappear, and other days I want to hear her laughter ring in my inner ear and feel her tenderness and innocence tucked safely inside of me. Don't desert me, little child inside of me. I need you on this journey through womanhood. Stay close to me, little girl within me. I need your childlike trust to give me the courage to believe in my own dreams. I will bring you along and show you what it is to be a woman, mature and willing to take on life. I bring you along so that my heart remains alive.

Stay with me, little child.

"To love deeply in one direction makes us more loving in all others."

—ANNE-SOPHIE SWETCHINE
The Writings of Madame Swetchine (1869)

Meditation

MEDITATION IS ONE OF THE BEST self-help tools going. It is an opportunity to give our stressed-out minds the rest they need to function well. It is centering, which helps with everything from relationships to standing in a grocery-store line. It teaches us to "witness" our own mental processes and get to know what's going on in our own minds. It allows us to use breath to calm our nervous systems and get our minds connected with our bodies. If meditation is new to you, it's a good idea to get some simple instruction on how to meditate. Join a class, buy a tape, or find a friend who can teach you. Your sitting position can simply be in a chair, if you can elongate your spine comfortably. You can even start by lying flat with palms up. Mantras help, but you can start by using a word such as "peace" if you wish. Breathe steadily and deeply and witness the content of your mind simply as an observer. Let it flow by without any thought of controlling or manipulating your thought process. Simply watch.

I train my mind to relax.

"Spirituality leaps where science cannot yet follow, because science must always test and measure, and much of reality and human experience is immeasurable."

—STARHAWK
The Spiral Dance (1979)

The Huntress
Exploring the World

⚓

Our deepest fear is not that we are inadequate. Our deepest fear is that we are powerful beyond measure. It is our light, not our darkness, that most frightens us. We ask ourselves, Who am I to be brilliant, gorgeous, talented, fabulous? Actually, who are you *not* to be? You are a child of God. Your playing small doesn't serve the world. There's nothing enlightened about shrinking so that other people won't feel insecure around you. We are all meant to shine, as children do. We were born to make manifest the glory of God that is within us. It's not just in some of us; it's in everyone. And as we let our own light shine, we unconsciously give other people permission to do the same. As we're liberated from our own fear, our presence automatically liberates others.

—MARIANNE WILLIAMSON
from *A Return to Love* (1996)

The Huntress

I AM THE HUNTRESS. I search the world for all that I need to create and sustain my life. I search myself for the speed, patience, and strength that will make my hunt a success. I prepare my tools. I sharpen my wits and hone my talents. The world is mine. I slip through, quiet, unnoticed until I sense my moment is upon me and then I spring into action. I take aim. I release my arrows and stand back as they meet their target. I love the hunt. I hunt for pleasure, for challenge, for survival. Some of what I capture I feast on, some I wear for warmth, some I store for later, some I share. I am creative in how I use the gifts of the hunt. I love and respect the world that mysteriously brings forth all that I need. I am captured by its beauty, inspired by its variety, and moved by its power.

I am power and patience and prayer.

"I long to put the experience of fifty years at once into your young lives, to give you at once the key to that treasure chamber every gem of which has caused me tears and struggles and prayers, but you must work for these inward treasures yourselves."

—HARRIET BEECHER STOWE
Letter to her twin daughters (1861)

*A*live

I ACCEPT. I have been cordially invited by God to attend my own life, and I will commit to coming. I have been given the invitation that is the grandest gift of all. Life. I will not squander this opportunity, and I appreciate my luck and privilege. I count my blessings. I don't wait for someone to come to my door and bring me to the party. I'll get there on my own steam. I'll find my way. I'll say please and thank you and be a good guest. Being alive is its own reward, and I recognize the beauty that is mine. If I don't show up for my own life, no one else can. It's mine and *only* mine. If I let it pass me by, if I don't embrace it and accept its challenges, it will simply be lost. My life is in my own hands.

I am deeply grateful to be alive.

"And reach for our lives . . . for *all* life . . . deep into the cosmos that is our own souls."

—SONIA JOHNSON

Signs

I NOTICE SIGNS that affirm my direction. The world is always talking to me, if I learn to listen. I look for the path that is passable. If I need to cut away at the underbrush or clear-fallen branches, I do so quickly and efficiently so that I can continue on my way. But I look for *my* path, the one that calls to *me*, the one that opens itself to me in a thousand mysterious ways. My path is the one that suits me, that is a natural fit, that allows for both my strengths and my weaknesses. The world gives me subtle signs to tell me I am on the right path, when I learn to read them. Another's path will not be my own, but I can learn from it. My path may be trod by many or by few, but I walk it in my own way.

I hear the world talking to me.

"Heroes take journeys, confront dragons and discover the treasure of their true selves."

—CAROL PEARSON
The Hero Within (1986)

The Power of Myth

I LOOK BENEATH THE SURFACE of life toward the metaphoric or deeper meaning that underlies any circumstance. As lover, I contain the hopes and dreams of a lifetime. As wife, I embody the steadfastness, security, and sense of home that over the centuries have shaped that role. I am a listener, reliable, and there for my friend. If I am a mother, I am also representing the archetype of mother, all that means mother. The needs and yearnings that we all feel. And so it goes, a daughter's love never dies. I am the grandmother, too, the point of security and love, the steadier, the giver of unconditional love. I am more than me. I carry with me the power, meaning, and responsibilities of the roles that I play.

I am all that my role contains.

"A myth is far truer than a history, for history only gives a story of the shadows, whereas a myth gives a story of the substances that cast the shadows."

—ANNIE BESANT
Esoteric Christianity (1901)

True Wealth

My heart is open. To life, to love, and to my greater good. Nothing can come to me if my heart is closed. Opening my heart doesn't mean laying myself out as a doormat. All my faculties are still engaged. I am not suspending my judgment and discrimination— I'm removing from my inner world that which blocks me from being able to receive and experience the simple pleasures of any given day. Life is happening all around me; the world is full of magic if I can recognize it and take it in. I can own everything my eyes can see, but if I lack the ability to be touched and moved by the beauty that surrounds me, I am still poor. I can own more or less of anything, but if I have the facility to take in the wonder that surrounds me, I am rich.

I experience this magical mystery tour called life.

"Spirituality is the sacred center out of which all life comes, including Mondays and Tuesdays, rainy Saturday afternoons in all their mundane and glorious detail. . . . The spiritual journey is the soul's life commingling with ordinary life."

—Christina Baldwin
Life's Companion (1990)

My Life, My Faith

I WILL STEER MY COURSE by the light of the highest star. Why not? It's not that I intend to reach it or even care. Only that my life has a higher meaning and purpose and it is that very conviction that makes it so. Let others give up, be naysayers, or devalue the experience of living. Not me. My life is a gift and I know it. I will not be beaten. As long as I have faith in my heart and in a higher purpose, I am where I am meant to be. Nothing will shake my faith. Nothing will take it from me. No one gives it to me and no one takes it away. It is mine. It springs from a well in my heart and my heart alone. I know where to find it, I know where to contact it, I know where it lives. I am the embodiment of a higher purpose, and I know it.

I live my life with purpose.

"Who has seen the wind?
 Neither you nor I
 But when the trees bow down their heads
 The wind is passing by."

—CHRISTINA GEORGINA ROSSETTI
"Who Has Seen the Wind?"
The Poetical Works of Christina Georgina Rossetti (1904)

Making a Mess

AN ARTIST WITH A DISHEVELED STUDIO or a writer with a basket full of crumpled paper may feel that chaos is a crucial part of the creative process. In the same way, I am willing to make a mess as part of my creative life-giving process. How can I go from numbness to life, from stagnation to spontaneity, or from boredom to pleasure without passing through a period of confusion and instability? If I choose life rather than the status quo, I will have to search out my own answers. That search can, at times, feel messy and disorganized. If I only play roles and forget to look into my heart and know myself, I am not truly tasting the banquet before me. There is so much about life that I would like to come to know better. I deeply appreciate all that life means, and I wish to allow myself the freedom to explore the world, even when my exploration feels fumbling or less than auspicious. In giving myself space to expand beyond my roles, I am also allowing others to be the benefactors of that space. I give us all room to be.

I am willing to make a mess.

"Everybody knows if you are too careful you're so occupied in being careful that you are sure to stumble over something."

—GERTRUDE STEIN
Everybody's Autobiography (1937)

The Creative Process

CREATIVITY IS AT THE CORE of a happy, meaningful, productive life. It is through our creativity that we bring order and meaning to our world. We use our creativity in how we create our homes, raise our children, build our careers, and continually reinvent a sustaining and joyous relationship. Cultivating creativity is as important to our souls as exercise and good nutrition are to our bodies, and they overlap, they work together.

Researcher Graham Wallas identifies four stages of the creative process. The four stages, adapted by Pierce Howard, author of *The Owner's Manual for the Brain,* are

Preparation: This is the time for research, fact gathering, assembling materials, gathering needed information before the creative act.

Incubation: This is the period of gestation, of letting go so that the mind, the unconscious, intuition, and emotion can mull over the information and put it into its own original perspective. Dreaming may be a part of this period.

Inspiration: This is the "Aha!" when the solution, illumination, or discovery either emerges or forces itself through into a coalesced form.

Evaluation or confirmation: This is the time to ask, Will it work, does it hold up next to other theories, does it logically fit with the original stimulus?

I am a creator.

"To fulfill a dream, to be allowed to sweat over lonely labor, to be given the chance to create, is the meat and potatoes of life. The money is the gravy. As everyone else, I love to dunk my crust in it. But alone it is not a diet to keep body and soul together."

—BETTE DAVIS
The Lonely Life (1962)

Spiritual Laws

ANYTHING I THINK about another person becomes true for me also. The good that I can imagine entering another person's life is the good that I am manifesting in my own, and the same is true of its opposite. What I see as true for another person is what I can see as true for me. Each thought I think about someone else will be thought about me somewhere, someday. The world I live in is governed by natural laws. Just as I cannot defy gravity, I cannot ignore the spiritual laws . . . do unto others as you would have others do unto you. The hate I carry in my heart toward others manifests in my own life, and so does the love, peace, and understanding. I'm not perfect, nor am I meant to be. I am meant only to be a better human with each new thing I learn.

I accept the laws of spirit.

"All the way to heaven is heaven."

—ST. CATHERINE OF SIENA, in Dorothy Day,
By Little and by Little

Stuck

PEOPLE WHO LIVE IN THE FORESTS and mountains of India have an age-old method of catching monkeys. They do not run after the monkeys, and they do not use ropes. Rather they rely on their understanding of a monkey's behavior. They carve pots with necks as long as a monkey's arm and a base large enough for a banana. The monkeys, eager to collect their food, put their arms down the neck of the jar until they have the banana in their tight grasp. Unable to pull it through the narrow neck, they sit holding their treasure, unwilling to release their grip for fear of losing it. Because they cannot give up the banana in their grasp, they remain immobilized, and the villagers simply pick them up. We are all afraid of letting go of what is in our grasp, that is why we become prey to the domination of others, whether that be advertising, other people's will pressed upon us, or mindlessly following the crowd. We take a leap of faith when we "let go," but in that leap of faith we might find our freedom in a variety of small or big ways. I will release what my mind is clinging to and refusing to let go of.

What I hold onto holds onto me.

"All human beings hold to the tools of their own destruction."

—BARBARA GORDON
I'm Dancing as Fast as I Can (1979)

Mental Picturing

TODAY I PICTURE MYSELF whole and happy in my own life. I see myself functioning successfully, moving day-by-day into and toward my own wholeness. I have a right to be me—to become the person that it feels right for me to be. I have a right to inner freedom—to follow my own pulse. How better will I succeed than by being in touch with my own inner wisdom? My best guide through life is the guide that lives within me—the guide that knows me from the inside out. I will trust that my inner wisdom and my inner guide are able to function well on my behalf.

I trust my inner wisdom.

"When I'm trusting and being myself as fully as possible, everything in my life reflects this by falling into place easily, often miraculously."

—SHAKTI GAWAIN
Living in the Light (1986)

Inner Mystery

I HONOR THE MYSTERY WITHIN ME. In my very being I am a part of two worlds, the known and the unknown. I am a passage through which life is expressed on this earth—a tunnel into eternity—a channel. Though I do not know from where it comes, I sense that life passes through me and is nurtured and sustained by my very essence. I am a carrier of life. Within me is coded a primal knowledge of how to live and love. I am in touch with a pulse—a rhythm beyond me. I am connected to something great, and my place on this earth is sacred. All the mystery that lies inside of me is also in others. Life makes no promises; it holds no guarantees. Though my life is real, it also comes to me as if from a dream. The close relationships in my world give life a quiet sense of grandeur. I don't really know how or from where my world manifests, but I am deeply grateful that it's here. I experience the beauty of my life. I treasure the mystery.

I am a part of a grand and beautiful scheme.

"We cannot take a single step toward heaven. It is not in our power to travel in a vertical direction. If, however, we look heavenward for a long time, God comes and takes us up."

—SIMONE WEIL
Waiting for God (1950)

Fostering Creativity

THREE ROLE DYNAMICS ARE CONSIDERED to be part of a creative personality: *the Explorer, the Challenger,* and *the Flexible.* The Explorer is characterized by "high openness," an attitude that recognizes possibilities and potential, that embraces and says "perhaps yes" rather than closes down. The Challenger is intense and not too relaxed. Sometimes the Challenger meditates before creative work. The Flexible is calmer, sees from many sides, and has the ability to adjust to change. Understanding these roles as part of any creative personality helps us to enter that state voluntarily, to create it. So many situations in a woman's life are enhanced by taking a creative approach. Homemaking, raising children, work inside of the home, careers and passions in the outside world all come alive, expand, and gain strength and purpose from applying this awareness.

I am an Explorer, *a* Challenger, *and* Flexible.

"When I can no longer create anything, I'll be done for."
—COCO CHANEL, in Marcel Haedrich, *Coco Chanel* (1972)

Nature's Timing

ANYTHING WORTH DOING is worth doing well. Nothing much happens overnight; and, if it does, it probably only seems that way. Upon closer examination, it is simply that the fruit that has been growing from a seed has finally come to fruition. Everything in nature teaches me this lesson. All things have their own season. If I try to eat an apple before it has had the time to ripen, it's not an apple. If I try to eat sweet corn in early July, I will be frustrated and disappointed with my inedible stalk. I need to learn to wait for the fruit to ripen and then to feast upon it and enjoy it when it appears. Everything has its season and, when I look carefully, each season has a purpose in the overall process that I can understand and appreciate. Even winter has its purpose. It is a time of deep rest and rejuvenation that, eventually, bursts forth in the yearly awakening of spring. I cannot push a tomato to ripen into perfection or lavender toward its burst of sweet aroma anymore than I can speed up many aspects of my life.

I will follow a natural rhythm.

"There is nothing in nature that can't be taken as both mortality and invigoration."

—GRETEL EHRLICH
The Solace of Open Spaces (1985)

Darkness

I EMBRACE THE DARKNESS WITHIN ME. What I deny about myself grows in strength and power. Just as I feared the darkness in my room as a child, today I fear the darkness in the depths of my own being. If I can learn to embrace this part of myself and even love it, I am giving it the opportunity to transform into another state—to change its level of vibration. I will befriend and love that about me which I have designated as unlovable. I can do more to alter my experience of life by loving the unlovable in myself than by finding reasons to keep it in hiding. When I do not run from what I fear within me, others do not frighten me so much. Their dark sides don't trigger my own. The inner strength that I gain from self-knowledge and acceptance allows me to live in an authentic, energized way.

I accept my inner darkness.

"Wonder and despair are two sides of a spinning coin. When you open yourself to one, you open yourself to the other. You discover a capacity for joy that wasn't in you before. Wonder is the promise of restoration; as deeply as you dive, so may you rise."

—CHRISTINA BALDWIN
Life's Companion (1990)

*H*idden *P*arts

IT'S NATURAL TO HIDE PARTS of ourselves that we fear might cast us in a bad light. Ask yourself these questions in your mind, or write about them in your journal:

- What is a part of me that I keep hidden, that I don't want anyone to see?
- What's in the way of this part of me healing; what limiting beliefs surround this part of me?
- If this part of me had a voice, what would it say?
- If this part of me were to heal, what would my life look like?
- Why has this part of me remained unhealed?
- Is there anything I need to give up if I move toward healing this part of myself?

Understanding ourselves gives us a kind of mastery and strength that allows us to be fuller, more alive, and more productive people.

I bring a part of me out of hiding and examine it.

"Hiding leads nowhere except to more hiding."

—MARGARET A. ROBINSON
A Woman and Her Tribe (1990)

ℒearned ℋelplessness

A DYSFUNCTIONAL OR TRAUMATIZING CIRCUMSTANCE may have taught me a debilitating lesson: that nothing I do can make a difference, nothing I do can help. Today I will examine where this learned helplessness might play itself out in my daily life. Do I give up too easily? Am I afraid to even try? Do I assume that, ultimately, all of my efforts will add up to little or end up in disappointment and that, consequently, allowing myself to really want something is pointless? Do I lose faith at the first disappointment or give up as soon as I reach a block in my path? Learned helplessness may indicate that I experienced something painful in my life that overwhelmed me, that was too much for me to cope with at the time. But today is not yesterday. I can do today what might have confounded me earlier in my life.

I will find a way to prevail.

"What am I doing? Nothing. I am letting life rain upon me."
—RAHEL VARNHAGEN (1810), in Hannah Arendt,
Rahel Varnhagen

Envy

WHEN I AM ENVIOUS OF SOMETHING that someone else has, such as money, talent, or success, I will ask myself, "Am I jealous of the object/experience or what I imagine that object/experience could give to me?" If I feel that I must be rich, famous, or successful in order to be entitled to happiness or a self, that happiness and self are somehow lodged in those things, then I will be jealous of anyone who possesses a piece of my "self," my "happiness." I will be making my culture's icons into my inner gods, and I will ever be a slave to them. It is not the possession of these things that will liberate me, but my recognition that my true sense of self and connectedness really comes from within. The relationship that I have with my higher self and the people in my life is what nourishes me today. My bank account can provide me with many important things, but it cannot buy me life or real, mutual love. When I place what I have before who I am, I isolate myself in a well-appointed, stylish jail. I will choose life.

I see beauty in the life I have.

"She wished all the faculties she did not share to be looked on as diseases."

—MADAME DE STAËL
Corinre (1807)

Changing Dynamics

I WILL BE OPEN TODAY to the shifting moods of my relationships with others. Dynamics are always changing; all is always in a state of flux. If I do not like the way that I am perceived by others or the way that I look at them, I will be open to change. My very act of being open creates favorable conditions for movement to take place. The waters beneath interpersonal dynamics are constantly flowing in all directions. When I see them as fixed, I keep myself in static relationships wherein the feelings lack spontaneity and what takes place has a strange sense of dislocation from the rest of my life, both inner and outer. When I am willing to allow the moment to have its voice—to do its work—life takes on a new sense of buoyancy and enjoyment. Situations that used to perplex me seem to work themselves out naturally.

I make an oh-so-subtle shift.

"When you're stuck in a spiral, to change all aspects of the spin you need only to change one thing."

—CHRISTINA BALDWIN
Solo Dancing on a Spiral Quest

Compromises

THINGS WILL NOT ALWAYS go the way that I want them to in relationships. I will need to adjust, to find a balance between giving up enough so that I am fair to others but not so much that I am not fair to myself. Compromise is not a dirty word, and when it is done well, there is great freedom in it for all sides. When I can compromise successfully, it means that I am able to look at both the self and the other with equal value. I am willing to see that another person has the same inner makeup as myself. This makes me feel less alone in the world and more understood, not only because I have extended these things to myself, but also because I have given them to another. The giving and receiving is all the same channel. The understanding I show to another person automatically returns to me from somewhere because that channel is open within me. The on/off switch is always in my own hands.

I open the channel.

"I've a theory that one can always get anything one wants if one is willing to pay the price. And do you know what the price is nine times out of ten? Compromise."

—AGATHA CHRISTIE
The Secret of Chimneys (1925)

*T*hink *H*appy *T*houghts

AN EXPERIMENT WAS CONDUCTED to explore how the thoughts going through the human mind all day affect the immune system. There were two groups in the experiment. Group One watched films of Nazi war crimes; Group Two watched films of Mother Teresa at her selfless work. After the viewing session, Group One showed depressed immunity, Group Two elevated. The effects lasted twenty minutes or so, and then the subjects' immune systems returned to normal. Next, the researchers asked the groups to play the movies over and over again in their minds throughout the day. The subjects in Group One had depressed immune systems *all day*. Group Two had elevated immune systems *all day*. The experiment suggested that what we think goes straight to our bodies. What we think shapes our ability to live healthy lives. What do you want to think about today?

I observe what goes through my mind (and change it for the better).

"Every thought vibrates through the universe."

—DOROTHY M. RICHARDSON
Pilgrimage: Revolving Lights

Enjoying the Process

I WILL LEARN TO ENJOY THE JOURNEY. Once I have set my life goals and created a structure to follow day by day, I will remember to take pleasure in each stage along the path. I understand that my happiness does not lie so much in the achievement of a goal but in the thousand tiny transformations along the way; the stretching, resolving conflicts, mastering small tasks, and daily showing up—meeting myself along the road in my kaleidoscopic variety. The payoff is what a commitment to a goal actualizes in me; the sense of inner awakening, purpose, and direction that it brings to my life. Without goals I can remain superficial—with goals I am called upon to dive deeper and deeper into what appears to be a subject but is truly my own psyche, heart, and will.

I take it a day at a time.

"I don't want to get to the end of my life and be asked what I made of it and have to answer, 'I acted.' I want to be able to say, 'I loved and I was mystified, it was a joy sometimes and I knew grief. And I would like to do it all again.'"

—LIV ULLMAN
Choices (1984)

Receiving

RECEIVING IS ANOTHER KIND OF GIVING. Isn't it actually selfish not to receive, graciously and gratefully, what another person gives me with their heart? It is another kind of vanity, a negation of the other person. Though it may masquerade, perhaps, as modesty, it's not. I need to receive with love what is given with love in order for another person to feel that I recognize them. That they matter. That their contribution is valued and important. When I can't receive, I will wonder what's going on with me; why can't I be touched? I can't enjoy my life if I can't feel it. I can't have mutually satisfying relationships if I cannot experience what another person is bringing to me. I am willing to be touched and in someone else's debt.

I am big enough to be grateful.

"In my belief, a harvest is also a legacy, for very often what you reap is, in the way of small miracles, more than you consciously know you have sown."

—FAITH BALDWIN
Harvest of Hope (1962)

Focus

I WILL BE INTELLIGENT in what I take on. I see people running from thing to thing and I recollect the Turkish proverb, "He became an infidel hesitating between two mosques." Similarly, if I take on too many goals, I am likely to succeed at nothing. I may frustrate myself simply because I have too much on my plate, and I'm not really able to do anything well. I may also deny myself the pleasure of going deep within; of digging into a life's work and developing a passion. Passion is something that grows and enriches as I give my energy, time, care, and attention to a worthwhile endeavor; as I shape it and it shapes me. I understand that faith requires a deep commitment that is the right size for me; that if I worship many gods, I miss the opportunity to delve deep into the God that lives inside of me.

I will dive deep into the healing waters of action.

"One who begins too much accomplishes little."

—GERMAN PROVERB

The Seductress

I AM THE SEDUCTRESS. I use my feminine wiles to draw toward me what I want. I am subtle and appealing. Others fear being ensnared within my orbit, caught in my web. I am confident of my abilities to get what I want, to find what I am looking for somehow, some way. I know the value of waiting for the right moment, of talking gently, of holding back my aggression. I fear both my own strength and the loss of it, my beauty and its waning, my charm and its effect. I see the world as something to be tamed; I want it to please me and meet my needs and desires.

I own that within me which seduces.

"Making love we are all more alike than we are talking or acting."

—MARY MCCARTHY
Characters in Fiction (1961)

*A*wake to *L*ife

IT IS CLOUDS AND INCLEMENT WEATHER that give the sun its meaning. And it's human nature to let the senses become dulled. I will not do this. I'll stay alert with my senses sharpened. I will not drown them in experiences that shut them off. I'll stay awake. I will keep my eyes open. I will listen. And wait. And when I know the moment is right, I will make my move quickly and with decisiveness. Then, if my action is sufficient, I will return to the active quiet of my own being. I will allow the still waters within me to be deep, and I will see through them into clarity. And when they are stirred and unclear, I will have clarity and alertness in reserve to carry me through until they settle.

I dive deep into the waters of life.

"It's only when we truly know and understand that we have a limited time on earth—and that we have no way of knowing when our time is up—that we will begin to live each day to the fullest, as if it was the only one we had."

—ELISABETH KÜBLER-ROSS
in *Parade* (1991)

*A*roma

WHAT WE'VE KNOWN INTUITIVELY is borne out by research. Aromas affect both productivity and helping behaviors, behaviors that are positive or nourishing toward ourselves and others. Bursts of fragrance such as lavender, lily of the valley, jasmine, peppermint, and lemon increase metabolism and alertness. Similarly, pleasant cooking aromas such as baking cookies or perking coffee elicit more helping behaviors. We are constantly interacting with our environment; we are biological beings in a biological world. Scents can calm us, arouse us, or lead to a flood of memories. We can use this knowledge in our own lives, creating pleasant aromas in our world, avoiding scents we don't like, and taking extra pleasure in the smells that are part of our surroundings, part of our day.

I honor my natural side.

"The smell of lilacs crept poignantly into the room like a remembered spring."

—MARGARET MILLER
Vanish in an Instant (1952)

Incubation

SOMETIMES THE LAND IS FALLOW; it does not bring forth. I will not lose faith. I know that seeds take time to germinate and grow—that simply because I cannot see them growing in the silence of the earth does not mean they are not there. They are not dead. Everything takes its own time. I cannot push a pear to grow any faster than nature allows it to, nor can I rush the circumstances of my life. They are alive too, part of an ever-growing universe. Like the pear, they will come forth in their own time. Incubation is as important as any other stage of growth. Without it, things grow halfway, lopsided. I am not looking for a shallow life, one without depth, a life where I move from surface to surface and then wonder why things feel meaningless. I can wait for what is real.

I can balance at the edge of time.

"Toleration is the greatest gift of the mind; it requires the same effort of the brain that it takes to balance one's self on a bicycle."

—HELEN KELLER
The Story of My Life (1902)

The Sister

"By now we know and anticipate one another so easily, so deeply, we unthinkingly finish each other's sentences, and often speak in code. No one else knows what I mean so exquisitely, painfully well; no one else knows so exactly what to say, to fix me."

—JOAN FRANK
"Womb Mates"
Desperate Women Need to Talk to You (1994)

"The desire to be and have a sister is a primitive and profound one that may have everything or nothing to do with the family a woman is born to. It is a desire to know and be known by someone who shares blood and body, history and dreams, common ground and the unknown adventures of the future, darkest secrets and the glassiest beads of truth."

—ELIZABETH FISHEL
Sisters (1979)

"If sisters were free to express how they really feel, parents would hear this: 'Give me all the attention and all the toys and send Rebecca to live with Grandma.'"

—LINDA SUNSHINE
Mom Loves Me Best (And Other Lies You Told Your Sister) (1990)

"More than Santa Claus, your sister knows when you've
been bad or good."

—LINDA SUNSHINE
Mom Loves Me Best (And Other Lies You Told Your Sister) (1990)

"We are each other's reference point at our turning points."

—ELIZABETH FISHEL
Sisters (1979)

Worry

WORRY IS A REAL ENERGY DRAINER. And most of the things that we worry about don't even come to pass. Also, worry can put us into a state of anxiety—we're worried and anxious about a person or situation—mad at ourselves for worrying—mad at the other person for being what we perceive as the reason we're worried, etc., etc., etc. It becomes a vicious cycle. Then we're easily irritated by little things, and we start to irritate those around us. Then we get irritated with ourselves because we're irritating them. They challenge us—we get defensive (After all, isn't our worry just a sign of caring? Don't they understand we're only being concerned people?). Soon, there is a fight—then we worry about the fight. The vicious cycle continues. While worry may help to bind a certain kind of anxiety or to contain it, too much worry breeds it.

I allow myself not to worry today.

"I always feel sorry for people who think more about a rainy day ahead of them than the sunshine today."

—RAE FOLEY
Suffer a Witch (1965)

cAccepting Support

AT SOME TIME IN MY LIFE, if I felt traumatized by something, whether it be test taking, a natural disaster, sickness, or emotional trauma, I may have learned to go it alone, to hunker down and plow through with whatever resources I could muster. While this may have gotten me through a tough situation, it is no way to live; it is a path to burnout. Part of my recovery is to learn how to ask for help, how to lean on someone, how to depend where appropriate, how to break my own isolation. There is a middle ground. There is such a thing as the right amount. I can be interdependent—neither codependent nor a loner. Somewhere in the middle I will find my right level—where I can depend to a normal, comfortable extent while standing on my own and taking appropriate proactive steps.

I can ask for help.

"Secrets of the heart are seldom news."

—JENNIFER STONE
"Beatific Blue"
Over by the Gates (1977)

The Task of the Huntress

As MUCH AS WE MAY have fantasies of being handed a wonderful life on a silver platter, they are, in truth, fantasies. Like it or not, we have to work for our lives. What we don't learn through our own awareness, deconstruct and process with our apparatus, and integrate into our internal world, is never really ours. It doesn't work with and for us because it hasn't been made sense of through our own eyes. It hasn't been assigned meaning as it relates to us, our needs and drives, our hopes and dreams, our sense of who we are and what life is all about for us. We live in our own minds. What is there is what we live in; it provides the filter that sorts through experience and the attitudes that are the engine that drives us through the world. Our own life is our most intimate adventure; no one can live it for us. It is the Huntress in all who looks for life, who yearns, listens, and seeks out a mission and purpose that feels right, that allows us to make our unique contribution to the world. We grow when we contribute in meaningful ways. This is how we stretch our souls. The Huntress is the researcher in all of us. The Huntress is the seeker, tester, and experimenter who looks everywhere until she finds the right fit, her place in the sun.

> "One can never consent to creep when one feels an impulse to soar."
>
> —HELEN KELLER
> *The Story of My Life* (1902)

£earning from £ife

THERE IS MUCH FOR ME TO LEARN from life by quiet observation. When I am patient and open, life unfolds itself and its wisdom to me. When my mind is cluttered with "shoulds" and endless desires, I keep life's beauty from entering my heart. There is no need to strain. All that I gain by strain comes with a price tag. I cannot force others to be different than what they choose to be without bending them out of shape. When I force myself to be someone other than I am, my real self comes back to haunt me. A relationship cannot be real if the two people in it are living a lie. What would be so wrong if we came to our relationships as ourselves and learned from one another? Our differences attract us to one another and create diversity and balance, but still we attempt daily to recreate one another in our own image. I like you the way you are. Why should I work so hard to change you? Where you are different from me, you are interesting. Where I don't like it, I don't like it. Big deal. Whoever said we had to be alike to get along?

I am me and you are you.

"One hardly dares to say that love is the core of the relationship, though love is sought for and created in relationship; love is rather the marvel when it is there, but it is not always there, and to know another and to be known by another—that is everything."

—FLORIDA SCOTT-MAXWELL
Women, and Sometimes Men (1957)

Mindful Moments

IN TODAY'S BUSY WORLD, life speeds by. Our days are often filled with too much activity and too little downtime. We can lose our ability to process, experience, and actually take pleasure from our day. But each day we have many opportunities to pull back and take stock of what's going on around us if we make use of them. Life is a series of moments. It's easy to throw them away and postpone living for weekends, vacations, or "later," but then, when we get there, we've forgotten how. Mindful moments teach us to remember. The magic of the world and life is deep and surrounds us all the time, but we have to stop, look, and listen. We have to remember a mindful moment is just taking a minute to sink into self. Mentally withdraw your attention from whatever is preoccupying you; breathe evenly in and out and take in the life that surrounds you. You will notice things that would otherwise have passed you by. You can take a mindful moment anywhere—at home, at work, on a bus, on a walk, while out doing errands. You may find that we are surrounded by a rich and beautiful world. This wondrous mystery surrounds us at all times, but we get wrapped up in surviving and we forget to live. Today I will pay attention. I will create mindful moments throughout my day so that I can appreciate the beauty that is mine.

There is no time like the present.

"Too many activities, and people, and things. Too many worthy activities, valuable things, and interesting people.
For it is not merely the trivial which clutters our lives but the important as well. We can have a surfeit of treasures—an excess of shells, where one or two would be sufficient."

—ANNE MORROW LINDBERGH
Gift from the Sea (1955)

Positive Self-Identity

LIFE IS CONSTANTLY RENEWING ITSELF and so can we. Whatever has happened to us may not be our fault, but it is our responsibility to get the help necessary to work through past experiences that may be damaging our lives today. Why should we take on a negative self-identity? If everyone who experienced problems or pain gave up on themselves, we would have no presidents, CEOs, senators, writers, actors, and therapists, to name a few. This is our challenge and our responsibility in life—to break our chains of self-defeating thoughts and behaviors and find a better way of living. We work slowly and methodically through the ways in which our painful experiences have affected us. Then, as new insights occur, we integrate a fresh perspective on old events. It is in understanding the events and the meaning we made out of them at the time—and may still be playing out—that we grow through them. "Putting things behind us" all too often includes a willful attempt to lock a part of ourselves in an unresolved period of our personal history. It sounds good, but it doesn't really work. I'm for integration versus amputation.

I will become willing to look at all of me.

"It takes a while to walk on two feet. Each one going the other way."

—DIANNE GLANCY
Iron Woman (1990)

Role-Speaking

"A ROLE IS THE TANGIBLE FORM THE SELF TAKES," according to Jacob Levy Moreno, father of psychodrama, sociometry, and group psychotherapy. In our busy lives, balance among our various roles can be tough to achieve. What variety of forms is your "self" taking these days? Try this: On a piece of paper, list the roles you play (for example, wife, mother, daughter, student, exerciser, worker). Write a journal entry "as" the role (for example, "I'm the student and I feel . . ." or "I'm the socializer and I . . ."). Are there any roles you need to add to your role repertoire in order to feel more complete? (This can be anything from journaler to jogger or doctor or lawyer, if you're feeling ambitious.) Are any areas in need of "role repair"? (For example, "I need to play more" or "I need to exercise or to learn something new" or "I need quality time with myself when I'm not feeling distracted" or "I need to do less of this and more of that.") When you allow your role to speak as itself, what is it saying to you?

I examine the roles that I play.

"It is the sweet, simple things of life which are the real ones after all."

—LAURA INGALLS WILDER
House in the Ozarks (1917)

Balancing Our Roles

EACH OF US CARRIES within us the roles we have learned. People who have well-adjusted lives tend to play a variety of roles, rather than being stuck in a very few. Playing a variety of roles allows for role relief and new stimulation. When we can experience a balance of roles in our lives, moving in and out of them with ease and fluidity, we guard against feeling burned-out, depressed, or sick of living. We can look at our lives from a role perspective and write out our own prescriptions for change or improvement by naming the roles that we play and seeing if they feel in balance. If they do not, there may be some role realignment to do. Are there enjoyable roles we do not give enough time to or roles that we wish to develop that we can add to our list? Do we need to reduce the time we're spending in some roles that aren't serving us well? We can then make a plan for how we might realistically add new roles into our lives in order to bring in more harmony and balance. Through action and interaction, we can affect positive change and growth.

I will live a balanced life.

"It is while trying to get everything straight in my head that I get confused."

—MARY VIRGINIA MICKA
Fiction, Oddly Enough (1990)

My Life Roles

HERE'S A ROLE EXERCISE YOU MIGHT TRY. First, list the roles you play in your life, for example, worker, socializer, daughter, mother, exerciser, grandmother, wife, friend, sister, and artist. Now, draw a big circle and create a pie-like graph of time spent in each role (the relative size of each section representing time spent in each role). Next, rate your level of satisfaction in each role from one to ten: one, not very satisfying; ten, very satisfying. Write your rating in the appropriate part of your graph. Finally, reflect on your life roles. Are you in balance or out of balance? Do you need to re-allot time spent in each role (more time in some, less in others)? Which roles are satisfying and which are not? Can you create more satisfaction in any roles? Seeing your roles lined out on paper can give you perspective on how they play out in your day-to-day life and give you inspiration to change where you may need to.

I analyze the way in which my roles play out.

"Making mental connections is our most crucial learning tool, the essence of human intelligence; to forge links; to go beyond the given; to see patterns, relationships, context."

—MARILYN FERGUSON
The Aquarian Conspiracy (1980)

If I Were an Animal

SIT COMFORTABLY AND IMAGINE the answers to the following questions, or write the answers in your journal. Imagination has many doors into it. We can see parts of ourselves emerge when we take a novel approach to exploring ourselves.

If I were an animal, what would I be? _____.

The qualities in my animal that I most admire are _____.

The drawbacks of being this animal might be _____.

The strengths of my animal are _____.

If this animal could talk, it would say _____.

My animal's favorite activity is _____.

My animal hates to _____.

My animal would like to be seen as _____.

Never call this animal _____.

As your animal, write a journal entry from the animal's point of view. You might write a brief autobiography of your animal life.

I see new sides of myself in metaphor.

"Writing forces consciousness."

—MELODY BEATTIE
The Lessons of Love (1994)

*H*appiness

I CAN AFFECT my happiness "set point." I can pay attention to my resting place for happiness. Where do I go on the inside most regularly? Do I visit a place of doom and gloom, or do I experience a basic sense of well-being and optimism? As I witness my own set point, I come to accept where mine generally rests. As I reflect on my life, does a low set point really benefit me or those around me? Does it change anything for the better? What influences have impacted my happiness set point? How can I work with myself in order to raise this set point a day at a time?

I can allow myself to feel happier.

"People have a 'set point' of happiness which explains why they return to a certain level of happiness even after tragedy.... It can be difficult if you've had difficult parents to feel good about yourself ... but you don't need to live out that script for the rest of your life ... you can change it. Those people who have a belief in something greater than themselves are those who come back much faster from sadness."

—DR. JOYCE BROTHERS
The Today Show, January 4, 2002

Going Home

I GREW UP IN THE COMPANY OF OTHERS, and who I am today was greatly impacted by all who surrounded me. I am a storehouse of my early experiences and the meaning I made out of them. I first learned to see myself in the mirror that those around me held up to me, and the way I was treated influenced the way I treat myself. What was the atmosphere of my home, of my parents' relationship, of my extended family? What was my role, and how did I experience myself within this system? What strengths did I inherit or develop, and what weaknesses? I can begin today to shape my own destiny both through the choices I make and through my fearless and humble inventory of self. I do not wish to live in the past, but I will examine it in order to better understand my present, knowing that my past is a part of who I am today.

I am willing to time-travel psychologically and emotionally.

"I was convinced you can't go home again. Now I know better. Nothing is more untrue. I know you can go back over and over again, seeking the self you left behind."

—HELEN BEVINGTON
The House Was Quiet and the World Was Calm (1971)

My Life Is My Responsibility

I WILL SEARCH FOR MY LIFE, my love, my meaning, and my purpose here on earth. I am not waiting for someone else to hand me a life. I will find it myself. I know it is out there waiting for me to contact it, just as I know that all things wait for me. I will do all that is necessary and more to prepare and ready myself. I will give more than 100 percent. When I take my life into my own hands and accept fully my responsibility to actualize it, a few things happen. I kick into gear and mobilize my own strength and talents, others recognize my effort and don't resent lending a helping hand, and I am carried along by unseen hands. Doors open, coincidences lead to an open path, and the waters part to allow me to pass.

I create my own opportunity.

"I was thinking of my patients and how the worst moment for them was when they discovered they were masters of their own fate. It was not a matter of bad or good luck. When they could no longer blame fate, they were in despair."

—ANAÍS NIN (1935)
The Diary of Anaís Nin, Vol. 2 (1967)

Giving Over to Passion

WE NEED TO CONNECT, or we'll find dysfunctional things to connect to. We need to connect with other people, and we need to connect with a personal passion that is bigger than us and reminds us that we're not alone. Something that allows us to make our own unique contributions to the world in which we live. Something that needs our souls. This is a way to self-actualize and to promote learning and personal growth that is good for us and the world in which we live. I will lose myself in my passion, allowing my spirit to widen, deepen, be tested, fall apart, and come back together again. I will give over. Surrender. Release and let go. I will trust the process and have faith in what I cannot see. I am entering new territory for me, opening up parts of myself that have never seen the light of day. The journey can feel both exhilarating and terrifying, rocky and smooth as silk. Now that I have allowed myself to think, to hope and dream, to set a goal, I will dive in and allow the surf, tides, and undertow to carry me as I swim toward my tomorrow.

I lose myself to find myself.

"Nothing contributes so much to tranquilize the mind as a steady purpose—a point on which the soul may fix its intellectual eye."

—MARY SHELLEY
Frankenstein (1818)

*P*remature *I*ndependence

I WILL NOT FORCE MYSELF into premature independence, the kind that is born out of fear of needing, fear of vulnerability. I have seen others declare their independence with such rigidity that it precludes any natural dependence. Then they live that life of alienation that masquerades as independence. I will not be that big a fool. I will listen to the feminine side of myself—my woman's wisdom—and allow it to lead me. My woman's wisdom tells me that a wise person can allow herself to need people, and she continues to expand her role repertoire throughout her life. To add rather than subtract. Interdependency is different from codependency. Depending on people and allowing them to depend on me is part of living, natural and appropriate. I have room in my heart for many people—people I don't even know yet—grandchildren, in-laws, and new friends. I have so much to look forward to.

I can have the strength for both independence and dependence.

"Nobody ever was—or ever again will be—as green as the day I landed in New York. That shade has been discontinued."

—CAROLYN KENMORE
Mannequin (1969)

Turning *It* Over

PSYCHOLOGIST CARL JUNG said that we don't necessarily solve all our problems—we just go to a mountaintop from where we can see them differently.

Let's try this simple relaxation/visualization. Sometimes going within, relaxing, and seeing something differently is enough to free ourselves from the grip of a problem that's bothering us.

Close your eyes. Sit comfortably in your chair. Lift your spine out of your waist. Lift your neck out of your shoulders. Lift your waist out of your hips and allow your legs to rest comfortably and in a relaxed position. Breathe in and out easily and completely without a pause between inhalation and exhalation and relax. Breathe in peace and serenity and exhale tension and negativity. Whatever is bothering you, depressing you, nagging at the corners of your mind . . . simply allow it to be . . . let it be. Give it space. Witness it without getting involved in it. Breathe in and out easily and completely without a pause between inhalation and exhalation and relax. I have a body but I am not only a body. I have a mind but I am not only a mind. I have thoughts and feelings but I am not only my thoughts and feelings. I am connected to all that is infinite, all that is eternal. I have a problem but I am not only my problem. I'm breathing in and out easily and completely without a pause between inhalation and exhalation and I am letting myself let go of whatever is preoccupying me, whatever feels unsolvable. I am going to a mountaintop inside my mind, and I am letting my problem just be. I am creating space between me and it. I am loosening my psychic grip so that I can see differently. I breathe in and out easily and completely as I release. I am aware of the pocket of peace within me, and I breathe into it and let it grow. Slowly I move my hands and my feet as I bring my attention back into the room. I open my eyes and see the same landscape through different eyes.

Enlightenment

Is it possible to be in this world but not of it? We are constantly surrounded by life. It is how we see it that makes the difference in whether we experience it as heaven or hell. There is a Zen saying, "Before enlightenment, till the soil and carry the water. After enlightenment, till the soil and carry the water." It's not the outer world but the inner world that changes with enlightenment. Enlightenment is a profound inner shift, a change in the way we see life, the world, and ourselves. We each have a reservoir of calm, wisdom, and insight within us. When we take the time on a daily basis to be with ourselves on that level, we expand our reservoir. Even if we only have a few minutes to set aside for quiet contemplation, the dailyness of the habit will reap rewards.

I dip within myself for sustenance on a daily basis.

"The world stands out on either side
  No wider than the heart is wide."

—Edna St. Vincent Millay
"Renaissance" (1917)

The Warrior
Confronting the Shadow

When danger knocks or the quivering hand of fear grabs for our throats or casts its shadow across our hearts, nature comes to the rescue. We are flooded with body chemicals that drive us to gather our young and band together with other women for safety or security. A groundbreaking research study at UCLA reveals that women, when under intense stress, produce oxytocin, which buffers the rush of adrenaline that is associated with the fight or flight response. In other words, we are like any other mother of any other species. And the more we touch and tend, the more oxytocin we produce, the more on task we become. Nature meant for us to respond to danger with an urge to protect. Integrating our aggressive and our protective instincts is a difficult dance. We are challenged to own our dark side so that it does not play itself out in the heart space of our little loved ones, so that our nurturing instincts are not colored or stuck in overdrive because of demons from within. Our fears, our angers and resentments, our unrequited loves, our traumas and dramas need to be accepted and faced and worked with so they come into our conscious control where they can serve us rather than we serving them. We accept, process, and integrate the shadow, knowing that its combustion and creativity will help to drive our engines in a uniquely feminine way.

—Tian Dayton
"Connect and Nurture When Stressed"
from *Making Peace with the Past to Live in the Present*

The Warrior

I AM THE WARRIOR. I marshal my strength. I channel my aggression. I seize my ground and hold it, protecting what is mine. I meet challenges head on. I stand and am counted. I am on equal ground with anyone. And I keep going. I live with and face my fear and work with it whenever it gets in my way. Understanding my rage, I use it to motivate me and give me power rather than destroy me. I empower myself to make my mark in this world, to go after what is mine and assign my borders. I do not retreat from my own strength nor do I aggress without reason. I strategize. I understand the ways of the world, and I neither resent nor resist them. I work with them with cunning and strength. I eat well, I sleep well, I take care of my body so that it will serve me and be at its best. I strengthen my mind through reading and meditation and seek learning so that I can think clearly. I am the Warrior.

I am at the ready.

"My passions were all gathered together like fingers that made a fist. Drive is considered aggression today; I knew it then as purpose."

—BETTE DAVIS
The Lonely Life (1962)

My Work

I AM WHOLE AND INTACT and as such I have a positive contribution to make now and in the future. My work needs me. Whatever my gifts are, I will cultivate and share them. I will not hold back, telling myself I am not ready, not smart enough, not good enough. Today is the day. This is as good a place to begin as any. I will dig deep into myself and find beauty and wisdom. I will produce good works and I will share them openly with others. As I expand my own consciousness, it becomes my responsibility to share what I learn with the collective. I am available to find my mission.

I will share my gifts.

"If not now, when?
If not me, who?
If not here, where?"

—ANONYMOUS

I Am Strong

I WILL SURVIVE. I will do more than that; I will survive and thrive. I will meet my tigers in the night with strength and confidence and give myself support from within to rise to the occasion. I have no intention of shrinking from the challenges that face me. Though I am fully aware of my fears and insecurities, I will not live in them. This hour is upon me, and I know that I have what it takes to move into it with serenity. Rising to a challenge is a process. It involves a combination of qualities. I am in tune with what is going on in my inner world and processing it so that it doesn't build up and explode on me. And I am preparing and doing what needs to be done in a reasoned, forthright manner.

I draw on an invisible source of strength.

"A woman is like a tea bag—only in hot water do you realize how strong she is."

—NANCY REAGAN
in *The Observer* (1981)

*C*haracter

PEOPLE THINK IT IS NATIVE INTELLIGENCE or talent that deter-
mines success in the end, but I think this is not so. It is strength
of character. What is character? Character is not just who we are
but who we decide to be. How sincere are we about maintaining
personal standards of honor, integrity, and compassion? It is a
delicate balance between discipline and release. Life is what we
make it, what we are willing to invest and invent, and who we
think and feel we are capable of being. But the bottom line is
character. A good life will not spring up and sustain itself from a
bad character. The infrastructure and drive will not be there to
hold it up. At the core of character is heart.

I will use my life to build character.

"It is not in the still calm of life, or the repose of a specific
station, that great characters are formed. . . . The habits of
a vigorous mind are formed in contending with difficulties.
All history will convince you of this, and that wisdom and
penetration are the fruit of experience, not the lessons of
retirement and leisure. Great necessities call out great
virtues."

—ABIGAIL ADAMS
Letter to her son John Quincy Adams (1780)

Channeling Pain for Good

I WILL TURN THE TRIALS of my life into fuel for motivation. The situations in my life that have hurt me can also inspire me. Some of the world's most successful people had to overcome something and in doing so they became deeper, better, wiser people. I can turn problems into riddles to solve and stepping-stones toward a higher place. I WILL NOT give up. What is life if not a challenge to meet, an adventure to live? I'm not going to sit around and wait for someone to give me an identity and a purpose. I want my own. One that suits me. One that I have built carefully and intelligently and that is tailored to me and only me. I am an original and part of what makes me me is what I have overcome—the tigers in the night I have met and struggled with, the battles I have fought in the privacy of my own heart.

My pain transforms and inspires me.

"Pain heightens every sense. More powerfully than any drug, it intensifies colors, sounds, sight, feelings. Pain is like a glass wall. It is impossible to climb it, but you must and, somehow, you do. Then there is an explosion of brilliance and the world is more apparent in its complexity and beauty."

—SUZANNE MASSIE, in Robert and Suzanne Massie, *Journey* (1975)

*F*ear

I CAN FACE MY FEAR. When fear rises up inside of me and grips me by the throat, I can work with it. I can do the inner work I need to do to get past my feelings of anxiety and panic. I can ask for help. I use my excitement for life to get through fear. I talk to myself in comforting ways. I find a friend to share it with or take some quiet time just for myself so I can get centered. Fear is part of my journey, and I accept that. It's natural. If I am to meet the challenge of living my own life, how can I avoid fear? Fear is also here to warn me if I am getting in above my head; to tell me to take another look. If I befriend my fear rather than run from it, I can learn to work with it in my life.

Fear can be my friend.

"I have not ceased being fearful, but I have ceased to let fear control me. I have accepted fear as a part of life, specifically the fear of change, the fear of the unknown, and I have gone ahead despite the pounding in the heart that says: turn back, turn back, you'll die if you venture too far."

—ERICA JONG
The Writer and Her Work (1980)

*L*ooking *I*nside

I WILL DIVE DOWN DEEP WITHIN MYSELF. In the quiet of the moment, I will let my mind wander and come to a restful place. Whatever helps me do this I will do. I will cultivate the quiet within me from where I draw strength. I can nourish myself if I take the time to sink into quiet and meditation. There is a secret world within me—a world to get to know, to explore, and to be in. This is the world that is mine and only mine but that paradoxically connects me with all that is infinite and divine. Through this inner world I connect with the spirit that dwells within me and around me. All that I need to arm myself for my journey through life begins here.

I dwell within.

"Being solitary is being alone well: being alone luxuriously is being immersed in doings of your own choice, aware of the fullness of your own presence rather than of the absence of others."

—ALICE KOLLER
The Station of Solitude (1990)

*A*ggression

AGGRESSION DOESN'T HAVE TO BE A DIRTY WORD in my vocabulary. It's okay for a woman to feel aggressive or to act aggressively. It doesn't mean I'm a bitch, someone no man would ever want, or cold and heartless. Why can't I be aggressive? When I deny my natural aggression, it leaks out in damaging ways. When I accept my natural aggression, I can channel it constructively; I can use it to further, rather than destroy, a situation. If I can accept that aggression is a natural part of my being, I can better work with it and allow it to come out in both moderate and powerful ways. I need my aggression so that I can operate and move forward when that is what is called for in this world.

I have my own, natural share of aggression.

"Historically, it appears that society has capitalized on what is at most a degree of difference between the sexes in order to institutionalize the polarization of aggression."

—FREDA ADLER
Sisters in Crime (1975)

*I*dealization

SOMETIMES PEOPLE WHOM WE IDEALIZE suddenly become simply human in our eyes and we then become angry at them. We want them to be perfect so that we can feel perfect in their presence—so that we don't have to experience our own fear and vulnerability. We may secretly harbor the wish that they will somehow enhance us and make us better than we feel we are. The more we assign qualities of perfection to someone, or need someone to be perfect in order to feel safe, the more we set them and ourselves up for disappointments. We set them up in a perfect-parent fantasy with ourselves as the child. We regress into a dependent state, and their actions become huge. Then, when they inevitably disappoint us, we're enraged—how dare they not be what we need and wish them to be to mend our own insides?

I will recognize the difference between respect and admiration versus idealization.

"Try not to have idols: they are interchangeable and lead to a wantonness that is easily mistaken for love."

—HILDEGARD KNEF
The Verdict (1975)

Anger in Its Various Forms

WHAT IS ANGER? A feeling that I am rarely comfortable with. One that is not often well modulated within me. A body sensation that can shoot through my limbs or ball up and tighten itself somewhere in my body. Sometimes I experience anger as a psychic traffic jam, a mental gridlock. Other times, anger is in the driver's seat, and I am following it on a wild goose chase. Still again, I can cower in fear underneath my own anger, beating myself up for having those feelings. Underneath anger is often hurt. Anger becomes the reaction to another more primary feeling that gets ignored. Like any infection that goes untreated, it festers and spreads. The more buried the hurt is, the more it goes unidentified. Then the anger takes over as the only feeling that gets spoken and nothing really gets resolved because only one feeling is being talked about. Anger rarely rides alone; it is usually among a collection of feelings. When we focus only on anger, a situation can so easily turn into a blame match, where words become blown up into exaggerated meaning. Anger fuels too much, and other feelings that would help to balance the situation go unexplored.

I will explore the feelings that are connected to my anger.

"Anger is a signal, and one that is worth listening to."

—HARRIET LERNER
The Dance of Anger (1985)

"The human heart does not stay away too long from that which hurts it most. There is a return journey to anguish that few of us are released from making."

—LILLIAN SMITH

*C*utting Off

WHEN I AM ANGRY, I will seek a solution rather than act out by disappearing, withdrawing, or cutting off. What will this accomplish, other than prolonging the pain? Cutting off is a relationship dynamic. When there is pain, the solution is seen as withdrawing or avoiding all contact. This sort of strategy passes through generations. The mother who cuts off the daughter teaches the daughter that this is the way to deal with emotional pain. Years of being shut out create a barrier of defense in the daughter that she carries into her relationships with her spouse and children. And so it goes. . . . Cutting people off and refusing communication cause great pain to both sides and actually cut off any possibility for resolution. It is not the same thing as wisely calming down and getting some emotional distance. It is an act of passive aggression. Cutting off is a temporary gratification, an acting out of a jumbled mass of feelings such as fear, hurt, and rage, and a wish to hurt another. But it only leads to more alienation and hurt.

I will explore and understand the emotions I'm going through rather than act them out in ways that perpetuate pain.

"The devil-ache of loneliness seldom deserts the bones of the angry."

—LUCY FREEMAN
Before I Kill More (1955)

Calming Down

SOMETIMES WHEN I AM ANGRY at someone, I lose sight of all feelings except my anger. I forget that this is a person I generally like. All I can feel is anger. I completely lose touch with all the other more benign feelings I have toward the person the rest of the time. Anger is blind. When I am lost in it, I can't see. Sometimes I think this kind of anger has a component of fear in it—fear that I won't get my point across, fear I will be blamed for something. When I can't get past my anger and fear, communication stops. At these times I will allow myself to calm down inside before I try to negotiate anything. I will take a deep breath and let myself feel my fear. Fear is natural; all people and animals experience it. When I allow myself to feel it, I am less controlled by it, and my awareness of the various components in the situation expands.

I give myself time to get calm.

"Beware of anger. It is the most difficult to remove of all the hindrances. But it is the alcohol of the body, you know, and the devil of it is that it deadens the perceptions."

—MARGERY ALLINGHAM
The Tiger in the Smoke (1952)

Emotion and Passion

EXCESS EMOTION IS NOT PASSION. Though passion can sometimes seem emotional, it is a deeper, more steadfast internal operation. Passion needs to be sustained with right action and well-considered thought. If I want to have a passion in life that will serve me and others over the long term, I need to let my emotions inform it rather than rule it. Emotions can serve as a source of information that allow me to know how I am affected by my life relationships and circumstances. When I am able to calmly witness emotions within my mind, they have a lot to teach me. When I get welded to them and act them out with no reflection, I am constantly at their mercy. I deprive myself of the insight they provide. Finding a life's passion isn't only finding emotion. It's finding what nourishes me, what I connect to and love, something that suits who I am and not who I think I should be ... something that touches me at a deep level. It is identifying an area in which I can make a contribution that also contributes to my sense of well-being.

I will devote time and energy to something I feel passionate about.

"We must have a passion in life."

—GEORGE SAND, in Raphael Ledos de Beautfort,
Letters from George Sand (1831)

"Passion is what the sun feels for the earth
  when Harvests ripen into golden birth."

—ELLA WHEELER WILCOX
"The Difference"
Poems of Pleasure (1888)

Trauma

TRAUMA IS A RUPTURE in a relationship bond, the result of which is a loss of trust and faith. The emotional and psychological symptoms created by trauma can inhibit our ability to construct and maintain healthy, mutually supportive relationships with others. Since, as women, we are relational beings by nature, the loss of the connections that engender good feelings about ourselves may undermine our inner stability, self-image, or ability to access and constructively use support. This, in turn, can impact our ability to be effective in life. Unresolved emotional and psychological pain often complicates our finding and sustaining satisfying, mutual, authentic relationships. Recovering from past trauma-related issues is important in order to have a present that is not undermined by unresolved pain from previous relationships.

I will face the full contents of my inner world.

"Underground issues from one relationship or context invariably fuel our fires in another."

—HARRIET LERNER
The Dance of Anger (1985)

Exploration of Relationship Connections

ASK YOURSELF THE FOLLOWING QUESTIONS. You may wish to write out your answers on a sheet of paper or in your journal. Remember, relationships are living, breathing things. We can affect how we live in our network of relationships and adjust our position, or how we see ourselves in our position, if we need to.

1. What is your network of support?
2. Where are your strong feelings of connection?
3. Where do your relationships disconnect?
4. How do you feel about your own place within your family system? Within your network of social relationships?
5. What needs to change about the way you experience yourself within your system?
6. What changes can you make in your network of relationships that might improve your sense of connection?
7. What does not need to change?

I examine the state of my relationships.

"If one is out of touch with one's self, then one cannot touch others."

—ANNE MORROW LINDBERGH
Gift from the Sea (1955)

*B*eing in the *M*oment

We HAVE COME TO VALUE TOO MUCH ACTIVITY. We have too little downtime. Then, when we get anxious, we see the solution as *doing* something else. We are afraid just to *be*. Empty spaces on our calendar make us feel unpopular or out of it. *But our bodies and our minds need rest.* We need high downtime to counterbalance high activity. Some of our anxiety may be because we have worked ourselves into a frenzy of constant activity without giving ourselves needed relaxation. If we want to sustain active, successful lives, we need to learn how to give ourselves rest. Maybe we can best understand what "being in the moment" is by understanding what it isn't. It isn't being preoccupied with racing thoughts to such an extent that we're not able to bring our unpreoccupied attention to what's going on in the moment. It isn't glancing around the room and only half-listening to the person we're with or using more of our mental and emotional energy on wondering what's going to happen in an hour than on what's going on right around us *now*.

I use the moment I'm in right now to practice being present.

"Maybe the tragedy of the human race was that we had forgotten we were each Divine."

—SHIRLEY MACLAINE
Out on a Limb (1983)

The Laws of Abundance

I BELIEVE IN AN ABUNDANT UNIVERSE, one that is in a continual state of creation, one that brings forth. I allow that abundance to be in my life. I can create success, wealth, a feeling of well-being. Quietly in my mind's eye I picture my life as I would like it to be and I release it. Over and over again in my mind's eye I actively visualize circumstances in my life that I wish for—however small or large the vision. I see it as if it is happening *right now*. I taste it, smell it, participate in it, and allow it to be mine. I realize that if I really am serious about creating abundance I do not hop from vision to vision but stay with a chosen few and take time to envision them over and over again over time. Then I look for the opportunities life presents me to actualize my visions, and I do the necessary work.

I create abundance in my own life.

"Abundance is, in large part, an attitude."

—SUE PATTON THOELE
The Woman's Book of Confidence (1992)

Witnessing and Being

I FEEL INSECURE—a strange mixture of fear and excitement, apprehension and self-confidence. I'm insecure about what I *can* do, while at the same time I feel I can do anything. I'm afraid of failure and success. Sometimes the world looks easy to understand and decode, and other times it's an intimidating mystery. I feel I have already lived so much. I have so many memories and experiences, but sometimes I still feel like an innocent. It takes a lot of my strength to sit with these ups and downs. Today I will try surrendering to the subtle changes of my inner world. I am taking on the challenge of making more out of my life—it's natural to feel all over the place sometimes. I have my life ahead of me. I will learn to ride the waves of my inner world without worrying about each and every change in temperature. I can ride and steer my course with strength and intelligence. I will take the right actions and let go of the results.

I witness my own internal process without manipulation or control.

"It is in our idleness, in our dreams, that the submerged truth sometimes comes to the top."

—VIRGINIA WOOLF
A Room of One's Own (1929)

The Bitch

I AM THE BITCH, relentless, harsh, and mean. I speak before I think and don't worry whom I hurt. I gossip and sow seeds of discord. I argue. I am unable to contain my negativity; it spills out all around me; it looks for relief and expulsion. I externalize and project feelings from inside me that are too painful to feel. I relieve myself of my difficult emotions at the expense of others. When I am feeling emotions that are painful to hold, I don't reflect on them; I don't sit with them and sort them through. I make them about someone or something else. I blame. I dump. I hate. I lead with my anger and rage.

I explode and look for a culprit.

"As chairperson, a biased ego recognizes only certain favored committee members. It silences others who express needs, feelings or viewpoints that it considers unacceptable by calling out of order. . . . Meanwhile, the perspective and priorities of out-of-favor goddesses are suppressed or repressed. They may be mute or may not even appear to be present on the committee. Instead, their influence is felt 'outside the committee room'—or outside consciousness. Actions, psychosomatic symptoms and moods may be expressions of these censored goddesses."

—JEAN SHINODA BOLEN
Goddesses in Everywoman (1984)

My Inner *Darkness*

MY DARKNESS IS WHERE MY TRUTH LIES. Mining its depths will set me free and release my power. If I deny my darkness, my shadow, I am pulled down into its treacherous undertow. If I ignore it or pretend it isn't there, my darkness summons me and finds its way into my life in a million small ways. It will not be denied. It will push on me from inside until it or I burst. It holds my spirit. Only by delving into it with courage and faith can I master its contents and release my own spirit from what ensnares it. Only through recognizing my own face in its shadowy depths will my inner world make sense to me.

I have the courage to face my own darkness.

"The heroine's journey is an individual quest. Traveling this path, the heroine may find, lose and rediscover what has meaning to her, until she holds onto these values in all kinds of circumstances that test her. She may repeatedly encounter whatever threatens to overcome her, until finally the danger of losing her selfhood is over."

—JEAN SHINODA BOLEN
Goddesses in Everywoman (1984)

Handling Loss

How I HANDLE LOSS in my life will go a long way in defining who I am and who I will become. Loss is a necessary part of life if I am to live in this human skin. Nothing lasts forever; all things change. It is what I do with this truth of my daily life and my deeper existence that matters. I will be the wise woman when I cope with life losses, allowing myself to pass through the stages of grief that are a natural part of significant separations from those I care about through moving, relationship fissures, divorce, or death. I can grieve for internal losses or parts of myself or periods of my life that feel lost to me. Maybe a job that I loved or needed or never attained is one of my losses. In any case, I will face the feelings surrounding the loss rather than run from them.

I accept the necessary losses that are a part of my life.

"When we think of loss we think of the loss, through death, of people we love. But loss is a far more encompassing theme in our life. For we lose not only through death, but also by leaving and being left, by changing and letting go and moving on. And our losses include not only our separations and departures from those we love, but our conscious and unconscious losses of romantic dreams, impossible expectations, illusions of freedom and power, illusions of safety—and the loss of our own younger self, the self that thought it always would be unwrinkled and invulnerable and immortal."

—JUDITH VIORST
Necessary Losses (1980)

Coping with Grief

WE CAN FEEL GRIEF over a variety of situations: job loss, a breakup, moving, losing a loved one to death or divorce, or early childhood wounds that surface later in life. Sometimes grief can overwhelm us; other times it can make us feel as if we are visitors in our own lives, going through the motions but not really there. According to British psychoanalyst John Bowlby, grief from loss can have four stages: (1) Numbness; (2) Yearning and Searching; (3) Disorganization, Anger, Despair; and (4) Reorganization. We all go through these stages in our own way, sometimes more than once, maybe leapfrogging some phases and lingering long in others. Where are you in these stages? What do we need in the way of support or help to usher us through? How can we bring that support toward ourselves? Remember, successfully working through grief issues will free us to get on with our lives. If we don't attend to them, they can turn into depression, anger, chronic guilt, or emotional numbness. Then these unresolved feelings leak into the rest of our lives, keeping us from living fully. Though it may hurt to process our grief, in the long run we'll be better off. And it clears the way for more peaceful feelings.

I face issues of loss and grief in my life.

"Let the crying stop when grief is fully expressed."

—CHINESE PROVERB

Falling into Negativity

I AM DETERMINED to have all I can in my life today. Negativity is all around and the temptation to fall into it is sometimes more than I can resist. Living up to negative ideals can be easier than living up to positive ones. Conducting myself with care and wisdom requires a discipline that I am not always able to come up with. It is not easy to make room for my real feelings without allowing them to overwhelm me on the inside or make me want to act them out in destructive ways. Thinking that I must surpass the circumstances in life that I grew up with or feeling inferior to them are traps that I can fall into. It takes courage and creativity to tailor my life to me. Some days accepting myself as I am, and others as they are, can seem almost too difficult. It requires that I sit with my own anxiety and fear rather than project these feelings onto others in the form of inhuman expectations or undeserved anger. Negativity is like a siren that calls to me to follow it. Today I will recognize that negativity only leads to more negativity.

I see my negativity for what it is.

pro jec' tion:
4. in psychiatry, the unconscious act or process of ascribing to others one's own ideas or impulses, especially when such ideas or impulses are considered undesirable.

—*Webster's Dictionary*

Regret

IF I HAVE DONE SOMETHING truly hurtful to someone, I will not run away from the pain and guilt I feel. Feeling those feelings is really the only way to clean them out of my system. When I will not allow myself to experience my regret fully, I set up a cycle in which I have to hurt someone else or myself as a way of getting rid of the feeling when it arises within me. I will also allow others the space to feel their own regret when they behave unkindly toward me. Often when others hurt me I react with anger, and I hide my hurt feelings. When that is all I let them see of me, we both focus on my anger and get lost in it. I don't get the understanding and comfort I need, and I provide fuel for focusing on my behavior only. I will stay with my real feelings when I am hurt so that others will have time and space to see the error of their own ways.

I allow the truth of my responses to reveal themselves to me and others. I see my side.

"Whenever you start measuring somebody, measure him right, child, measure him right. Make sure you have taken into account what hills and valleys he came through before he got to wherever he is."

—LORRAINE HANSBERRY

Holding onto Resentment

I RECOGNIZE THAT HANGING onto anger and resentment harms only me. Though I have a fantasy that it is somehow a way of getting back at another person, I see that this is not really the case. In fact, I have no control over another person's response. The only person's response I can control is my own. Angry, resentful thoughts and feelings, even if they are justified, have a powerful impact on my body and my mind. It is one thing to allow myself to experience my anger—to know that I am angry and not deny it. That's healthy. That's part of healing and staying honest and present with myself. It's quite another to nurse a grudge and keep resentment alive over and over again. Denying my anger means I hang onto it unconsciously. Fomenting angry thoughts leads to living in anger. I will find a way to face and work through resentment so that it does not turn my own insides sour.

I allow my anger to dissipate.

"If you're going to hang onto resentment, you'd better dig two graves."

—CHINESE PROVERB

*H*istory

WHEN I WAS YOUNG, I grew up in the environment of my family relationships. I imprinted what I saw at a very young and deep level. What I imprinted remains stored in my brain as my own personal "how-to" archive on relationship behavior. I was taught by example to handle situations from family meals to money to in-laws. What came easily to my parents often comes easily to me, and what was difficult for them can be difficult for me as well. I will ask myself when I have problems with intimacy if I am living in the present or acting out what I learned from my family of origin. Am I repeating what I experienced as a child whether or not it is appropriate now? If the answer is yes, I have some work to do. I will survey from where I stand. My circumstances are vastly different from those of my childhood. When I mindlessly repeat old behaviors, I am not living in the here and now of my life. Consequently, my actions may lack appropriateness for my current circumstances.

I learn from my history.

"From the moment of his birth the customs into which [an individual] is born shape his experience and behavior. By the time he can talk, he is the little creature of his culture."
—RUTH FULTON BENEDICT

My Own Life

I NEED TO MAKE MEANINGFUL, nurturing connections all around me with the people in my life, with a passion, and with my Higher Power. When I limit my source of potentially meaningful experiences to what is known, I deny new possibilities from entering my world. I can become pessimistic in my outlook on life if I reduce my scope of vision to the few objects and people closest to me. I hem myself in without knowing it. I need to seek a balance between overdependency and an inability to need or depend on others. My overdependency on people, places, and things can actually lessen my feeling of safety because I constantly fear losing them. But dependency is not a dirty word; it's part of what makes my life worth living. Healthy, comfortable interdependency is a gift in life. But I need to fit myself in, too, to depend on me while I am looking to others. To take in love from others and let it feel good and sustaining and to give love back. I need to have a secure relationship with myself. I will seek to anchor myself within. I will trust life to continually be there for me.

I am open to new ways of seeing and thinking.

"Freedom means choosing your burdens."

—HEPHZIBAH MENUHIN

Keeping Myself

IF I AM TO FEEL GOOD about my life, I need to see it as my own. Too often I give myself away to whoever will have me. When I give my own life away, I want another in return to fill the void. If I find myself excessively preoccupied with another person— even living in their skin—I will ask myself what parts of me I have given away. How much of my autonomy have I turned over to another person without even being asked? I take each day into my own hands and enter into it with full ownership and energy. This is my day to co-create with a Higher Power—to live, engineer, and appreciate. I am responsible for my day.

I take action on my own behalf.

"I do not want to die . . . until I have faithfully made the most of my talent and cultivated the seed that was placed in me until the last small twig has grown."

—KÄTHE KOLLWITZ (1915)
The Diaries and Letters of Käthe Kollwitz (1955)

Need

NEEDING CAN BE SCARY. I can lose what I love, get hurt, or be left wounded. But if I can't risk needing, I can't get truly intimate with myself or another person. If I've had painful experiences with needing, I might have learned some negative lessons. Ouch. Needing hurts. And needing from people who sometimes gave too little and other times gave way too much may have made me feel crazy in heart and mind. Eventually, I reasoned that needing anything was not such a good idea. When I feel too vulnerable or dependent, I am uncomfortable. It's tough to be intimate, however, without sometimes feeling vulnerable and dependent. I need to rebuild my inner world so it is strong enough to risk needing another person. I will feel solid enough within myself to weather disillusionment and disappointment without falling apart.

I can survive my own needy feelings.

"God forgives those who invent what they need."

—LILLIAN HELLMAN
The Little Foxes (1939)

Journaling Powerful Feelings

MOST OF US HAVE TROUBLE knowing what to do with our "negative" feelings. Sometimes we act them out in irrational ways. Or we hide negative feelings from ourselves, burying or denying them, but they still live inside us. Burying feelings gives them a real power over us because they never get processed. Instead, they pop "out" in funny ways like criticism, control, passive aggression, or constant complaining. Or they pop "in" and make us depressed, our muscles tight or sore, our stomachs churn, or our backs ache. Next time you have anger, hurt, jealousy, or whatever emotion that you don't know what to do with, try this: Journal "as" that feeling. For example: "I am Jean's anger and I live in . . ." or "I am Anna's jealousy and I feel furious when . . ." or "I am Maria's hurt and I am rising up like yeast. . . ." You might find relief, compassion for yourself, and an honest perspective of your situation.

I will pick up my pen and put it to the page.

"I write entirely to find out what I'm thinking, what I'm looking at, what I see and what it means. What I want and what I fear."

—JOAN DIDION, in Janet Sternburg, *The Writer on Her Work,* Vol. 1 (1980)

Emotion Map

MAKING AN EMOTION MAP can help you deal with an uncomfortable emotion or situation. Make a diagram like the one below in your journal or on a sheet of paper. In the center of the circle, write a word or two describing a current situation or an emotion that you're having trouble with. Next, on the jutting lines, write any associations you have that come to mind—any thoughts that arise around the central emotion or situation. Sometimes it's not the emotion but your emotions about the emotion that get you stuck. Try this out and see if it helps!

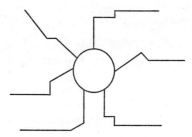

Reflect on what emerges and share it with a trusted person or journal about the feelings.

I am curious and wish to explore my emotional responses in depth.

"Anger and jealousy can no more bear to lose sight of their objects than love."

—GEORGE ELIOT
The Mill on the Floss (1860)

Intensity and Commitment

I'M GOING TO RIGHT the world's wrongs today. Why not me? Why shouldn't I empower myself to be part of the solution? I have courage and strength. I believe in this world, and I wish to protect it with all that I am. I am going to be a part of what gets this world to work. It will start with me. I will get *my* life to work: *my* relationships, *my* career, and *my* leisure. If I can't figure out my own life, I can hardly expect to be effective elsewhere. Once I understand what it takes—qualities such as commitment, integrity, passion, and love—I will practice those principles in all my affairs. I have the power to set things right in my world.

I will learn about life and the world through the vehicle of my own life.

"The fiery moments of passionate experience are the moments of wholeness and totality of the personality."

—Anaís Nin
The Novel of the Future (1968)

Balance

I WILL SEEK BALANCE. Running from extreme to extreme in order to maintain inward and outward balance is a fool's paradise. I have more wisdom than that. I recognize the high cost that I pay mentally, emotionally, and spiritually when my feet travel faster than my mind and heart. Yes, running from end to end does achieve a sort of anchoring to a mid-ground but at what cost to my serenity? I can test my limits and push the envelope using the strength and power that I get from a balanced life rather than from the speed I get from running toward an extreme. I will last longer this way, and I will be able to keep my eyes open as I go.

Balance is a source of strength.

"Mystical experiences nearly always lead one to a belief that some aspect of consciousness is imperishable. In a Buddhist metaphor the consciousness of the individual is like a flame that burns through the night. It is not the same flame over time, yet neither is it another flame."

—MARILYN FERGUSON
The Aquarian Conspiracy (1980)

*A*nimus and *A*nima

I HAVE AN ANIMUS AND AN ANIMA—both a male and a female aspect—inside. This is biologically, psychologically, and emotionally true. Animus, the masculine aspect of me, may be aggressive, assertive, single-minded, and even combative; while anima, the feminine aspect, tends to be nurturing and nest-building. I can move in and out of each role throughout my day. There is no reason to limit myself in this modern society where women work outside the home and men care for small children. I can expand into all roles, extend myself, and broaden my consciousness, and allow the men in my life to do the same. I am capable of playing a wide variety of roles, and the more society modernizes, the more I am called upon to broaden my role repertoire. People who play a variety of roles feel happier and more refreshed than those stuck in a single role. Roles cross-fertilize and energize each other. They provide variety and counterbalances. My male aspect gives me its own type of strength and power. My female aspect helps me to build a comforting home. I wear out when, in playing a variety of roles, I overextend myself trying to be all things to all people. I rebuild and renew myself when I allow my role focusing to shift naturally throughout my day.

I carry the seeds of all aspects of being inside me.

"If I may venture to be frank, I would say about myself that I was every inch a gentleman."

—CATHERINE THE GREAT (1759)

*A*ction

EACH OF US PLAYS ROLES IN OUR LIVES. In this exercise we're exploring how playing a particular role affects us. Try filling in the following blanks mentally or write out your answers in your journal:

In my role as _____, I feel _____.
It seems I always want to _____ and I never get to
_____. When I
_____ in my role as _____, I feel
_____. I am constantly thinking
_____,
which leads me to _____.
In my role as _____, I feel
_____ and I think of myself as
_____.

I examine the ways in which the roles I play shape my thinking, feeling, and behavior.

"Sow an act and you reap a habit; sow a habit and you reap
a character; sow a character and you reap a destiny."
                    —FRANCES E. WILLARD, in Anna A. Gordon et al.,
                    What Frances E. Willard Said (1905)

Words

WHAT I SAY HAS POWER. Words have power. When I consider not only what I say but also the person who is hearing it, I speak in a way that takes their essence into account as well as mine. Good communication isn't only about saying the right thing; it's also being able to mentally reverse roles with the listener, to understand how she might be experiencing me. Manipulation is not good communication. When I use words to batter or control or manipulate, I'm on the wrong track, the hurtful track. When I try to outsmart or gain an unfair edge through what I say, I stop and reflect on what's coming out of me. Communication is a two-way street. When I'm communicating well with someone, each of us feels taken into account, each of us feels that there is room for us to express ourselves and be heard by the other. When communication is not happening, we can experience our self as shrinking or even disappearing in another's presence. I want to consider both sides of the street.

I consider the listener.

"You may choose your word like a connoisseur,
 and polish it up with art,
 But the word that sways, and stirs and stays,
 is the word that comes from the heart."

—ELLA WHEELER WILCOX
"The Word"
Pastels (1906)

Diversity

I SEE UNITY IN DIVERSITY, perfection in what is. Nature is full of variety, full of opposites that create balance: the sun and the moon; winter and summer; a rainstorm followed by a clear sky. I accept all people and cultures in the same way that I accept rich and varied plant and animal kingdoms. There is a subtle ecosystem wherein all is interdependent. Everything has a purpose toward maintaining a healthy whole. I trust God's plan. People are a part of nature, too, as diverse as any other aspect of the world. Differences are part of a divine plan, a balanced world. I will learn to work with variation in an open-minded, constructive manner, keeping in mind that differences in point of view and style are part of overall harmony.

I see the whole.

"Diversity is the most basic principle of creation. No two snowflakes, blades of grass or people are alike."

—LYNN MARIA LAITALA
"In the Aftermath of Empire"
in *The Finnish American Reporter* (1992)

Multicultural Living

IN A RESEARCH STUDY, Kevin Dunbar of McGill University observed that researchers in the "more creative scientific laboratories thrive in the presence of colleagues with dissimilar backgrounds and specialties." Their variety of perspectives and diverse
approaches to analogous situations lead to novel approaches.
Laboratories staffed only with those of similar backgrounds lack
this rich variety of points of view. Living in a melting-pot culture forces us to see the same thing in different ways. We're
challenged to stretch beyond our personal stereotypes and to
push our boundaries. Respect for and curiosity about different
cultures have proven benefits.

I am willing to entertain diverging perspectives.

"Mankind will endure when the world appreciates the logic
of diversity."

—INDIRA GHANDI
Freedom Is the Starting Point (1976)

Strength

GIVE ME STRENGTH. Strength to suffer fools and bear up to unfairly inflicted personal injury. Give me strength to consider the source when someone hurts me rather than to take anger into my soul. Help me to listen to the person's words and honestly evaluate their truth in relationship to me. But keep me safe from drinking another person's poison or from taking into my heart a blackness that is not mine. Give me strength. I cannot do your work if I cannot bear up to the anger and pettiness that will inevitably come my way when I touch people's deepest wounds. I wish to know and accept myself and others in the light of day, warts and all. Truth can hurt but eventually it will set me free.

Give me strength to live with truth.

"Character cannot be developed in ease and quiet. Only through experience of trial and suffering can the soul be strengthened, vision cleared, ambition inspired and success achieved."

—HELEN KELLER

The Feeling Body

OVER AND OVER AGAIN RESEARCH HAS DEMONSTRATED the most effective ways to keep emotional responses level. These strategies include, first, staying in good physical condition by eating a healthy diet, having an aerobic exercise plan, and getting plenty of sleep and, second, developing emotional, psychological, and behavioral strategies for managing stress. These strategies influence not necessarily the *kind* but the *intensity* of our emotional responses. Feelings are physical; they run through our bodies through neurotransmitters and are affected by hormone levels. When we're "off" in terms of meeting our bodies' basic needs, our hearts and minds are off too. Then we get testy and depressed and create conflict. We look for the reason outside of ourselves to make sense of it. But sometimes we're just letting ourselves go and our emotions are paying for it.

My body has its own needs.

"The body is wiser than its inhabitants. The body is the soul. We ignore its aches, its pains, its eruptions, because we fear the truth. The body is God's messenger."

—ERICA JONG
Fear of Fifty (1994)

Fullness

I WILL FILL UP FROM WITHIN. Stillness. Awareness. A recognition that what is within me in this moment is "enough." And, when I allow it to be enough, the room I'm in fills up in a mystical, serene way. It becomes full of life, of the moment, of energy and awareness. This is me and I am this. I fill up in this way; it is from an invisible source. I don't fill up on mere intensity of my personality. I fill up on that energy and aliveness that always surrounds me and is within me—that energy that comes to life through resting in quiet awareness and that fuels my own sense of life and aliveness and "me-ness." My world becomes enough when I allow it to; when I let it be. This is how I contact God, or my Higher Power. God is not separate but a force of life or aliveness that is in all cells and atomic particles. God is life.

I am full.

"and he said: you pretty full of yourself ain't chu?
so she replied: show me someone not full of herself
and I'll show you a hungry person."

—NIKKI GIOVANNI
"Poem for a Lady Whose Voice I Like"
ReCreation (1970)

Relax, Relax, Relax

NOTHING MUCH GETS DONE if we're in a tense state. Our minds don't work well, we waste more energy than we use, and we make mistakes. Tension makes everything feel harder. We get tired, sick, and nonproductive. We lose sleep. We lose serenity. We act in ways that push people away and create interpersonal messes. We get less done. Scrambled brains produce scrambled lives. We need to relax. Tension isn't going to help—it will only make things even more tense. Instead, let's try developing an attitude of relaxation. Let's imagine the situations in our lives working smoothly. We make necessary plans and then let them go, assuming that things will fall into place easily when the time comes. We leave time in the day for relaxation and letdown. We get exercise so our bodies stay loose. We breathe deeply and fully so our brains, blood, and organs get oxygen and our mood stays even.

I am responsible for my level of tension.

"No temper could be more cheerful than hers, or possess, in a greater degree, that sanguine expectation of happiness which is happiness itself."

—JANE AUSTEN
Sense and Sensibility (1811)

The Task of the Warrior

A COMMON RESEARCH FINDING IS that women find it difficult to express emotions that are typically considered masculine, such as anger and aggression. And most people, men and women, have trouble with the "darker" emotions, such as grief, hate, jealousy, and rage. Nonetheless, these emotions are part of us to greater or lesser extents and pretending they aren't there gives them more power over our inner worlds, not less. When we actively confront and work with the parts of our self that we may split off from conscious awareness, a few things happen. We get to know ourselves and who we really are on the inside, which becomes a source of tremendous freedom and power. We become less afraid of taking on challenges because we sense our creative talents and know our limitations, so life feels less daunting. We harness our own power, creativity, and aggression and use it consciously. By feeling and understanding parts of ourselves that we have relegated to our shadow sides, we transform them with new insight and awareness into something less threatening and more under our conscious control. We integrate them into our larger personality. This allows us to be deeper and more-conscious people capable of responding to life more fully. It gives us choices, which research has proved elevates our immune systems and gives us greater vitality toward life.

I am willing to confront, experience, accept, and integrate the darker parts of me.

"Only in growth, reform, and change, paradoxically enough, is true security to be found."

—ANNE MORROW LINDBERGH
The Wave of the Future (1940)

cA Letter toward Forgiveness

LET'S CLOSE OUR EYES and allow ourselves to bring into focus someone against whom we hold resentment, someone we are unable to forgive. Let's allow ourselves to make this whole emotional situation conscious to whatever extent is comfortable; feel the associated feelings; and let the words that have gone unspoken begin to form and have voice in our minds. Let's write a letter (not to be sent, but for personal use only) to the person against whom we are holding resentment, fully saying all that has gone unsaid, getting off of our hearts the resentments that we carry, saying what—for one reason or another—we have not been able to say before. Let's write whatever needs to be said to this person to bring emotional closure within us and then sign the letter in whatever way feels appropriate. A variation of this activity can be to write a letter that we wish we had received from someone asking for *our* forgiveness. In other words, reverse roles with that person and write the letter to us as them. We may read this letter to ourselves for greater emotional clarity or share it with a trusted person.

I use letter writing and journaling to relieve myself and sort through my powerful feelings.

"If you haven't forgiven yourself something, how can you forgive others?"

—DOLORES HUERTA, in Barbara L. Baer,
"Stopping Traffic: One Woman's Cause" (1975)

*D*reamwork

DREAMS CAN BE A WINDOW into our unconscious. They can mirror ourselves back to us in creative and insightful ways. They can reveal what may be going on beneath the surface of our minds. Try this exercise as a way to explore your own dreams. Allow a dream that you had recently—or one that you remember—to come to mind. Picture the dream moving before your inner vision. Watch it, and let it envelop you. Feel the atmosphere of the dream and let it move into the foreground of your consciousness. For each significant person, element, or object, write a brief soliloquy in the first person. For example, "I am a star in a dark sky. I shine even when I cannot be seen. . . ." Amplify each aspect of your dream that feels important and then continue to explore even those aspects that seem pushed into the background or unimportant. When finished with this process, answer the following questions: Is there one character, object, or element that seemed to have the most to say or to speak the loudest? What was it saying to you personally? Why do you think you had this dream at this particular time? What do you feel this dream was trying to say to you?

My dreams open a window to my inner world.

"During the day, our souls gather their . . . impressions of us, how our lives feel. . . . Our spirits collect these impressions, keep them together, like wisps of smoke in a bag. Then, when we're asleep, our brains open up these bags of smoke . . . and take a look."

—MARSHA NORMAN
The Fortune Teller (1987)

The Lover

Seeking a Soul Mate

How do I love thee? Let me count the ways.
I love thee to the depth and breadth and height
My soul can reach, when feeling out of sight
For the ends of Being and ideal Grace.
I love thee to the level of every day's
Most quiet need, by sun and candlelight.
I love thee freely, as men strive for Right;
I love thee purely, as they turn from Praise.
I love thee with the passion put to use
In my old griefs, and with my childhood's faith.
I love thee with a love I seemed to lose
With my lost saints—I love thee with the breath,
Smiles, tears, of all my life!—and, if God choose,
I shall but love thee better after death.

—Elizabeth Barrett Browning
"How Do I Love Thee?"
from *Sonnets from the Portuguese*

The Lover

I AM THE LOVER. I am powerful; I seduce and entice. I play with nature's gifts and adornments that make me beautiful and give me power. I am the Lover. I surrender and am overtaken. I sail with delight on the private waters of pleasure with my beloved. I am beast and angel, lust and heavenly caresses. I connect with God and humanity through each pore and nerve of my body. My lover and I become bound through mutual satisfaction and play. I am a coquette and the hand of mercy and comfort, deep and frivolous, generous and tormenting. I search the world over for love and turn myself inside out when it captures me within its tender yet vice-like grip. I toss and turn. I am torn in pieces and pieced together again. I run; I stand in total stillness. I am troubled and profoundly contented. I yearn for the touch and presence of the one I love.

I am the feminine, the girl, the woman.

"I believe in the curative powers of love as the English believe in tea or Catholics believe in the miracle of Lourdes."

—JOYCE JOHNSON
Minor Characters (1983)

The Now

I WILL EXPERIENCE THE HERE AND NOW of our relationship. What is happening is what is. We do not exist in a separate reality but in one that functions from day to day. Who we are in our minute-to-minute interactions is a mirror on the surface of the water reflecting the depths of all that we are. The moment is important. It is the palette that I hold in my hand with which we paint our portrait. It is the clay, the film, the pen and paper; it is our substance with which we create our very being. I will not waste the moment.

I am present in the here and now.

"Normal day, let me be aware of the treasure you are. Let me learn from you, love you, savor you, bless you before you depart. Let me not pass you by in quest of some rare and perfect tomorrow. Let me hold you while I may, for it will not always be so. One day I shall dig my nails into the earth, or bury my face in the pillow, or stretch myself taut, or raise my hands to the sky, and want more than all the world your return."

—MARY JEAN IRION
Yes, World (1970)

Journey Inward

OURS IS NOT AN EXERCISE OF THE MIND but a journey of the soul. When we mistake the tasks and trials of our courtship for superficialities, we divide ourselves from a deeper purpose. You are the perfect vehicle through which I can better vindicate and experience myself; a mirror of my hunger and thirst. As I chose you, I chose a path to me. You are the wind that pushes at my shadowy depths, the siren's song that draws me to the edge of the precipice of my own being and the immortal mind that holds my body in its arms.

I am on a journey.

"We are not unlike a particularly hardy crustacean.... With each passage from one stage of human growth to the next we, too, must shed a protective structure. We are left exposed and vulnerable—but also yeasty and embryonic again, capable of stretching in ways we hadn't known before. These sheddings may take several years or more. Coming out of each passage, though, we enter a longer and more stable period in which we can expect relative tranquility and a sense of equilibrium regained."

—GAIL SHEEHY
Passages (1976)

Being Human

YOU ARE NOT HERE to live up to my fantasies of romance or to make my life worthwhile. I am not here to satisfy your expectations or give you a reason to live. We each search out our own meaning and build our own inner worlds. I will share mine with you and will be mindful of your inner world so that when you unzip your heart to me, I will walk with awareness into that place. You should be an answer to my dreams not my fantasies. We will not be perfect with one another. We may be insensitive and unaware some of the time. It doesn't mean that we are not right for each other; it only means that we are human.

I am willing to be human.

"We do not grow absolutely, chronologically. We grow sometimes in one dimension, and not in another, unevenly. We grow partially. We are relative. We are mature in one realm, childish in another. The past, present and future mingle and pull us backward, forward, or fix us in the present. We are made up of layers, cells, constellations."

—ANAÍS NIN (1946)
The Diary of Anaïs Nin, Vol. 4 (1973)

Debunking Myths about Relationships

- If you choose the right person, there won't be any problems.
- If you're in a relationship, you won't be lonely anymore.
- Healthy couples think alike.
- No conflict is a sign of a good relationship.
- If you are well suited, problems will be easy to work through.
- If you choose the right person, the rest will be easy.
- Conflicts mean you're with the wrong person.
- You shouldn't have to tell a well-suited partner what you like sexually.
- Good partnerships stay the same—they don't change.

Myths and fantasies construct impossible expectations.

"The liberating encounter with God/ess is always an encounter with our authentic selves resurrected from underneath the alienated self. It is not experienced against, but in and through relationships, healing our broken relations with our bodies, with other people, with nature."

—Rosemary Ruether
Sexism and God-Talk (1983)

Inner Work

I AM WILLING TO DO THE INNER WORK that it will take to have a meaningful and loving relationship in my life. Every endeavor that is worthwhile takes work. Why should my relationship with you be any different? I will not become arrogant, taking you for granted and overrating myself, nor will I underrate myself and get lost in pleasing you. I will keep in front of my eyes all that we mean to one another and not debilitate our growing love by harping endlessly on the areas where we are less than ideal. Everyone has problems and disappointments in life. It doesn't mean people stop living. No relationship is perfect, even wanting it to be is its own phobic reaction. When I am afraid of life, I separate it into unrelated sections. I want each section to prove itself to me in order for me to feel secure and worthwhile. Life is meant to be lived hour by hour, day by day. It is not only an act of endurance but also one of surrender.

I apply myself and commit myself.

"The important thing is not to think much but to love much; do, then, whatever most arouses you to love."

—ST. TERESA OF AVILA (1577)

Being Enough

TODAY I WILL WORK TO MAINTAIN a sense of self within the context of our relationship. I am so quick to organize my insides and outsides according to what I imagine you would like me to be. By doing this I enter into a mythical relationship with people neither of us knows or can know because they are constructions of dreams and fantasies rather than the Real McCoy. When I try to change myself to suit what I perceive to be your wishes and desires, the next person I want to change is you. I consider it the appropriate trade-off. When you do not or cannot change, I grow disappointed and disillusioned. I rob myself of the experience of us and of being with myself as I am, and I grow fearful of discovering a hidden you. I become fear-driven in our togetherness, silently waiting to be found out for who I really am. I need to trust that who I am will be enough for me and enough for you.

I am enough.

"I read and walked for miles at night along the beach, writing bad blank verse and searching endlessly for someone wonderful who would step out of the darkness and change my life. It never crossed my mind that that person could be me."

—ANNA QUINDLEN
"At the Beach"
Living Out Loud (1988)

A Holding Environment

TODAY I WILL BEAR WITNESS to my own thoughts and feelings. I will create a quiet "holding environment" within myself where my essence can be contained in safety and support. If I expect you to be my holding environment, I will be at loose ends when you are not present. You have enough to handle being present for yourself on a consistent basis. How can you do for me what you can only just do for yourself? I will hold myself. At times I can look to you to help me when I cannot help myself—but only at times. If it becomes my way of life, neither of us will be able to sustain it. I have quiet within; I have a heart and a spirit and a mind. All of these parts of me can work together to make serene inner space where I can be held in safety and comfort. From there we can hold each other.

I experience containment.

"What others regard as retreat from them or rejection of them is not those things at all but instead a breeding ground for greater friendship, a culture for deeper involvement, eventually, with them."

—DORIS GRUMBACH
Fifty Days of Solitude (1994)

Myths

OFTEN I HOLD AN IMAGE of a relationship in my mind that is an impossible dream disembodied from real life, unattainable and unreal. When I ask our relationship to conform to something that is not possible and cannot be sustained in day-to-day life, the discrepancy between who we are and who I think we should be divides us from ourselves. We get depressed and discouraged about what we are not and disconnected from all that we are. When I ask us to be in good form all the time, I ask too much. I insist on the impossible and I use, as my measuring stick, relationships that are not even real. They are a construction of someone's ideas about people who in reality do not exist. I will examine the parts of our relationship that I hold hostage to my fantasies of how a relationship "should" be. There is no crime in just having the relationship that we have; we don't need to follow a prescribed pattern to be all right.

I will let us be who we are.

"If only you were you and yet not you."

—JESSIE REDMONT FAUSET
The Poetry of the Negro (1949)

*H*iding

OUR RELATIONSHIP IS NOT A PLACE TO HIDE, either from myself or the rest of the world. If I use our relationship for this purpose, it will shrink in size and in its ability to nurture me. I will start to expect what it cannot give me, and I will drain it of its energy. I need to engage fully in life on my own two legs. This relationship I am developing should not be a crutch to hold me up. I can lean on you as you can on me, but we also need to carry our own weight. Our love is not a place to hide from ourselves. If we try to use it in this way, we will look for ourselves in one another, and we will be disappointed when we do not find ourselves there. We can only find ourselves within. We can offer each other refuge and support, but hiding will create darkness and darkness can lead to blindness. We are here to help each other see.

I face who I am becoming in the context of our relationship.

"Take love when it is given,
But never think to find it
A sure escape from sorrow
Or a complete repose."

—SARA TEASDALE

Sexuality

I WILL BRING MY FULL SEXUAL SELF to our bed and ask you to do the same. It is not your job to make me sexual nor vice versa. My sensuality is my own; my openness, receptivity, and willingness to experiment and be free with you are qualities that I find inside of myself, then talk about and agree upon with you. For me to come to you and wait to be turned on and led through a sexual experience by you is missing the point. We are in this together, and we each need to do our part. Our sexual life is deeply bonding and profoundly intimate. It is not about how we perform for each other, but how sensitive, clear, and open we are willing to be with one another. What I can have with you is not easily replaced because sex is not only about sex but also about love and intimacy. It is a moment when our spiritual and animal selves can be freely expressed and enjoyed. It connects us to each other and to our selves.

I allow myself to feel sexual.

"with each touch of you
I am fresh bread
warm and rising."

—PAT PARKER
Movement in Black (1978)

Being Different People

WHEN I FEEL MY OWN FEELINGS and let you feel yours, it does not necessarily mean that we will not get along. You are not here to satisfy my needs. What I did not get is not up to you to supply. Your job is not to finish up my insides or to be hostage to the deficits of my past. What you give me you give because at some deep level our needs speak to one another. We call out in the silence of our unfinished selves, to grow through one another's gifts and desires. We cannot but serve each other's inner movement, if we allow the unconscious match between us to do its work.

I am open to the transformative experience of love.

"Out of the corner of one eye, I could see my mother. Out of the corner of the other eye, I could see her shadow on the wall, cast there by the lamplight. It was a big and solid shadow, and it looked so much like my mother that I became frightened. For I could not be sure whether for the rest of my life I would be able to tell when it was really my mother and when it was really her shadow standing between me and the rest of the world."

—JAMAICA KINCAID
Annie John (1983)

Perfectionism

I WILL NOT ASK each day of this new and growing relationship that it be the perfect cameo of health and bliss. If I do that, I will be asking us to live a lie because life doesn't work that way. Relationships are tied to reality and subject to those forces. Allowing our relationship to ride the waves of life will give it fortitude and flexibility. Trying to force it to be better than life will undermine it. Beauty is in the eye of the beholder. I will attempt to see beauty in things as they are, rather than as I feel they should be. When I hold us to my image of how we should be before I allow myself to feel secure, I sentence myself to a state of frequent insecurity. Nothing is exactly as I want it to be. That is the nature of life. I can learn to feel contentment with things as they are instead of always trying to get them to conform to my ideals.

Too much perfectionism locks life out.

"Our consciousness rarely registers the beginning of a growth within us anymore than without us: there have been many circulations of the sap before we detect the smallest sign of the bud."

—GEORGE ELIOT
Silas Marner (1861)

Rejection

BECAUSE, AT TIMES, I FEEL REJECTED by you does not mean that I have to reject myself. You may be rejecting me for reasons that have nothing to do with me. Perhaps you felt rejected by a parent and get frightened when you get too close to another person. Maybe you don't feel good about yourself, and you act out that painful feeling by rejecting me. Whatever it is, I need not always take it personally. When I reject myself because I feel rejected by you, I lose myself and only deepen a painful dynamic. I become filled with self-doubt and insecurity. I hold myself responsible for things I have nothing to do with, and I give up my serenity to your changing moods. There is a way for me not to allow you to hold the scorecard in your hand when it comes to my own self-acceptance. I will create a space in which I hold myself safe, secure, and unconditionally loved.

I will not reject myself.

"Oh seek, my love, your newer way
  I'll not be left in sorrow
  So long as I have yesterday
  Go take your damned tomorrow!"

—DOROTHY PARKER

We Touch at Points

I WILL NOT NECESSARILY AGREE with all that you say. Why should we as two adults have to see eye to eye before we can feel comfortable in each other's presence? There is room enough for separate, if not diverging, points of view. Before I blindly accommodate, I will first take my own counsel. Too often when I force myself to be compliant, resentment builds up underneath. We touch at points, you and I. I cannot grow in your shadow nor you in mine. I will not think that by sheltering you from me or me from you, I am helping either of us. Rather, I will seek to grow beside you and let you grow beside me, resisting the urge to hang on too tightly at the root. I will let you take in a full breath of you, and I will take in a full breath of me.

We each can be our own people.

"Love will not always linger longest
 With those who hold it in too clenched a fist."

—ALICE DUES MILLER
Forsaking All Others (1937)

Pushing You Away

I CAN PUSH YOU AWAY WHEN I NEED TO. I worry so about being pushed away by you that I play the victim and cast you in the role of the aggressor. I am not just a reactor; I am also proactive. When I need space, I can have it. I have a right to some room to breathe if I feel cramped or hurt or misunderstood. I can stand on my own for a few hours without my life falling apart. I can say, "I need a break." When I am not able to decide to give myself the room I need to process my uncomfortable, upsetting feelings, I may create a crisis in order to get away. I do not need your approval to have a little quiet time, nor do I need your permission or blessing. You may not even need to know what I am doing. But I will know. I am giving myself room to feel.

I can set my own boundaries.

"You gain strength, courage and confidence by every experience in which you really stop to look fear in the face. You are able to say to yourself, 'I lived through this horror. I can take the next thing that comes along.' . . . You must do the thing you think you cannot do."

—ELEANOR ROOSEVELT

Jealousy

WHEN I FEEL JEALOUS OF YOU, I will look at myself closely. Why should I keep you from your own happiness and personal satisfaction because it threatens me? Being jealous is not good for our relationship, and it is not good for me as a person. When I feel myself getting tied up in all of my worst fantasies, I will step back and examine ways that I might move away from a painful, destructive position. Am I jealous of you because I feel you are achieving more than I am? Or are you able to allow yourself more freedom to enjoy your life, your relationships, and your passions than I allow myself? Perhaps I can take steps to move closer to my own dreams or abundance. Though I may have things about which to be jealous, will it really benefit me to indulge myself in that feeling? It is a beautiful thing to be able to feel joy in another person's happiness. Not only does it expand me as a spiritual person, but also it gives me more moments of pleasure in my own life and connects me with others in a positive light.

What you contain and obtain need not diminish me.

"Of all the idiots I have met in my life, and the Lord knows that they have not been few or little, I think that I have been the biggest."

—ISAK DINESEN

The Task of the Lover

Do WE FIND LOVE or does love find us? Do we find a person so that we can learn to become intimate, or do we learn to be intimate so that we can be in love? Our being in love begins with our first love, the love of our parents. Our first romance is with those people who seemed like genies opening a strange and mysterious world to us, carrying us on their magic carpet into a wondrous and complex land. We carry these magical expectations, wishes, and dreams with us into our own lives and look for a love that restores us to that state of wonder, that brings us home. We crave arms to enfold us and make us feel safe and secure. We long for passion to awaken our sleeping souls and give life purpose and meaning. We bond with the familiar, someone who mirrors our own insides, who pulls out what is hidden, massaging the sore spots and giving wings to our heart. Our love is an opportunity to meet our own self. Love calls us to the edge of our being if we are willing to go there and asks us to take a flying leap without a net. To risk abandonment, loss of self and hurt. To be a fool. To let go. And it is in the losing that we find and in that leap through darkness that we gain a new kind of sight. Love is a paradox. It destroys and gives life. It burns away the underbrush so that new growth can happen.

I risk inner birth.

"We love because it is the only true adventure."

—NIKKI GIOVANNI, in *Reader's Digest* (1982)

Telling All

I WILL LEARN when to keep my mouth closed. It's very tempting for me to say all—to tell you each hurt, each bit of anger or mistrust. But there's a difference between opening my heart to you and opening my mouth. When I open my heart, I have two-way vision, and I can empathize with both of our positions. When my words come only from my mouth without being first felt and considered, they feel different to both of us. Our conversations become less of a sharing and more of a debate. You do not need to know everything that goes through my mind. Living with another person will always have irritating features. We will rub up against one another in ways that annoy us both; it's to be expected. Whether we bother one another is not a sign of our rightness as a couple—only part and parcel of being two grown adults trying to integrate complicated lives. A certain amount of discomfort is natural and needn't always be worked out—only accepted.

I can be discriminating.

"Love has nothing to do with what you are expecting to get—only with what you are expecting to give—which is everything."

—KATHARINE HEPBURN
Me (1991)

Perspective

WHILE I BELIEVE, as Plato said, "The life which is unexamined is not worth living," I will not confuse self-examination with excessive scrutiny. Looking too closely can produce the same lack of understanding and perspective as not looking enough. If I want to view a painting, I move back so that I can see all of it. If I am too close, I miss the full picture. If I am too far, I can't see the forms or colors clearly. The best seats in a theater are a little back from the stage. The front row puts me so near to the play that I get lost in the actor's torn sleeve or his perspiration. The back row makes me miss too much of the emotion and sound. So it is with my relationship. When I look too closely, detail takes on too much meaning, focus, and attention. When I don't look closely enough, I disengage from what is really going on. I will look for the right distance from which to examine you and my relationship with you.

I keep our relationship in perspective.

"In love, gallantry is necessary. Even when the first wild desire is gone, especially then, there is an inherent need for good manners and consideration, for the putting forth of effort. Two courteous and civilized human beings out of the loneliness of their souls owe that to each other."

—ILKA CHASE
In Bed We Cry (1943)

Scrutiny

BEING YOUR LOVER can make me anxious. Am I expecting too much or too little, giving myself away too soon or taking a chance on happiness that is right for my future? I make the little things into too much and the big things into too little. I ignore what I should pay attention to and pay attention to what I should ignore. But, I guess, everything you do need not meet my scrutiny. If I tried to squeeze you into a shape that meets my approval, I would be cheating both of us. I would lose the real you, and you would be giving up your real self for an image in a mirror. I will not ask you to take that flight from yourself. Your soul belongs to you. When I try to get you to be who I want you to be, I rob you of your dearest possession—your essential self.

We can still be connected even though I recognize that you have a right to your own life and I to mine.

"You are discontented with the world because you can't get just the small things that suit your pleasure, not because it's a world where myriads of men and women are ground by wrong and misery, and tainted with pollution."

—GEORGE ELIOT
Felix Halt, the Radical (1866)

Being Right

BEING RIGHT used to seem so much bigger with you than it does now. I used to feel if I lost ground that I was giving up something very important. I can't remember now what it was that I was afraid of losing. Today I know that each of us has our own truth or way of seeing a situation that is right for us. If I try to take away your sense of what feels right to you and make you live with my sense of the situation, it doesn't fit for you. If I allow your visions and definitions of life to drive me and tell me who I am, it doesn't fit for me. Each of us needs to be with our own experience first and then share it with the other. That is ultimately what will provide us with a sense of security, self, and communion. Relationships are not about cloning but about sharing. If communication is prescripted by either party or by society at large, we'll never plumb our own depths. How then can we bring depth to our relationship?

I would rather be happy than right.

"The best thing for everyone concerned . . . is what people always say when they have arranged something exclusively to suit themselves."

—SHIRLEY HAZZARD
The Bay of Noon (1970)

*A*ll the *T*hings *Y*ou *A*re

LOVE IS THAT ENERGY that allows the juices of life to flow. Love makes, at least, my world go round. I will enjoy this experience of love and sense the intrinsic beauty of your presence in my life. All that you give that is unseen will not go unnoticed, unfelt, or unknown. I will not be fortune's fool and learn too late what I have. I will know it and appreciate it while it is mine. Life holds no guarantees. But you are here now, I love you now, I am fed and held by your love now—this day is ours.

I count your alive presence as enough today.

"A commercial society urges its citizens to be responsible for things, but not for people. It is the unquestioned assumption of a mercantile culture that things need and deserve attention, but that people can take care of themselves."

—MARGARET HALSEY
The Folks at Home (1952)

Over and Over

OVER AND OVER AGAIN in a silent corner of my heart I observe your presence within me—you have traced your image across the landscape of my life and etched your being into my psyche. You are a part of me in ways I hardly understand and still forever a stranger—a person apart while at the same moment living within my inner vision. You are a thousand times me and a million times yourself. So frightening in your power to hurt me; so endearing in your love that makes all the rest disappear at your touch or the sound of your footsteps.

We two are bonded by a thousand invisible threads.

"It is the way of lovers to think that none can bless or succor their love but their own selves. And there is a touch of truth to it, maybe more than a touch."

—MARY WEBB
Precious Bane (1924)

*D*istance

I WILL LET THERE BE DISTANCE in our relationship without bolting. Without distance neither of us can take in a full breath of ourselves. An appropriate distance gives each of us room to be our own person, pursue our own interests, and follow our own uniqueness. In this way, when we come together, we bring ourselves, not only our expectations. Too much distance creates loneliness and isolation, but too little can have a similar effect. In each other's presence, we become lonely for ourselves and the people we used to be. Then, as a reaction, we need too much distance to find ourselves again. There is space enough in our relationship for each of us to be.

I allow you some distance without withdrawing my love.

"Union is only possible to those who are units. To be fit for relations in time, souls, whether of man or woman, must be able to do without them in the spirit."

—MARGARET FULLER
Woman in the Nineteenth Century (1845)

Meeting Needs

Because I have learned to identify my needs does not mean that I will hold you responsible for meeting them. My needs are my own, and it is up to me to see that they are met in a variety of ways. When I look to you to meet too many of them, I create a lopsided life for myself and a kind of codependency that is not good for either of us. You meet many basic needs for me just by being my partner in a steady, reliable relationship. When those basic needs are well met, the rest of life looks different. I will attempt to be reasonable in what I expect from you and likewise reasonable in what I expect from myself. Holding each other responsible for one another's needs is a breeding ground for resentment and a never-ending job. I will realistically assess what I get from you that really counts at a deep level and then look at what is fair to expect and give from there.

I will not hold you hostage.

"People talk about love as though it were something you could give, like an armful of flowers. And a lot of people give love like that—just dump it down on top of you, a useless strong-scented burden."

—Anne Morrow Lindbergh
Locked Rooms and Open Doors (1974)

*P*ersonal *G*rowth

WHEN I GET LOST in the struggles of our relationship, I forget that ultimately the reason for me to seek the most positive, constructive path is to liberate myself. Our relationship offers me incredible opportunities to grow as a person. If I can see the changes that I make in myself not as something I am doing to please you, but as changes I make in order to become a fuller, more expressive, empathic person, I will be keeping the locus of control where it belongs, within me. A relationship is a wonderful opportunity to expand one's understanding of self. It acts as a mirror for our deepest patterns of behavior and brings to the surface unconscious material to be worked out in the present. I will use this relationship as an arena in which to grow myself. I am in this relationship to expand myself.

You bring more of me into focus.

"Growth is not concerned with itself."

—MERIDEL LE SUEUR
"Formal 'Education' in Writing" (1935)
Harvest Song (1990)

"Till it has loved, no man or woman can become itself."

—EMILY DICKINSON (1879), in Mabel Loomis Todd,
Letters of Emily Dickinson

Resolving Conflict

WE DO NOT NEED TO RESOLVE all of our conflicts. Hearing each other out and acknowledging that each of us has a right to our own truth is often enough. If resolving things means seeing eye to eye or somehow ending up with the same point of view, we could spend all our time at it and still never feel satisfied. Because we are in a relationship together does not mean that we own each other's inner reality. I am not with you to collect on an invisible debt or to get you to sign on the dotted line. I am here to enjoy your companionship and the support of your presence in my life. Working through conflicts involves a lot of hearing each other and sharing our own truth in a considerate and responsible manner without blame, insult, or projection. When we can leave the blame out and talk about our own fears, anxieties, and concerns, our discussions become positive and constructive, and we reach a place of feeling good more quickly.

I will accept the things I cannot change and change the things I can.

"No human being can destroy the structure of a marriage except the two who made it. It is the one human edifice that is impregnable except from within."

—GWEN BRISTOW
Tomorrow Is Forever (1943)

Greener Grass

MY FANTASY LIFE is full of potential lovers. It seems every time we have a conflict or I feel disappointed with you, me, or us, I want a brand-new relationship. I want to start all over. That is, I experience another conflict or disappointment. But just once, I will not be betrayed by the illusion of something better always around the corner. I will learn to work with and value what I have. Anything requires tending. A beautiful garden untended will turn to weeds in three years—so will a beautiful relationship. Anything that I ignore or abuse will only last so long. To cast it aside and start all over again is missing the point. I need to look at myself and what in my own actions has brought something wonderful into a state of disrepair. A relationship, like a garden, needs to be handled with care and regular attention. Even if I have been hurt, the way back to myself is not through hurting back or being tough. If I feel hurt by you, I will get further if I quietly remove myself and let you sit with your own offensive behavior. Eventually you will see the error of your ways just as I do under the same circumstances and, if we don't, at least we will not escalate into something too ugly to come back from. We can forgive and forget quite a lot, but we can also go too far. I will exercise some caution.

I will make my life right here.

"Monogamous heterosexual love is probably one of the most difficult, complex and demanding of human relationships."

—MARGARET MEAD
Male and Female (1949)

Hope

IT IS ALL RIGHT FOR ME to have hope for our relationship and to harbor that hope deep inside of me in the silence of my heart. There will be times when I cannot share it with you—times when each of us may be too distracted by life or our changing insides to even remember what it means to have a relationship. There will be long periods when I am not getting what I need from you in order to feel secure. Being your lover can leave me in a strange sort of limbo, neither wife nor girlfriend, committed but insecure about what we really mean to each other. This does not mean that I have to give up hope or that it is foolish to hope. What's foolish is not what I really feel. Hope is something that I have a right to—no matter what. It is also something that I can feel and then let go of so that I do not cling to it and maintain myself in that state. Anxious wishing and attempting "to hold on until" will only keep me locked into a cycle of hope and despair. There is another kind of hope that just abides because somehow it has confidence in the ever-present beauty of life.

I believe in life's ability to repair and renew itself.

"Hope is the thing with feathers
 That perches in the soul
 And sings the tune without the words
 And never stops—at all!"

—EMILY DICKINSON

*C*o-obsession

ALL RELATIONSHIPS require experimentation and practice. What I learn in one relationship is mine to take to another one if I choose or need to. We go to school to learn to read; we have relationships to learn how to have relationships. You and I will go through many periods of change in our time together. It will be enough for me to handle my own changing without becoming tied up in yours. When you become obsessed by something, it is time for me to back up and give you and me more space. If, instead, I see your obsession as a time for me to move in close, I will become wrapped up in an obsession that has its roots in another person's psyche. I will not have the benefit of playing something out within me that needs to be seen—I will just drive myself and you crazy with my obsession about your obsession. Obsession with anything is not healthy or balanced. I experience losing you in your preoccupation, just as you are losing yourself to it. Then I try to find you by getting involved. Soon we are both out of balance. Next time, when you are obsessed with something, I will stay centered. That way, at least one of us will be locatable. I will live and learn.

I have the right to remain secure within my own center.

"It's a sad day when you find out that it's not accident or time or fortune but just yourself that kept things from you."

—LILLIAN HELLMAN
Pentimento (1973)

Bringing Out the Best

I HAVE TO LEARN to bring the best out of myself over and over again. In turn, I will bring out the best in you. If we bring out the worst in each other, we may need to take a closer look at ourselves. Having a successful relationship is not just about finding the right person but *being* the right person. First I find someone with whom I think a relationship is possible. Then I work on it for years and years—I have to be bigger than I was to include all that is new. What will I do with the unfinished business from my inner depths when it gets triggered into the middle of my relationship? What I do with the unresolved hurt, pain, or distorted perceptions from my past that I bring to my relationship will be key to its success. Our relationship is an opportunity to see more of me, to grow in my ability to understand how I function in relationships and what they're all about.

What I bring out of you is also a reflection on me.

"To be together is for us to be at once as free as in solitude, as gay as in company. We talk, I believe, all day long: to talk to each other is but a more animated and audible thinking."

—CHARLOTTE BRONTË
Jane Eyre (1847)

Owning My Side

IN ORDER TO FEEL peaceful inside, I need to own my part of a conflict. My fear is that the other person won't do the same, and I will be left holding the whole bag. So, I stay stuck feeling annoyed with myself for not being open and honest and with the other person for not coming forward in, what feels to me, a fair and decent manner. It occurs to me, though, that maybe I can find a way to manage this from my end. I can own my part and not expect the other person immediately to recognize that they have a part too. I can say something like, "I think we both have a part in this. I'll do my best to come clean with my side and then you can clear up your side, okay?" That way, regardless of what the other person does, I will have made it clear that we share responsibility.

I can participate in setting up a situation in which I feel comfortable.

"Resentment is an evil so costly to our peace that we should find it more cheap to forgive even were it not more right."

—HANNAH MORE
Thoughts on Importance of the Manners of the Great to the General Society (1788)

Humor

OUR HUMORS MATCH, and this is no small thing. Humor is multilayered, and the fact that we find the same things funny or see amusement in a like manner indicates that we see life in a compatible way. I laugh at your jokes, and you think I'm funny. What a cherished bond this creates; what joy-filled moments. Humor is also our healer, when we can share laughter in addition to pain or turn an annoying situation around and see it through the lens of levity. Sharing laughter and joy creates an incredible intimacy, strong enough to hold our pain and face life's challenges. It challenges us at the deepest level to open up and see difficult circumstances in a new light.

I invite you in and let you see me not through sarcasm but through genuine humor.

"Anyone can be passionate, but it takes real lovers to be silly."

—ROSE FRANKEN
Another Claudia (1943)

Stretching Beyond

I WILL STRETCH BEYOND what I perceive to be my limits with you. When I feel that I have given enough and understood enough yet still feel stuck, I will not run from this place. I will feel this "stuckness" fully, observe it, and let it have its day. By letting myself stay with it rather than walking away, I give myself the opportunity to experience the feeling. It will change—it will transform—it will break apart into many separate little emotional images, all of which will provide me with more information about myself. Inner windows will open up and I shall see further into the variables that created the emotional traffic jam in me and in our relationship. Next time I feel as if there is no way out or around, I'll wait a little while, relax, and allow things to change. I don't need to force my way through and control the outcome. What is the outcome anyway—why does it have to be the way I picture it? Why should I limit it? Spiritual growth comes in many ways. Meeting the challenges of my relationships sincerely and honestly is one way available to me to grow in spirit.

I can move a little further.

"I have found the paradox that if I love until it hurts, then there is no hurt, but only more love."

—DAPHNE RAE
Love Until It Hurts (1980)

Modeling

WHERE DID I LEARN about how to have a relationship, what to look for, and how to live inside of one? What do I see when I look at my parents' relationship and how does that shape my thoughts, feelings, and behavior? I had no greater teachers than my own parents. What I experienced growing up in the cradle of their partnership formed my understanding of relationships. What do I see when I look at my siblings, my grandparents, my aunts and uncles? What have these people taught me about what relationships can mean in my life and how to go about having them? What did I learn when I was young from my peers about how I fit in a group? The models that I grew up with were my relationship teachers. They, by example and interaction, showed me what relationships were all about and how I should conduct myself within them. What I saw as possible for them may be what I feel is possible for me. In what ways have the lessons I learned from them, both positive and negative, translated themselves into how I live inside my relationships today? What do I imagine is possible for me—or not possible—based on my past experiences and how they affected me both in positive and negative ways?

I examine the models of my past.

"There's a period of life when we swallow a knowledge of ourselves, and it becomes either good or sour inside."

—PEARL BAILEY
The Raw Pearl (1968)

$\mathcal{F}$lexibility

I HAVE BEEN LOYAL to a search for selfhood, but in my finding and standing by myself I will not forget that you exist also. I will not use my personal quest as an excuse to shut you out or take care of myself at your expense. That would only be replicating dysfunction or putting a new face on abuse. If I push you away in order to protect myself without taking your feelings into consideration, I am creating a wound in you and in our growing relationship. By my behavior, I may cause a rupture that could divide us or from which we will have to heal at some later time. My goal in life is self-reliance, not a life of emotional isolation. If I am not willing mentally and emotionally to reverse roles with you and see things through your eyes also, how can I ever really understand you? Building a relationship requires me to do a lot of bending and stretching. Balance involves more than one object. Understanding requires flexibility.

I can bend and flow.

"Sometimes I think we're all tightrope walkers suspended on a wire two thousand feet in the air, and so long as we never look down we're okay, but some of us lose momentum and look down for a second and are never quite the same again: we know."

—DOROTHY GILMAN
The Tightrope Walkers (1979)

Autonomy in Relationships

EACH OF US NEEDS OUR OWN LIFE. I cannot live yours and you cannot live mine—it doesn't work that way. When we try, each of us experiences a loss of identity and connection with the self. Our connection with the rest of the world is through the self. Through our personal soul we access a universal consciousness and the soul force or consciousness of another person. In order to do this I have to live in my own skin and allow you to live in yours. Though on the surface this may decrease our connection, on a deeper level it increases connection. Through our highly developed selves or souls we can truly have our most meaningful and satisfying sense of relatedness.

We connect on unseen levels.

"I will work in my own way, according to the light that is in me."

—LYDIA MARIA CHILD

Projecting My Needs

FALLING IN LOVE WITH YOU makes me feel strong and happy and infuses new meaning into my life. It also brings up feelings of dependency and vulnerability in me. Our intimacy draws needs, longings, fears, and pain from my unconscious self. When these feelings are too painful for me to feel, I sometimes project them onto those close to me. It is the way that my unconscious self tries to see its contents. I need to recognize that these are not your feelings but mine that I am seeing. Once I own them, I can do something about them. The very act of seeing that they are about myself, rather than you, is perhaps the biggest step in healing. It is easy for me to own my good feelings because it doesn't hurt to feel them. The ones that hurt are those I project outward in an attempt to get rid of them. Unfortunately, when I am not aware that they are my own, I genuinely see them as being about someone else. I get caught up in convincing another person that what I feel is actually true for them, and I miss the opportunity to better understand myself.

My needs are my own to discriminate and deal with.

"In some families, *please* is described as the magic word. In our house, however, it was *sorry*."

—MARGARET LAURENCE
A Bird in the House (1963)

Expectation

I WILL NOT EXPECT so much of love today either from me or from you. When I expect love between each other to look a certain way—my way—I get into trouble. It is then hard for me to accept you as you are if you are not doing what I want you to do. How much of this is my need for control? Where does it get me to exert that control over you? Controlling other people's behavior never really works. It backfires. We all need to follow the outline of our own personalities and work with who we are. We can improve and become the best version of us, but we cannot happily abandon our basic nature and become someone who is alien to our natural selves without losing our sense of comfort in life.

I allow you to be you and me to be me.

"Ah! there is nothing like staying home for real comfort."

—JANE AUSTEN
Emma (1816)

*U*nderstanding *C*onflict

I DO NOT NEED to give myself away in my relationship with you. My conditioning sometimes taught me that the best way to avoid conflict is to fuse my identity and desire with another person. Over time I became resentful for having put my wants aside, and I long for the person I used to be, the one I have chosen to ignore. Today I understand that a good relationship is not without conflict. Conflict is natural throughout the course of a day. A close relationship will inevitably include plenty.

Conflict does not necessarily mean that I'm in the wrong relationship.

"There can be no reconciliation where there is no open warfare. There must be a battle, with pennants waving and cannon roaring, before there can be peaceful treaties and enthusiastic shaking of hands."

—MARY ELIZABETH BRADDON
Lady Audley's Secret (1862)

Release

I RELEASE YOU. I trust life and the universe to hold us both. The ocean of life is buoyant enough to keep us both afloat—to support each of us in our voyage through life. We will be held up and rocked on the waves of the world. This is natural and meant to be. You need both arms free to swim and so do I. This has nothing to do with finding or losing each other. We lose each other when we can't release—when we hang on—when we mistrust. That is when we risk drowning. We can swim near each other but not for each other.

I swim and you swim.

"The story of a love is not important—what is important is that one is capable of love. It is perhaps the only glimpse we are permitted of eternity."

—HELEN HAYES
in *Guideposts* (1960)

It Works If We Work It

YOU ARE NOT HERE to fulfill my fantasies or be the person who will make my life finally work. We shape one another in subtle and not so subtle ways by our presence in each other's lives. We need to remember that we also have to shape ourselves. For me to shape myself according to what I perceive to be your expectations of me would be a loss to both of us. I would deprive myself of a sense of becoming and feel less and less connected with my own insides. You would lose the person you fell in love with. Two would-be people make one would-be relationship. Somehow I don't think it would have the lasting power that two real people coming together in honesty might have.

I take responsibility for my own life.

"Perhaps loving something is the only starting point there is for making your life your own."

—ALICE KOLLER
An Unknown Woman (1982)

Conscious Living

OUR RELATIONSHIP IS UNIQUE. Our needs, desires, likes, and dislikes are particular to us. I wish to create a safe space in which to understand and express my own uniqueness and allow that same experience for my lover. The sense of safety and security we give each other supports me in moving into life with love in my heart. You are part of my inner world and my support network. Having a consistent kind of relationship in my life is about more than us. It's part of what provides me with a sense of security and bearings in my life so that I can better enjoy the world and feel productive and whole.

I acknowledge the importance of you in my life.

"She knows what she sees. She has her eyes in the right place."

—JOHANNA SPYRI
Heidi (1880)

Being Myself

ONCE I THOUGHT INTIMACY MEANT that I lived inside of another person's skin and had rights from that position. I thought that to understand others meant to finish their sentences for them rather than to let them finish their own. I felt that to be close to someone meant signing away my own rights to individual personhood. I didn't know that I could be an individual with my own feelings and remain cared for, even if what I thought and felt differed from those I loved. I thought that to be loved I had to please. I see today that I can only honor you if I honor me. That I can only see you if I see me. That I can only appreciate and love you if I appreciate and love myself.

I see me and you.

"It was as if I had worked for years on the wrong side of
a tapestry, learning accurately all its lines and figures, yet
always missing its color and sheen."

—ANNA LOUIS STRONG
I Change Worlds (1935)

Different Paths

TODAY I RELEASE YOU from all false contracts—quiet little ways in which I hold you hostage to my own needs and fantasies—whether or not they concur with your own. What am I doing trying to recreate you in my image of who and what I think you should be? You have a right to your own particular variety of fulfillment and enjoyment. If I try to get you to live life as I feel you should live it, I will drain away your spirit. Then, after it has disappeared by inches, I will long for the person I fell in love with. When your ways of doing things threaten me, I will remind myself that that is part of being close to another person. You have the right to be you. If we can each remain ourselves, we will have more to bring to one another than if we have reorganized our personalities to fit the job description of the other.

I will let you be who you are.

"People who are always thinking of the feelings of others can be very destructive because they are hiding so much from themselves."

—MAY SARTON
Crucial Conversations (1975)

Being Whole in the Presence of Another

THE GREATEST GIFT that I can give you is to be whole myself so that when you come to me you actually find me. If I am not willing to be whole in my own right, I am not fully actualizing my own potential. This puts a pressure on us that causes us to move off balance. I cannot say that you get to be whole while I quietly remain half. It takes two whole people to make one whole relationship. Part of the gift of a relationship in my life is to pull on parts of me that I have forgotten about, to bring more of me to the surface. When this happens, though it may feel overwhelming at times, it can also be self-actualizing. The more of me I have access to, the bigger a person I can be. I need to face, embrace, and work with what parts of me surface in my relationship with you.

I am whole and you are whole.

"Everyone must row with the oars he has."

—ENGLISH PROVERB

The Wife
Tending the Hearth

❧

"When you love someone ... you do not love him or her
in exactly the same way, from moment to moment. It is
an impossibility. And yet this is exactly what most of us
demand. We have so little faith in the ebb and flow of life,
of love, of relationships. We leap at the flow of the tide
and resist in terror its ebb ... The only real security in a
relationship lies neither in looking back in nostalgia, nor
forward in dread or anticipation, but living in the present
relationship and accepting it as it is now."

—ANNE MORROW LINDBERGH

The Wife

I AM THE WIFE. I endure. I commit. I go to the fountain of my own love and draw water to share. I exercise patience and forbearance knowing that the storms of today will give way to sunlight and the sunlight will give way to showers and so on and so on throughout life. I see the horizon stretched long and wide and keep the larger picture before me in my mind's eye. I listen and follow. I lead. I walk in time. I sustain and nurture and accept the same. I am the everlasting friend of my everlasting friend. I have traveled the complex corridors of love and intimacy and understand the deepest kind of union. When hope is gone, I dig down into my own spirit, call to the heavens, and search the world around me until I find it again. I abide. I reap the countless, delicious, and nourishing fruits that have grown from careful sowing of a thousand tiny seeds. I celebrate and give thanks for the bounty and treasure that are mine.

I am committed to our love.

"We love as soon as we learn to distinguish a separate 'you' and 'me.' Love is our attempt to assuage the terror and isolation of that separateness."

—JUDITH VIORST
Necessary Losses (1986)

My Garden

MY RELATIONSHIP HAS A LIFE OF ITS OWN. It exists in the space between two individuals and is fed by those people. Like a garden, it is a growing thing and needs to be tended. What is sown is what will grow and the quality of nurturing will reveal itself in the health of what comes forth. There will be storms, forces of nature that will visit their destruction on my garden; sometimes it will seem as if the entire acre needs to be redug, resown, and grown anew. At these times I will remember that this ground is sacred to me. It is the earth that I have loved and tended for years, that has fed me and brought me pleasure. It is my little plot, a part of my life and heart. I will dig my hands deep into this soil, into this relationship, and I will look for life. When the storms come, I will remember the fruit, and when the fruit comes, I will remember the storms. If my relationship is alive, it is subject to the elements.

I am nourished and sustained by my garden.

"Nothing in life is as good as the marriage of true minds between man and woman. As good? It is life itself."

—PEARL S. BUCK
To My Daughters, With Love (1967)

Bonding

I AM BONDED TO YOU by what cannot be seen; by the thousands of hours we have passed in pleasure; by the countless small encounters; by all of your complaints that I have listened to and my tears that you have wiped away. I am bonded to you by our companionable silence, by the endless details that we know about each other. The bond that is between us is deeper than I am conscious of. It reaches into places that I forget are there. I will not undervalue or underestimate what it means to my life, my heart, and my psyche to have this type of ongoing bonding experience. Replicating it would be no easy task and eliminating it would be impossible. It is a part of me forever. Respecting it and nurturing it are what will keep it growing and alive.

I respect the power of the bond between us.

"I used to believe that marriage would diminish me, reduce my options. That you had to be someone less to live with someone else when, of course, you have to be someone more."

—CANDICE BERGEN
Knock Wood (1984)

Choosing

I CHOOSE YOU. I choose you with my mind, my soul, my heart, and my body. I come to you with all the fear and vulnerability of one who loves and hopes to be loved in return. I allow you to see me quite unadorned, very raw, very pure. I choose you to be my partner in life, to work through petty annoyances, deep sorrow, and monumental love. You are the person with whom I have cast my fate, who will influence me in a thousand invisible ways, day after day. We are building selves together, struggling to be more of who we are, comrades in laughter, adversaries in pain. At war, at peace, or on a quiet afternoon, I choose you. We make our home together; we are family, a safe harbor from which to sail and return.

Marriage is a choice.

"Take each other for better or worse but not for granted."

—ARLENE DAHL
Always Ask a Man: Arlene Dahl's Key to Femininity (1965)

Our Tapestry

WE HAVE WOVEN A TAPESTRY of our life together. Whether or not we are pleased, it is what we have woven. It represents us and what we have put into being us. To me it is beautiful and valuable and precious. I could not give it up without giving up a part of my heart, my soul, who I am. So much of me has been woven into you and so much of you has been woven into me. Pulling the threads apart would tear me inside. I cannot pretend that my relationship with you is less than it is. Some days I feel as if we live in a world that doesn't understand relationships or really support them. If I am not getting all that I want, the world I live in tells me to get out, to get my needs met, to ask for more. All that is valid, but it is only part of the story. Life is long and, if I am to be with you for the duration, there will be times when my needs aren't met and I'm not getting what I want. Just as my life will not always go smoothly on my own, how can it always go smoothly with you?

We are woven into the fabric of each other's lives.

"Pains do not hold a marriage together. It is threads, hundreds of tiny threads which sew people together through the years. That's what makes a marriage last—more than passion or even sex."

—SIMONE SIGNORET

As You Are

OVER THE YEARS I have grown to know you, to appreciate you, to love you not for who I thought I wanted you to be but for who you are. This is the greatest gift I can give to you and the most precious one I can receive. To love and be loved as we are. I will walk beside you. Our steps in time, our steps out of time. Walking over the same path in different ways, each at our own pace.

I will tell you what you mean to me every day.

"I like not only to be loved, but also to be told that I am loved. I am not sure that you are of the same mind. But the realm of silence is large enough beyond the grave. This is the world of light and speech, and I shall take leave to tell you that you are very dear."

—GEORGE ELIOT (1875), in J. W. Cross, ed.,
George Eliot's Life as Related in Her Letters and Journals

Our Love

OUR LOVE HAS A PURPOSE of its own. It shelters us from the elements. It is a shared experience, a feeling that surrounds something deep that is generated between us. It can be felt by ourselves and others. It heals. It makes ordinary time pass in a quiet kind of beauty. It allows. It defines. It motivates. Our love does not have boundaries, and yet it sets limits through its caring. It stretches me beyond myself. It connects us with something that is larger than either of us. It anchors us in the world. Our love for each other teaches us to reach beyond our own selfishness in search of generosity. When we feel there is no hope and cannot think of another possible way to look at a problem, it opens an unexpected door. It teaches us to wait and spurs us on to action. It is something worth taking care of, worth fighting for. Our love gives meaning and truth to our lives.

I find deep and sustaining meaning in loving you.

"and if i ever touched a life, i hope that life knows.
  that i know; that touching was is and always will
  be the only true revelation."

—NIKKI GIOVANNI

Holding

I CHERISH THE SPACE BETWEEN US, walking side by side without touching—being in the same house, each in a different room. Your presence in silence acts on me like a warm, summer afternoon. You have your own Higher Power, and I have mine. I will not seek to be yours, nor will I allow you to act as mine. If, at times, we drop each other, I will trust life to hold us up. Having you in my life as a constant and steady presence allows me to relax and move along in my life in other areas. I feel secure going out into the world knowing that I can come home to you. I am happy with myself. I like having my own life, my own thoughts, my own essence. And I like knowing that at the end of the day we belong to each other. Our connectedness gives me this security to go out into the world and find my paths. I am quiet inside knowing that you love me. I don't feel indentured by that love. I feel freed up by it because I know I can count on it. Then what happens in the world isn't so very critical because there is this place that holds me no matter what. And the place is you. Home. Us. It.

I am held by our love.

"A long-term marriage has to move beyond chemistry to compatibility, to friendship, to companionship. It is certainly not that passion disappears, but that it is cojoined with other ways of love."

—MADELEINE L'ENGLE
Two-Part Invention (1988)

The Bottom Line

I AM PART OF A STREAM OF LIFE. My choice of you as a partner was greatly influenced by my past, how I grew up, who was important to me, the nature of my relationship with my parents, and a million other factors that went into building my psyche. In this sense my past is continued through my union with you. We pass ourselves on through any progeny we may bear or through those lives that we touch. You live within me much in the way my parents or siblings do, at a deep and indelible level. You are part of my sense of continuity in my life—this is the way it is passed on—through those you love and touch and shape your lives and spirits with. Leaving you would be leaving that part of myself. It can be done, but there would be a price to pay. A good negotiator always makes sure that the gain is greater than the loss. A good negotiator looks at the bottom line.

We are a part of each other's inner world.

"In the true marriage relation, the independence of the husband and wife is equal, the dependence mutual and their obligations reciprocal."

—LUCRETIA MOTT (1880), in Theodore Stanton and
Harriott Stanton Blatch, eds.,
Elizabeth Cady Stanton as Revealed in Her Letters,
Diary and Reminiscences, Vol. 2 (1922)

Love and Hate

I WILL SEEK A BALANCE in our relationship. If I insist on too much love, it may seek to balance itself out with too much hate. Familiarity breeds contempt. Pushing any feeling beyond its natural course gives rise to its opposite. I will do what comes naturally. Our love is there like a water table beneath the earth. We don't have to prove it over and over again. If I make each little thing a proof of your love, then I risk making each little thing a proof of your contempt. We do not need to be as shallow as that. We can rest in quiet knowing that we are there for one another in the depths of our souls. Gushiness does not mean love; rather, it can be a compensation for what I unconsciously fear is not there. Excessive attentiveness has its opposite flip side. It gives way to a need to run, to ignore, and to hide. Then, over-attention returns to compensate. It's a love/hate dynamic and painful at both ends. Love is a quiet thing. It abides, it need not be shown off or overdone. It can just be.

I look for a healthy, middle path.

"A man is very revealed by his wife, just as a woman is revealed by her husband. People never marry beneath or above themselves, I assure you."

—CAROL MATTHAU
Among the Porcupines (1992)

Connected in So Many Ways

It's not the big things but the little ones, not the splashy moments but the simple ones, not the trips to the moon but the walks to the corner that bond me to you. We are woven into the fabric of each other's lives—breath in each other's lungs—time in each other's days. You are my person; the person in the world who carries my history. You know me in ways no one else could and I know you the same way. We live from the inside out. Our relationship is spirit made flesh. I carry you inside of me; I wear you on my face. Your presence in my life and your love give me a quiet kind of strength and courage. I am not afraid to need you.

You are my person.

"Those who have made unhappy marriages walk on stilts, while the happy ones are on a level with the crowd. No one sees 'em!"

—John Oliver Hobbes
The Ambassador (1898)

Influencing

WHEN I WAKE UP in the morning, I see you. If you have already gone, then I see where you slept. You are next to me at night and next to me in life. Our dreams mingle at night and in our shared hopes and visions and deeply held beliefs. We have made us into the people we are. We have grown each other up and shaped the adults we have become. I chose wisely when I chose you to be my partner for life; to be my fellow traveler in each other's growth and soul journeys. You and I have influenced each other in so many ways. Who we are today has everything to do with each other. I am glad it's been you, and you are glad it's been me.

We co-create each other day by day.

"The sign of a good marriage is that everything is debatable and challenged; nothing is turned into law or policy. The rules, if any, are known only to the two players, who seek no public trophies."

—CAROLYN HEILBRUN
Writing a Woman's Life (1988)

Familiarity

YOU HAVE BECOME so familiar to me, almost as if I have always known you—your movements, your touch, the feel of your skin, the sound of your voice, all so much a part of the fabric of my mind, the well-worn image of you. When your moods change, they don't shock me so much anymore. There is so little of you that I have not seen. We have worked our way into each other's lives in a manner that goes beyond time. It is hard to imagine life without you. I remember it, but the feeling of having you around has enveloped me. I do not choose to think of a life without you today. Your ways are too close to my heart and your presence too dear to me. If you went away, I could pretend in the day not to notice but somewhere in the night I would call out your name. I will live both as if we had a thousand years to spend together and as if our lives (as they do) hang constantly in the balance. This life with you has been worth all the work, the heartache, and the pain of misunderstanding. Being with you is enough.

I cherish your presence in my life.

"Sometimes idiosyncrasies which used to be irritating become endearing, part of the complexity of a partner who has become woven deep into our own selves."

—MADELEINE L'ENGLE
Two-Part Invention (1988)

Staying with It

I COULD TRADE YOU IN. I could re-choose, look for another model, try to improve my lot in a variety of ways. But would I be improving or only exchanging for a different set of problems? Are relationships about placing my original order just right or learning to love and stretch and go beyond what I thought were my natural limits? Who can give me just what I want when I hardly know what that is myself half the time? How can I ask another person to know me better than I know myself or to want to be with me more than I care to be with me? My life with you is an opportunity for growth—a chance to experience myself not as I wish I were but as I really am. If I embrace it as such, I will recognize that both of us are a process, not a product. We can help one another to heal past wounds and become better, fuller people, or we can use our relationship as a dumping ground for all that ails us. The choice is ours.

My relationship is part of my spiritual path.

"I have come to believe that giving and receiving are really the same. Giving and *receiving*—not giving and taking."

—JOYCE GRENFELL
(1976)

A Long-Term Relationship

IF WE ARE TO HAVE a relationship stretched long over time, we will have to allow each other to change. What is appropriate for one stage of life does not necessarily work for another. When we have a family, our attentions go toward building a life, a home, a place to be. Later, we face different challenges. How can we develop a relationship that is secure and trusting yet gives each of us room to pursue our own lives? How can we find a balance between enough togetherness and enough independence? What needs to happen for us to feel sufficiently connected so that we can flow freely in and out of each other's space without losing one another? Where do I begin, where do you leave off, and vice versa? What do we really need from each other to feel safe and which expectations are excessive? If we are to last, we need to be flexible and willing to throw out what doesn't work and to try new things. We can experiment and take little risks—we can change and grow.

I take small, calculated risks.

"Marriage is not a finished affair. No matter to what age you live, love must be continuously consolidated. Being considerate, thoughtful and respectful without ulterior motives is the key to a satisfactory marriage."
—PAMPHLET FROM CHINESE FAMILY PLANNING CENTER

Ritual

I WILL RESPECT RITUAL in our life together. There are daily rituals beginning in the morning. Evening rituals—things we do apart or together that we count on to anchor ourselves. There are events that we share that draw on our humanness and create a bond, a sense of belonging to a community. Rituals appear as habit, but for us they are not empty. Rather they deepen our sense of self and connectedness. Some rituals are sacred and bring us into an experience of God. They are consciousness changing. Others may just assist with transitions in our day. The rituals that we share are important. They act as a catalyst into shared space and experience. They center us and, having done that, set our minds free to explore. They have a quiet level of grandeur all their own. Ritual serves as a gateway into a deeper experience of the self, a more profound level of connectedness. When we engage fully in rituals, we are anchoring ourselves to life and a greater purpose and meaning.

I respect our rituals together.

"When a man, a woman, see their little daily tasks as integral portions of the one great work, they are no longer drudges but co-workers with God."

—ANNIE BESANT
Theosophy (1912)

Maturity in *Partnership*

PART OF A GOOD PARTNERSHIP includes maturing into understanding the real impact that our relationship has on those closest to us and maturing out of blaming, acting out, and dumping. Along with making significant improvements, we have set some standards that make everyone feel as if they are failing at intimacy. If we're not feeling close, fully understood and fully intimate at all times, we think we're in the wrong relationship. But relationships ebb and flow throughout the day, month, year, and decade. We will have close years and more distant years, ups and downs. If we make all life problems about our relationship, we'll overburden it and deeply wound each other. In a healthy, intimate relationship, eventually we learn that wounding each other is wounding our self. Trashing our relationship is trashing me because you and our relationship are a part of me. We learn to be separate and connected, to retain a sense of self in the presence of each other—this helps to strengthen self. We have the satisfaction of a job well done and the pleasure of passing on something that is of real value in this changing world.

I mature within my relationship.

"Were marriage no more than a convenient screen for sexuality, some less cumbersome and costly protection must have been found by this time to replace it. One concludes therefore that people do not marry to cohabit; they cohabit to marry."

—VIRGILIA PETERSON
A Matter of Life and Death (1961)

Unfinished Business

ALL THAT REMAINS UNFINISHED within me seeks to play itself out in the intimate arena of our relationship. The feelings of vulnerability and fear of dependence—along with the unexpressed pain of past situations that never came to a comfortable closure—will be activated by the closeness that we experience together. When we love one another, the intensity of that love is like light in a dark room. It illuminates what heretofore lay in the shadows of the unconscious. The light that it sheds can be beautiful and harsh and painful; it awakens our deepest dreams and our sleeping monsters. When the monsters wake up, they rise to their full and terrifying size, frightening us both and making us think the other is responsible for them. When the dreams wake up, they allow us to feel an innocence, security, and love that ignite our spirits. These are the forgotten elements of our own souls coming to us to see, to feel, to release, and to love.

I take responsibility for the contents of my unconscious.

"A happy marriage is the union of two forgivers."
—RUTH BELL GRAHAM, in Julie Nixon Eisenhower,
Special People (1977)

$\int$pirituality in $\mathcal{R}$elationships

I WILL LEARN TO SEE a Higher Power within you, within me, and at work in our relationship. Our relationship has an alive and spiritual feeling to it. It is an arena in which I can experience divine expression, if I choose to use it as such. It can help me to grow—to learn to be a more tolerant and loving person. It is an opportunity to see who I really am in relation to another person. Our relationship can give me perspective on myself as I see myself reflected through another person's eyes. I learn to balance that outer reflection with my inner one. Intimacy teaches me that I cannot control another person. Rather I need to learn to maintain a sense of newness, wonder, and spontaneity. Our relationship can help me to connect with more than just you or me—it can be a door to other places.

The door of intimacy leads many places.

"There are very few human beings who receive the truth, complete and staggering, by instant illumination. Most of them acquire it fragment by fragment, on a small scale, by successive developments, cellularly, like a laborious mosaic."

—ANAÍS NIN

Riding the Waves

JUST AS I WOULD NAVIGATE a boat to avoid choppy waters, I will not steer myself straight into the waves of our relationship. When the sea is rough, I will turn my motor off and focus on staying afloat. I will ride it out, knowing that I may end up in a different place from where I started. Life is like riding a boat on a changing sea. I am my own boat and I can do what is sane and sensible. Resisting the inevitable flow of the water is neither wise nor prudent. Knowing when to just stay in the boat and float takes as much dynamic energy as covering vast distances. There are days for traveling and days for riding the waves. I cannot control the sea, but I can navigate it. To understand when to act and when to remain still is to meet life on its own terms. To know in our relationship when to act and when to let it be is to live with the potential for grace and wisdom to enter our lives.

I change my tack according to our needs.

"I suspect that in every good marriage there are times when love seems to be over."

—MADELEINE L'ENGLE
Two-Part Invention (1988)

Forgetting and Remembering

I REMEMBER YOU—you're my husband. You were my boyfriend. I used to get really excited when we did things together. You were the guy who answered my prayers, who rode into my life on a white horse, and who carried me away happily ever after. I remember, you were the man I said YES to with all of my girlish hopes, all of my womanly charms, all of my unspoken dreams. I remember you; you're fun. I chose you for a thousand reasons that I too often lose track of. Have you been here all this time? We really get task-oriented and stretch our couple-space to its limits (and sometimes beyond). I remember you; you're the man I adore. I want to be with you now and focus on you and let you focus on me. Let's do things just for us; just because we feel like it. Living life with you as my primary focus has a beauty all its own. We get to have each other and our lives with all they entail.

Let's boogie.

"I can't actually see myself putting make-up on my face at the age of sixty. But I can see myself going on a camel train to Samarkand."

—GLENDA JACKSON, in John Robert Colombo,
Popcorn in Paradise (1979)

Releasing the Past

I WILL ATTEMPT TO ALLOW the past to be the past. So often when we argue, each of us dredges up painful material from the past to illustrate and reillustrate our points. Some of what we go over doesn't even apply anymore. At times what we bring up has long since been worked through, but neither of us can resist the opening to drag it out again. It is one thing to bring something forward because it needs to be healed and quite another to recreate pain and drama over and over again due to a morbid attachment to them. Just for today I will leave well enough alone and see how that works. I will assume that our relationship can work out and not burden it with excess baggage from past circumstances. Just for today I will be kind to myself and let that kindness take the form of keeping myself out of unnecessary trouble. Just for today I will know that my serenity comes first, and I will let dissension go.

I am capable of shutting my mouth.

"Love lights more fires than hate extinguishes."

—ELLA WHEELER WILCOX
"Optimism"
Poems of Pleasure (1888)

*A*ll *T*hat *I F*eel about *Y*ou

UNLESS I ACCEPT WHO YOU ARE, I will not know how to live around you. If I don't look clearly at your difficult sides, I will not protect myself from them. If I don't credit your strengths, I will not be able to benefit from them. When my energy goes into changing you rather than accepting you, I enter into a life-long obsession in which I rarely succeed in altering you; but I do succeed in losing myself in the trying. Trying to change you is a vain attempt, and I am the biggest loser. I not only devote my time and creative energy to remaking you in a different image, but I try to remake myself and our relationship as well. I need to give myself space to feel all of my feelings about you. I don't like it when I don't like certain things about you. I find it threatening, and so, in order not to have to sit with those uncomfortable feelings, I imagine changing you into something different, much like a child would fantasize turning a mean parent into a nice one. I will do better in the long run if I can face all of my feelings about you, positive and negative.

I accept you as you are.

"A successful marriage requires falling in love many times, always with the same person."

—MIGNON MCLAUGHLIN
The Second Neurotic's Notebook (1966)

A Quiet Kind of Love

OURS IS A QUIET KIND OF LOVE. We two know one another. Your unconscious movements are etched into my unconscious. The sound of your voice lives within my inner hearing. Your touch is part of me. I feel it when you are not there. I know it in my very depths. I take your heart into my hands. Your life into my life. Your soul into my soul. You live at my very center and yet we are two—very separate—closer than close. Both are meant to be.

I rest in the peace and tranquility of our union.

"There is nothing more lovely in life than the union of two people whose love for one another has grown through the years from the small acorn of passion to a great rooted tree. Surviving all vicissitudes, and rich with its manifold branches, every leaf holding its own significance."

—VITA SACKVILLE-WEST
No Signposts in the Sea (1961)

The Depth of Friendship

YOU ARE MY FRIEND, an amiable presence in my life, someone with whom I can pass time in comfort. We make plans together that sound appealing. We chat. We listen to one another and spill out our innermost thoughts. We share the shallow, the first impressions, the nonsense. I am so used to you that I hardly know the thousand tiny ways in which I know you. I understand you not with my thoughts but with my being. I would have a hard time describing you to someone because so much of you has integrated into me. Though we are two, we are connected at a level that is indescribably deep. I have passed countless hours in your presence and heard as many of your words spoken as any one person has. I have seen you in endless situations, observed how you break your bread, how you sip your tea, how you stroll along a garden path. Your movements, your voice, your touch are all drawn into my memory like paintings on a wall. They span time; they span my life as I know it. You are a part of me in so many ways, so very many ways.

I appreciate you.

"A great love is an absolute isolation and an absolute absorption."

—OUIDA (1884), in Sydney F. Morris,
Wisdom, Wit and Pathos (1884)

*H*ealing

I BELIEVE IN HEALING. The wounds that we may have caused each other can heal if we allow them to. When they begin to heal, I will not keep picking and pounding at them, making them hurt all over again. Just as a body needs rest and quiet to heal, so does our relationship. I will create optimum conditions of calm, support, and love so that we can feel safe and well again. Anybody can get sick for a while. Any relationship can too. Just as I would not turn in my body, I will not turn in my relationship. It just needs a little rest and relaxation until it is back to normal. If we need help, we can ask for it. Why should we be any different than anything else in this world? I will take care of what I have, remembering that it is as subject to disruption from the environment as any other living thing.

Our relationship is human.

"I know our marriage has just as good a chance of being
   wonderful as it does of missing the mark."

—WHITNEY OTTO
How to Make an American Quilt (1991)

Recognizing the Divine in Our Relationship

RECOGNIZING THE DIVINE in our relationship is understanding that God dwells in each and every heart and that it is this power, or life force, that unites us. This power helps relationships because it connects each person to something bigger than themselves and bigger than each other. Being petty is a fairly normal part of relationships but too much pettiness can erode respect, intimacy, and our enjoyment of life together. When we see the divine in each other, it helps to lift us into a vision of each other and our relationship that is centered around a higher truth.

I appreciate the workings of spirit in my marriage.

"Marriage with love is entering heaven with one's eyes shut, but marriage without love is entering hell with them open."

—MRS. ALEC TWEEDIE
Behind the Frontlights (1904)

The Gift of Love in My Life

TODAY I WILL LEARN to see our relationship as a gift. Wasn't it my prayer to find love? Well, here it is. This is the answer to my prayer. When I see my partner and children as gifts from God or a divine source, something magical happens, something transformative. I not only need to receive love, I also need to give love. Giving and receiving are the same channel. When I open myself to one, the other comes along with it. It's a co-active flow, a being in touch with another person at a deeper level, a level in which spirituality is present, in which trust is built, in which spirit can enter.

I see the divine at work in my relationship.

"A great marriage is not so much finding the right person as being the right person."

—MARABEL MORGAN
The Total Woman (1973)

Long-Term Commitment

WE ARE WOVEN TOGETHER by tiny threads. Spirituality can grow in the belief that our relationship is serving a larger purpose—that it's creating joy and sustenance in today's world and for our children and grandchildren. A loving relationship leaves a legacy of love and tolerance. A sound, caring, and intelligent relationship doesn't just happen. We create it; it is a deeply creative process to be in an ongoing partnership with each other. We are carriers of each other's history in partnership. If people knew how good it can be to share our daily lives, both deep and superficial issues, the world would see more long-term commitment. We deepen both the container of the relationship and all we are capable of experiencing together. We expand ourselves to include the selfhood of each other while growing, as well, into more of us.

I recognize the value of long-term commitment to my own journey.

"To mature is in part to realize that while complete intimacy and omniscience and power cannot be had, self-transcendence, growth and closeness to others are, nevertheless, within our reach."

—SISSELA BOK
Secrets (1983)

Giving 100 Percent

THE MORE LOVE I pour into our marriage or partnership, the deeper the pool of love from which I can draw comfort, strength, and security becomes. Love begets love. Real love is not for sissies. It demands the best I have to offer and then asks for more. But in the giving, in meeting the challenge, is the growth. Because a committed partnership challenges us at our very core, it sheds light on our weakest spots and motivates us to work on them. It provides a secure base from which we can move out into the world to meet our needs and find creative expression. It gives us a safe harbor to return to each day to sustain us and give us the rest and will to meet the challenges of another day.

I throw my hat into this ring.

"After marriage all things change, and one of them better be you."

—ELIZABETH HAWES
Anything but Love (1948)

Retribution

WHEN YOU BEHAVE in hurtful, insensitive ways, I see the great temptation to behave that way myself in return. I realize that in getting even with another person, I am getting even with myself; I lose my own serenity, and any possibility of changing the interaction for the better is lost. If you are acting in ways that are hurtful, it is because you are in a bad place. When I behave in kind, I am joining you. I am clearheaded enough to realize that the way in which you're acting is undesirable, and I need not do the same.

I focus on what's working.

"I begin to see what marriage is for. It's to keep people away from each other. Sometimes I think that two people who love each other can be saved from madness only by the things that come between them—children, duties, visits, bores, relations—the things that protect married people from each other."

—EDITH WHARTON
"Souls Related"
The Greater Inclination (1899)

Telling Us Apart

YOUR ACTIONS ARE NOT NECESSARILY a reflection on me, nor mine a reflection on you. In partnership I forget that other people are capable of telling us apart. Though we may reflect each other, we are different people. It is an important distinction to keep in mind. When I see each thing that you do in your life as saying something about me, I become a frantic monitor of your every action. If you have an activity I do not like, it is your activity, not mine. If you act in a way that is inappropriate, you are embarrassing yourself. Though I may also feel embarrassed, I need to remember that I am not you and you are not me. Even when other people confuse us for each other, it is important that I keep our identities straight. If I do not, I will be living for two, thinking for two, and reacting for two. It is hard enough to do these things for myself without the added complication that arises when I weave you into me.

I can tell us apart.

"Get rid of the tendency to judge yourself above, below, or equal to others."

—ABHIRUPA-NANDA (6 B.C.), in Susan Murcott,
The First Buddhist Women

Real Value

I WILL VALUE WHAT I HAVE. In this world of object worship, it is so easy to forget that the only true wealth is inner wealth and what we share with one another. Life is relationship. I do not wish to lose you in order to understand your importance in my life. I will treat us well and respect the meaning of your presence. Just by being in this committed, loving relationship with me, you are a powerful source of support. We are thousands of things to one another. I look around and see a society that overvalues objects and undervalues people. At the end of the day I cannot hold hands with a bank account, success, or even a profession. I cannot reach out and touch these things in the night. The objects of this world serve me only when I can keep them in perspective. When I cannot, they rule me. I will remember today what is really important—what truly matters.

I value the meaning of an intimate relationship.

"A simple enough pleasure, surely, to have breakfast alone with one's husband, but how seldom married people in the midst of life achieve it."

—ANNE MORROW LINDBERGH
Gift from the Sea (1955)

Separating Past and Present

I WILL NOT MAKE my relationship with you the container of all my painful history. When I have a powerful overreaction to something that you do, is it you I am reacting to or some deep hurt from my past that has never fully healed? When I allow resentment, anger, and mistrust that have their origins outside of our relationship to overwhelm our presence together, I neither heal my past nor allow us to have our own separate partnership. When I react too strongly, I will ask myself what I am really reacting to. Is it something you have done that bothers me, or has something you have done triggered unhealed pain from my past? I will make every effort to separate you and us from my own personal history.

I grow in and through our relationship.

"Love opens the doors into everything, as far as I can see, including and perhaps most of all, the door into one's own secret, and often terrible and frightening, real self."

—MAY SARTON
Mrs. Stevens Hears the Mermaids Singing (1965)

The Temporary Nature of Things

To BE WITH YOU FULLY, I need to live with the fear of losing you. Life holds no guarantees. If our relationship is alive, anything can happen. Nothing is permanent—though events and circumstances appear stable, they can be turned upside down when I least expect it. There is nothing anyone can do about impermanence. When I accept the temporary nature of life and relationships, two things happen. First, aspects of us that could be troublesome seem less serious because I understand that nothing is forever. Second, I treasure you more because I know that each day with you is a gift. It is important to be in touch with a deeper nature of life to understand the meaning of things. I will give myself the quiet, rest, and meditative solitude that I require in order to get in touch with all that lies beneath the surface.

I am capable of living without you.

"Losing is the price we pay for living. It is also the source of much of our growth and gain."

—JUDITH VIORST
Necessary Losses (1986)

Taking Care of Our Relationship

IN THIS WORLD of object worship and me-first living, I will not lose my head and forget that the real riches in life are relationships. Taking care of "number one" does not mean that I have a right to forget that you have feelings also. If I take care of myself in a way that does not take your humanity into account, I am training you to treat me that same way. I am just giving selfishness a new name and face. Once again I am doing something that sounds good but feels bad. When taking care of myself means that I shove your insides aside, I will remember what it feels like to have that done to me. I will keep in mind that I am in relationship to you and that there is such a thing as taking care of that relationship as well as myself. There is a way to take care of myself as a separate person within our relationship without forgetting that your inner world and the relationship also need to be considered.

There's me and you and a third entity called us.

"There is always something left to love. And if you ain't learned that, you ain't learned nothing."

—LORRAINE HANSBERRY
A Raisin in the Sun (1959)

ℒiving

YOU NEED NO LONGER FULFILL my dreams for life. That would not be fair. It never works anyway. Have dreams of your own. Dream them in the privacy of your own mind and let your imagination talk to your spirit and move forward into more of you. Have a cup of tea with me. You need no longer step in time while I call out the beats. Find the beat that is right for you and move to it. Let your body lead you into places you have not gone as yet. Take a walk with me. You need no longer justify my life for me; I will find it for myself. I will formulate my own questions and search out the answers in the quiet of my own heart. Let's chat a while. You need no longer breathe life into my lungs. I will draw my own breath from the infinite supply available to me always—there patiently waiting. I will let you be who you are and me be who I am and in this way we will both find our place in the natural order of things.

I do not live through you but next to you.

"Love is a context, not a behavior."

—MARILYN FERGUSON
The Aquarian Conspiracy (1980)

Enjoyment

I WILL ALLOW YOU TO HAVE FUN—fun that has nothing to do with me—knowing that the positive energy you receive will eventually be shared with me in one form or another. I will let myself have enjoyment and meaningful connections with people in my own life. The experience that I collect in a life separate from you will enhance what we have together. If we are really connected, then being separate need not threaten us. The connection we make is through acceptance and understanding, mutual respect and a sense of place and belonging. The fun you have apart from me need not diminish what we have together. Rather it should enhance it. When we fill our cups from all that life has to offer, we are less demanding of one another. I can trust that my enjoyment apart from you and yours apart from me does not divide us. I can better allow us both the space to engage more fully in our own lives, knowing that it needn't mean that we will not be there for one another. There is more to life than each other, but your presence in my life makes all the rest feel sweeter.

Enjoyment is what makes life sweet.

"Love is a fruit in season at all times."

—MOTHER TERESA
A Gift for God (1975)

Growing Together

THE PART OF ME THAT CHOSE YOU is deeper than I know. The depths of my unconscious self reached out to yours. At some unspoken level I chose you to assist me in the continuous process of my own soulmaking. Parts of me that came to you may be outside of my immediate vision. The unrequited yearnings, the unfinished childhood, the hidden dreams, all reached out to you for completion and illumination. Being with you is an attempt to see myself—to be with those parts of me that are pulled on by you. If I am wise, I will use our relationship as an opportunity to grow. Growth is messy and painful—it can be confusing and make me doubt myself and you—but growing through my difficult feelings has its own reward. I experience my expanded self, which I take to my life and to all my relationships. You were not an accidental choice. At a profound level I knew what I was doing, and I chose not only someone with whom I liked to be, but also someone in whose presence I saw myself; someone with whom I felt I could grow.

I recognize the depth of my choice.

"I am sure there is Magic in everything, only we have not sense enough to get hold of it and make it do things for us."

—FRANCES HODGSON BURNETT
The Secret Garden (1911)

Pleasure

I WILL REMEMBER the importance of enjoyment—spending lots of time in easy, pleasant recreation. This is the art of living. Relaxing with a cup of tea, savoring a delicious dinner, taking a walk. Really the world is here for us to enjoy—not to identify with, control, and possess, but to experience. What is the use of prosperity if we do not take time to enjoy life? What is the point of owning things if they do not bring us pleasure? What we share with others bonds us at an important level. Little pleasures accumulate and provide a sense of deep contentment. They allow something down inside of us to relax and let go. They abide within as a connection to each other and to life.

I take pleasure into my being.

"The deep, deep peace of the double-bed after the hurly, burly of the chaise lounge."

—MRS. PATRICK CAMPBELL, on her recent marriage, in Alexander Woollcott, *While Rome Burns* (1934)

Apology

I WILL NOT BE AFRAID TO SAY, "I am sorry." Entrenching myself in a position and refusing to move is not an enlightened way in which to live in relationship. Relationships are give-and-take, compromise and understanding. Clenching my jaw and setting my chin are not taking care of myself or the relationship. Stubbornness is a subtle form of self-abuse and blindness to another person. Taking care of myself is much more demanding than shutting a door on another person. It requires full honesty, vulnerability, and self-disclosure. It asks me to take responsibility for my real thoughts, actions, and motives. When I take care of myself by denying or ignoring your feelings, I am creating sickness, hurt, and mistrust. Unhealthy positions are black and white, overly understanding and solicitous, or rigid and distant. Health is somewhere in between. Our relationship happens in the space between us. It is our common goal, our shared purpose, our commitment, and our good will. It is an entity that we create.

I am big enough to apologize.

"There are two ways of spreading light; to be the candle or the mirror that reflects it."

—EDITH WHARTON

Meeting Needs

PARTNERSHIP IS NOT ABOUT meeting needs in isolation. Rather, it's about creating a safety net so that we can risk flying. When I demand that you meet each and every one of my needs, I set up a situation of frustration and disappointment. Partnership is meant to meet our most basic and fundamental needs for belonging, trust, love, and comfort. Let the proverbial toothpaste tube be squeezed in any direction; it is love we need not control. The little things aren't that important when compared with the deep security of having love in our lives. Loving is a daily, active endeavor. We love each day all over again. When we pour the best of ourselves into our partnership, we co-create a thriving and alive relationship that actually generates warmth and love.

I recognize what's truly important to my life.

"How helpless are we, like nettled birds, when we are caught by desire."

—BELVA PLAIN
Evergreen (1978)

Faith

I WILL HAVE FAITH in our relationship. When you feel far away from me, I will have faith that you will return, stronger, newer, with more of you. When I feel that you are disappearing under the weight of change, day-to-day living, and your own search, I will know that you are still there even though I cannot see you. When my heart wanders and looks for what it feels it cannot find with you, I will remind myself that my heart is big enough to include more than just you or just me. You need not be each and every thing I want. And when you go to others to find what you cannot find with me, I will remember that I cannot be all to you—that your having other sources of sustenance is natural and good and need not in any way reduce your love for me. In fact, when you and I know that we can reach out for sustenance and passion outside of our relationship, we have more to bring to each other, more to share that can enrich and nourish our partnership.

I say a prayer for us.

"The best marriages, like the best lives, were both happy and unhappy. There was even a kind of necessary tension, a certain tautness between the partners that gave the marriage strength, like the tautness of a full sail. You went forward on it."

—ANNE MORROW LINDBERGH
Dearly Beloved (1962)

The Task of the Wife

WE HAVE COME TO WORSHIP the idea of romantic love. Then, when our partners inevitably reveal their clay feet, we may feel disappointed and disillusioned. Sold a bill of goods. But long-term relationships serve a very deep purpose in our lives that goes beyond the particulars. They provide a sort of basic architecture, a framework, and a foundation upon which we can build our world. Working toward a fuller, deeper relationship is a good thing, but holding our current relationship hostage to our unfulfilled childhood needs and fantasies and projecting our unfulfilled sides onto it is not such a good thing. A relationship doesn't have to be perfect in order to be "good enough." There is really no such thing as a perfect relationship because there is no such thing as a perfect person. Instead we want to create alive, nourishing, resilient relationships that can grow and change and will roll with the punches. We want relationships that are flexible enough to incorporate children, relatives, and friends and solid enough to thrive on their own. Our partner in life becomes what psychologists call a "self-object." Our partner's presence, accommodation, and "fit" maintains our sense of self, our emotional stability, our continuity of identity. Deep, committed love relationships, though they may seem at times to fence us in, can ultimately lead to great freedom to explore ourselves and our world.

I commit myself to a long-term relationship a day at a time.

"Everyone wants love to follow them down their road.
Where is it that Love wants to go?"

—JUDY GRAHN
The Queen of Swords (1987)

A Quiet Place

YOU LIVE IN A QUIET PLACE inside my heart. I find you there when I least expect you. You sit in the rooms inside my unconscious self. You swim in a river inside my soul. I turn a corner, and I see you there. I expect you. I wait for the sound of your footsteps. I hold you in the silent memories that I keep in a basket beside my bed. You live there with me. We are together in all those places. Though letting go is part of how I love you, part of what I owe you, I can keep you with me in my reverie. You are part of my inner world, my joy, my purpose. You are part of my place in the scheme of things and my identity. All of this remains tucked safe inside my memory. All of this is mine forever.

I cherish your place within me.

"Where thou art—that—is home."

—EMILY DICKINSON

Getting to the Root: Identifying a Pattern

SOMETIMES WE USE our present-day relationship as a place to work out unresolved issues from the past. While this is natural, it's important that we understand which unresolved issues from the past might be undermining our relationship today. To do this, we need to become conscious of how old issues might be playing themselves out in today's partnership. Try this exercise as a way of making a connection between yesterday and today, as a way of understanding how we might have felt at one time in our lives, and how those feelings are surfacing today.

Relax, get comfortable, and allow a problem or concern that occurs over and over again within the context of an intimate relationship to come to your mind. Let the situation unfold in your mind's eye, and let yourself feel what comes up for you as this occurs. Answer the following questions in your mind or in your journal: What words describe or capture the way you feel at this time? Scrolling back in your mind, when do you recall feeling this way before and who was it that you felt this way about? If you could say what you were unable to say then to that person, what would it be? Now, coming back to the present-day situation, do you see any correlation? If so, what? How might this earlier situation be affecting your present-day circumstance?

In your journal, divide a page into three columns. At the top of the first column, write the word *Present*. At the top of the middle column, write the word *Feelings*. At the top of the third column, write the word *Past*. In the first column, briefly describe situations that occur regularly in your intimate relationships that you find problematic. In the second column, corresponding to each situation, write words that describe how you feel when that situation occurs. And, in the third column, write situations from your past intimate or family relationships in which you felt those same feelings. Then look at what you have written in your columns. See if you can tell how the past might be influencing the way you experience or view your present-day circumstances.

The Mother
Nurturing Life

If children live with criticism, they learn to condemn.
If children live with hostility, they learn to fight.
If children live with fear, they learn to be apprehensive.
If children live with pity, they learn to feel sorry for themselves.
If children live with ridicule, they learn to feel shy.
If children live with jealousy, they learn to feel envy.
If children live with shame, they learn to feel guilty.
If children live with encouragement, they learn confidence.
If children live with tolerance, they learn patience.
If children live with praise, they learn appreciation.
If children live with acceptance, they learn to love.
If children live with approval, they learn to like themselves.
If children live with recognition, they learn it is good to have
    a goal.
If children live with sharing, they learn generosity.
If children live with honesty, they learn truthfulness.
If children live with fairness, they learn justice.
If children live with kindness and consideration, they learn
    respect.
If children live with security, they learn to have faith in
    themselves and in those about them.
If children live with friendliness, they learn the world is a nice
    place in which to live.

—Dorothy Law Nolte
"Children Learn What They Live"
Children Learn What They Live: Parenting to Inspire Values

The Mother

I AM THE MOTHER. I bring forth life. I love for love's sake. I protect and nurture. The lives of my children are given to my charge. Nature has designated me as the channel through which new life enters this world. My children come first. I sacrifice my well-being for theirs. The nourishment that enters my body nourishes them and then, me. This love and commitment I feel toward my children is bigger than I am; it is part of nature's and God's design; part of the dance of life in which I play my role. I am here to ensure that our species endures. I have this in common with all forms of life. My babies captivate and delight me. They call on my deepest and most ancient need to love and protect. They adorn and give meaning and purpose to my world. They are my heart and soul made manifest.

My children are God's gift to me, and my gift to the world.

"In search of my mother's garden I found my own."

—ALICE WALKER
In Search of Our Mothers' Gardens (1983)

The Transformative Experience of Mothering

As MOTHERS, for a moment, we are Peter Pan, able to fly back to Never Never Land where we "never, never grow old." The place that's "not on any chart, and you must find it with your heart." Reentering this land of childhood allows a transformation to take place in us as mothers. We learn to see through two sets of eyes, our child's *and* our own, and the world is born again within our vision with all of its beauty, excitement, and wonder. We are with our children in a sacred place. We create transformational space that allows two souls to connect. We also create a "holding environment" where learning, development, and psychological and emotional growth can take place. It is where we build the self and study and learn how to "be" in a relationship. And here is a key—it is a space that goes two ways. The transformation happens in both, child and mother; the learning, love, and leaps of faith are mutual. The self of the child grows out of the relationship. And the self of the mother is illuminated, strengthened, challenged, deconstructed, and reconstructed through this experience of motherhood. Once we are on this train, we travel. Once we enter this journey, we come to recognize that all of life is a journey, and our job is to travel it well, to be open and honest, strong and true.

I enter the mystery of motherhood.

"Mother, in ways neither of us can ever understand, I have come home."

—ROBIN MORGAN
Matrilineal Descent Monster (1972)

The Journey of Motherhood

MOTHERHOOD IS A JOURNEY of self-discovery, the "toughest job we'll ever love." No one holds a mirror up to our insides like our own children. They see into us with laser-like precision and illuminate the areas within us that need repair like a black light. They test our patience, our nerves, and our souls. Because we are so intimate with them, they warm up all of our experiences of intimacy. The deep love, the hurt and disappointment, the need, the vulnerability—all are restimulated in the intimate arena of our relationships with our children. I will do my best not to act out on that vulnerability, making this little person's heart the unwitting container of my unhealed pain. I will not remedy a former sense of helplessness by seeking power over my child. I will accept the journey and sincerely and fully examine the issues that arise as belonging to me *before* I make the issues about them.

I will look within.

"You might not have thought it possible to give birth to others before one has given birth to oneself, but I assure you it is quite possible; it has been done; I offer myself as evidence as Exhibit A."

—SHEILA BALLANTYNE
Norma Jean the Termite Queen (1975)

Personal Growth

MOTHERHOOD CHANGES ME EVERY DAY. It carves out new spaces inside of me. It calls to places in me that I have forgotten are there. It challenges me to grow. My dead spaces hurt and bewilder my children. They can't find me if I can't find me. They feel like failures if they feel that they can't please me, that they don't make me happy. I am their world when they are small. When they feel they cannot please me, they feel that they cannot please the world. I owe these little beings my willingness to grow past my own limitations. My limitations become the unseen boundaries around their own souls. What I think of them becomes what they think of themselves. And what I think of myself lives in the atmosphere between us. I must keep growing if I am a mother. Not only do I raise my children, but also they tug on what still needs raising in me.

I will grow as a gift to my children and myself.

"Pregnancy doubled her, birth halved her, and motherhood turned her into Everywoman."

—ERICA JONG
Parachutes & Kisses (1984)

Mother Love

FIRST, FOREMOST, AND ALWAYS my job as mother is to love my children unconditionally. Though unconditional love may seem difficult, a spiritual attitude can help. My children are God's gifts to me and my gift to the world. I am the custodian not the owner of their lives. They belong, as I do, ultimately to God. When I constantly set conditions and expectations on my children, I don't really see them for who they are. Rather, I am seeing them through the lens of who I think they should be. This is not to say that I have no expectations for my children. Only that I understand that I am the person who will love them no matter what. I am their mother. There is no other me. If I do not hold this role, who will? Who can? We all need to feel loved unconditionally in life by someone so that we can relax at our core and feel good about ourselves. In times of trial and self-doubt, unconditional love is the port in a storm that our children can rely on. "My parents love me so I must have value, I must be a good person, I must have a right to a decent life." The way I love my children is the way they will learn to love themselves and their children.

I will pass on a legacy of unconditional love.

"To her whose heart is my heart's quiet home
To my first love, my Mother, on whose knee
I learnt love lore that is not troublesome."

—CHRISTINA GEORGINA ROSSETTI
"Sonnets Are Full of Love"
A Pageant (1881)

The Importance of Childhood

VIRTUALLY MOST RESEARCH ATTESTS to the importance of children's early experience in building the persons they will one day become. The truths that we accept about ourselves in childhood form the cornerstone of our self-image and the way we look at life. How our parents and family see us becomes how we assume and expect the world will see us. We incorporate their view of us into our own self-image. Our maturation and development wrap themselves around these core beliefs. Each new stage of growth is built upon who we are up until that moment. New information is filtered and made sense of through the lens of how we see ourselves and our world. The contours and strength of the foundation we build as children set the architecture for how we shape ourselves upon it. Our early experience forms the template out of which we think, feel, and behave as life moves along. The way our brain gets wired in childhood is the wiring we live with throughout our lives.

I understand the power and resonance of my role as mother in my child's life.

"When we talk of leaving childhood behind us, we might as well say that the river flowing onward to the sea had left the fountain behind."

—ANNA JAMESON
A Commonplace Book (1855)

ℱloor 𝒯ime

DR. STANLEY GREENSPAN, child psychologist, talks about daily "floor time" with kids. Floor time is when we're on the floor with our children connecting at their level, seeing through their eyes, and doing what they want to do. If we allow for floor time every day, we help to set a foundation for both healthy development and intimate connection. We get to know our kids at their level. We show them through our behavior that we value them, want to be with them, are there for them. Floor time translates into other forms of together time throughout life. It is a way of truly being together in a focused, intimate, connected manner. It is a way of expanding the container of the relationship so that it can hold a greater depth of emotional and psychological connection. It is a gift that keeps on giving and growing.

I take daily floor time with my kids.

"If a child is to keep alive his inborn sense of wonder . . . he needs the companionship of at least one adult who can share it, rediscovering with him the joy, excitement and mystery of the world we live in."

—RACHAEL CARSON
The Sense of Wonder (1965)

Surrendering and Mothering

I NEVER KNEW THE TRUE MEANING of anxiety and fear until I had children. The idea of anything happening to my children sent shivers not up my spine but through my soul. I will never forget walking through the woods with my husband when a cacophony of screeches shot through the silence like a car alarm during a black night. "What was that?!" I said, frozen in amazement. "Oh, it's a partridge. She must be a mother who feels her young are being threatened," said my husband. I was transfixed. I knew just how this bird felt, and her screech could easily have come out of me under similar circumstances. It seemed clear to me that we mothers are all wired pretty much the same, whether we have feathers, fur, or skin. I was so moved by that mother partridge. I felt she understood and spoke for my experience; my desperate need to protect my young. She also understood that I would prefer to be shot at myself rather than to endure the pain of watching my child suffer. This is why *surrender is learned better in motherhood than practically any other time.* My fear of something happening to my children is so big that only a true surrender, a genuine letting go of the illusion that I can control all eventualities, can bring me relief when caught in fear's grip and restore me to inner peace.

I give my children into the loving hands of a benevolent God.

"She knew how to make virtues out of necessities."

—AUDRE LORDE
Zami: A New Spelling of My Name (1982)

A Noble Purpose

I HONOR THE POWER OF PURPOSE. I recognize the quiet joy and contentment that are mine when I apply myself daily to a worthy endeavor. My purpose needs to be a balance of giving and receiving. This is a spiritual paradox. If we can only give but cannot receive, we won't be able to take in support and love from others so that we can relax, refuel, and feel cared about. We also deny someone else the pleasure of giving to us when we cannot humbly and gratefully receive their love. Things are not always as they seem. Sometimes, as St. Francis said, "It is in giving that we receive." And at times, receiving is a sort of giving. It is part of the mystery of connection, part of the truth that we are all issued from one great source and we are made up of the same particles of life.

I recognize the hand of God in life.

"Many persons have a wrong idea of what constitutes true happiness. It is not attained through self-gratification but through fidelity to a worthy purpose."

—HELEN KELLER
Helen Keller's Journal (1938)

Fitting Myself In

ONE OF THE PROBLEMS mothers have is adding themselves into the equation of family needs and demands. In putting children first much of the time, rather than putting ourselves second or even third, we put ourselves nowhere. When we disallow our own needs, dreams, and desires for too prolonged a period, we stop building self. We set up an all-or-nothing situation. Our dreams, needs, and desires get relegated to our shadow side, where they grow in darkness. They leak out. We feed them surreptitiously through others. Rather than understanding our needs and desires and meeting them constructively and openly, we repress and deny them. Then, when they finally burst forward, they are like a hungry beast who cannot feel full. While child rearing does ask us to sacrifice, and rightly so, we still need to attend to ourselves. If we don't, we run the risk of trying to fill up our empty self on the self of another.

I count too.

"Nothing else will make you as happy or as sad, as proud or as tired, for nothing is quite as hard as helping a person develop his own individuality—especially while you struggle to keep your own."

—MARGUERITE KELLY and ELIA PARSONS
The Mother's Almanac (1975)

Emotional Refueling

CHILD PSYCHOANALYST Margaret Mahler speaks of the small comings and goings of the toddler from her mother's knee as moments of "emotional refuelings." The toddler wanders off and engages in separate play, frequently returning to the mother's side to reconnect. Each successful reconnection reassures the child that it is possible to leave and return without sacrificing the care and presence of her mother. If the mother consistently undermines the child's wish for independence, the child may learn that she must sacrifice her mother's approval if she wishes to move away from her. If the mother allows the child her curiosity in a safe and supported manner and then welcomes her back with care and interest, the child learns that she can have a separate self *and* a loving connection with her mother. She can go into the world and come home for refueling throughout her life.

I will allow my child to be separate while connected.

"Who ran to help me when I fell
 and would some pretty story tell
 Or kiss the place to make it well?
 My Mother."

—ANN TAYLOR
"My Mother," in Jane Taylor and Her Sisters,
Original Poems for Infant Minds (1804)

Constancy

MOTHERHOOD CAN ABSOLUTELY CHALLENGE me to my core. It is truly one of the hardest things I've ever done. I'm on duty twenty-four/seven and I am certainly not 100 percent all of that time. I wish there were two of me so I could always be fresh, rested, and in good form. Somehow, though, I'll do my best and my best will just have to be good enough. I will do my best to be stable, constant, and reliable. In your young years you totally depend on me for your survival. I understand that if I am careless with you at this tender, vulnerable age, if you cannot depend on me, you may feel you cannot depend on life. I am your connection to this world. Without me you cannot access it on your own. I am your world. Though the responsibility of this feels awesome to me, though I may, at times, feel overwhelmed by the reality of these words, there is really no way around it. You need me to come through for you so that you learn that life can be trusted. One way I will show you love at this stage is by being there for you in a consistent manner. If your world revolves around me, then I will do my best to be a stable and loving presence.

I will do the best I can with what I have to work with.

"... undemanding, unambitious; she is receptive and intelligent in only a moderate, concrete way; she is of even temperament, almost always in control of her emotions. She loves her children completely and unambivalently. Most of us are not like her."

—JANE LAZARRE
The Mother Knot (1976)

My Children's Special Knowledge

MOTHERHOOD HAS CHANGED ME, grown me up, softened my edges, and taught me to be more. The person that my children really want to get to know is me. They sense me; they know who I am. Their eyes see through to the other side. Most of the time they keep this vast understanding to themselves so as not to invade my privacy. They stand guard at the door of their mother's unspoken secrets. My children know me as well as I know them, and they love me as much as I love them. They try not to embarrass me by telling too much truth. They protect me from myself in their minds. Isn't it funny to realize how much they really know?

My children know me, and I know them.

"Motherhood is the one experience in life that puts everything else into a different place."

—LINDSAY WAGNER

Sharing My Stories

TELLING OUR CHILDREN our personal stories is a way to transmit our values and a sense of morality to them. Stories inspire and instruct in a way that captures the imagination and leaves room for our kids to use them without feeling overly controlled. We can get across many of our views on life by telling stories from our own lives, lessons on living that our children can tuck away to use when they need them. Personal stories illustrate what is important to us, what we care about, what moves us, what brings us joy, and what sustains our faith in life. They can also reveal the mistakes we made along the way and what we learned from them. I tell my children lots of stories in which I am the antihero, did dumb things, goofed up, or took a wrong direction. In this way, I let them know that they don't have to be perfect or measure up to things that took me much of my life to accomplish. I show them the warts and bumps along the way so they won't come as such a shock. Our stories will live on in our children's minds and hearts, and they can draw strength and inspiration from our stories for years to come. Stories are the spoken history of our families.

I share who I am as a person and who we are as a family through stories.

"Yes, mother . . . I can see you are flawed. You have not hidden it. That is your greatest gift to me."

—ALICE WALKER
Possessing the Secret of Joy (1992)

The Calling of Motherhood

FOR ME AND FOR MANY WOMEN I KNOW, motherhood is more a calling than a role. From the deepest recesses of my spirit and the cells of my body, I am called by all that is living to be a mother. My children feel like the answer to a silent prayer that I have been whispering in my heart since girlhood. They feel as if they could belong to no one else. They are the trusted carriers of their parents' hearts and the culmination of our love. I feel that the universe has sung its sweetest song to me through their being—that we have been embraced and included in an eternal circle of love and life through, as poet T. S. Eliot puts it, "this grace dissolved in place." It is their presence in life and the process of building a family that has taught me surrender and humility. They are nature's way of teaching me my right size, my place in the scheme of things.

I surrender to the power of motherhood.

"If you bungle raising your children, nothing else much matters in life."

—JACQUELINE KENNEDY ONASSIS (1994)

Lighthouse

I AM MY CHILDREN'S LIGHTHOUSE. I stay in the same location so that whether in the light of day or in the dark of night they can locate themselves when they see me. I hold the shore. I mark the spot. If I move around, if I am too hard to find, if I hide, disappear, or misunderstand the value of stability in their lives, I will do them a great disservice. They could get lost looking for me. Or they might spend so much of their energy trying to find me that they won't have enough to get their own lives going. Because my children sail away from me, because they seem not to need me as they used to, I sometimes feel I am no longer vital to their lives. This is not, nor will it ever be, the case. I will show the wisdom and love of being easy to find, easy to see.

I locate myself where I can be easily accessed.

"You can never go home again, but the truth is you can never leave home, so it's all right."

—MAYA ANGELOU
The Maya Character (1987)

Turning It Over

MY CHILDREN HAVE THEIR OWN HIGHER POWER, and it's not me. When my anxiety overwhelms me, I will remember this. As I release them, I will understand it. I cannot control the outcome of their lives. Ultimately, I have to take what I perceive to be the right steps and let go of the results. I can pray, beseech, bargain, and micromanage but, ultimately, their lives are in God's hands, not mine. I am not always able to disengage my self-interest or my image of their self-interest enough to see the big picture. When I release my children to the loving care of their own Higher Power, I also release them from my tenacious grasp. I recognize that I am not all-powerful. Though I have tremendous power over my children, I cannot play God in their lives without overstepping healthy boundaries.

I pray for my children's well-being.

"If it can be verified, we don't need faith. Faith is for that which lies on the *other* side of reason. Faith is what makes life bearable, with all its tragedies and ambiguities and sudden, startling joys."

—MADELEINE L'ENGLE
Walking on Water (1980)

Stress

I FEEL PULLED in so many directions. There are days when I wish that I could clone myself just for a decade or so. How can I possibly meet all the demands of motherhood, partnership, and career? If I need to put something on hold for a while, what is it? Anything I put on hold, seems to me, will suffer. I am stretched taut and some days can see no way out. I wind up feeling like a control freak, that no one can step in and help because it's just too complicated to keep it all straight. Ahhhhhhhh! Maybe I need to do what, at the moment, seems impossible; to take a deep breath, relax my shoulders, and see if anything here can be subtly shifted in priority or delegated, put off for a bit, or supported by someone else.

Somehow this will all work out.

"At work, you think of the children you've left at home. At home, you think of the work you've left unfinished. Such a struggle is unleashed within yourself: your heart is rent."

—GOLDA MEIR, in Oriana Fallaci,
L'Europea (1973)

Being Present to Our Relationship

I WILL BE WILLING to go all the way. I will not hold back or trim round the edges in my commitment to my relationship with my children. If I hold back, I teach them to hold back. If I keep parts of myself hidden, I teach them to hide parts of themselves. If I am present in body and words, saying and doing the right or expected things but withholding my authentic self and presence, how can they learn what it feels like to be present, to have an open heart, to feel and experience another person? I value the time we are together. We are not ships that pass in the night. We are here, now. We're together, in each other's mind and heart space. If this is an alive universe, then the space we occupy together is alive too. It carries our thoughts and feelings back and forth.

I am with my children.

"How we spend our days is, of course, how we spend our lives."

—ANNIE DILLARD
The Writing Life (1989)

Helping Children with Painful Feelings

WE ALL GO THROUGH painful circumstances—it's part of life and cannot be avoided. We sometimes learn about ourselves and the deep meaning of life through pain. We develop through struggle. Don't tell your children *not* to struggle; teach them *how* to struggle well with dignity, with depth, and with a desire to grow from it; to reach down into themselves and pull out something they didn't know was there. They will build self and feel strong.

- Let them voice their feelings; let them talk about what's on their minds. Try to have enough emotional distance so that they can emote without your wanting to fix, explode, control, or disappear.
- Don't say, "Don't worry." They do worry, and they need to learn how to work with what's upsetting them. They worry about the world and they worry about their lives and about us. Don't interpret silence as meaning they're not bothered inside.
- Let them draw or journal or write letters (not to send) to get their feelings out. This type of expression can help them feel empowered, especially if they're young and have limited language skills.
- Recognize that, with your help, working through tough issues builds character, mastery, and self-confidence. Talk to them at their level and listen to them at their level.

I can do this.

"Even without wars, life is dangerous."

—ANNE SEXTON
Hurry Up Please, It's Time (1990)

Holding a Place

I WILL HOLD A SPACE for you in which to be; my gift to you. A place in the world that is sacred beside me. I will honor that space and protect it; and, if you hold a place for me, I will accept and value it. We can do each other a great service here on earth while we are alive. We can give each other shelter. We cannot change the wind or the rain or devastation of storms. We cannot make what will happen not happen, but we can provide a feeling of safety in each other's presence. This is what family can do that is such a gift in this busy world. It can provide a safe space to be loved, accepted, and valued simply for being a family member.

I am deeply grateful for our deep and sustaining bonds.

"I wonder why you care so much for me—no, I don't wonder. I only accept it as the thing at the back of all one's life that makes everything bearable and possible."

—GERTRUDE BELL (1892), in Elsa Richmond, ed.,
The Earlier Letters of Gertrude Bell (1937)

Age-Correspondence Reaction

THE AGE-CORRESPONDENCE REACTION can have a powerful impact on parenting. For example, Alice's mother divorced Alice's father when Alice was ten years old. Alice becomes an adult with her own marriage and child. According to the age-correspondence reaction, Alice may feel like divorcing when her daughter reaches ten years old. In other words, Alice's daughter becoming ten stimulates unconscious memories in Alice from when she was ten. Unconscious memories related to age can be stirred up in a variety of situations. If we had a tough year in seventh grade, we may worry irrationally about our children when they are in seventh grade. We may project our unconscious stuff onto them, assuming they are experiencing difficulties that, in some way, mirror our own (even if they're fine). Our children's age triggers what may have been important to us at that time in our own lives. Next time we seem as if we might be overreacting to something about our children or the situations they're in, let's think back to that age in our own lives and what was going on with us. Do we find anything interesting?

My child holds a mirror up to my own past.

"If it's hysterical, it's historical."

—TWELVE STEP PROGRAM SAYING

The Parents' Unlived Lives

SOMETIMES WE WANT our children to be who we never were. We live through them and not with them. We want our unlived lives to be lived through them. On a piece of paper or in your mind answer these questions for yourself:

- What unlived part of me longs for expression?
- What is a block in the way of this expression?
- Why do I hide this part of myself?
- What are my greatest fears in letting this part of me out?
- What do I imagine my life would look like were I to let this part of me express itself?
- What are the old messages I carry that make me think I need to hide this part of myself?
- How might my unlived life be impacting my child's life?

I will examine my unlived lives.

"Parents teach in the toughest school in the world—The School for Making People. You are the board of education, the principal, the classroom teacher and the janitor."

—VIRGINIA SATIR
Peoplemaking (1972)

Healing My Past

IT IS SO IMPORTANT to heal early childhood wounds so that we do not pass them on, either in the form in which they were passed on to us or in an opposite reaction. This is the process of breaking the chain of generational pain. It is getting free enough of old, deep hurts so that we do not act them out with our children. When the mother who was demeaned by her own mother demeans her daughter, she may be acting out the unresolved pain of her own childhood. She is *showing* her pain because *talking* about it is too painful for her. If she talks about it, she will have to allow herself to remember how hurt and how vulnerable she felt and to experience once again her feelings of sadness and betrayal. But, if she is not willing and able to sit with the child who lives within her, her inner child—to talk and feel out the pain— she puts herself at great risk for treating her little girl the way she was treated.

I will examine myself.

"Always there remain portions of our heart into which no one is able to enter, invite them as we may."

—MARY DIXON THAYER
Things to Live By (1933)

Seeing and Attunement

MOTHERHOOD FOLLOWS NO SET COURSE and comes with no set of instructions. Just the thing that works perfectly in one situation or at one age lays a big goose egg somewhere else. When our children are small, we are the lamps that light their hearts—they cannot get enough of us; they want us around constantly and cry when we're not close. Then they hit the teenage years and want us out of their face. So there are no hard-and-fast rules that work across the board. Attunement allows us to come up with the appropriate response to a given situation. It means tuning in so that we can come up not with the perfect-for-all-time-response nor the *pro forma* one, but with the tiny, simple response that is right for this small moment. The art of raising a child well is to pay attention to a million and one small encounters.

Motherhood is in the details.

"I had the most satisfactory of childhoods because Mother, small, delicate-boned, witty and articulate, turned out to be exactly my age."

—KAY BOYLE, in Robert McAlmon,
Being Geniuses Together (1968)

Interaction and *F*eedback

I WILL TAKE JOY in my children. I will show them that their mother takes pleasure in their presence, in their being. I will let my face light up when they walk in the room and a tear come to my eye when they are hurt; I will fall down in peals of laughter at their jokes. I will be their best audience, allowing them to affect me. If I were to be impassive, cool, or aloof, what would that do to them? Their confidence and sense of who they are is built through a myriad of tiny interactions that we share. My variety of responses to them is how they learn about who they are and what kind of place the world is. I am their litmus paper, their market research, their feedback upon which they decide their strategies on how to be and succeed in the world.

I understand my role.

"The heart outstrips the clumsy senses, and sees—perhaps for an instant, perhaps for longer periods of bliss—an undistorted and more veritable world."

—EVELYN UNCERCHILL
Mysticism (1955)

Exploration

I WILL ALLOW MY CHILDREN to explore their universe. When they are tiny, I will keep them safe while they touch, step, vocalize, and look. As they grow older, I will stand by them as they experiment with behaviors, ways of being, and new activities. I can be a good sous-chef and provide the raw materials for their creations. And later I'll give them some space in their search for self as they push on the boundaries of the world and our relationship. As they grow into adulthood, I won't withdraw my love and support. I need them, too, for my life to feel whole and meaningful. If I ditch them when they need my understanding and support, I will surely damage our relationship, their future and mine. We just need to learn how to be separate and connected. My children can challenge me, need me, distance from me, and I will work it through with them, asking for their respect and consideration but not their blind obedience, not their souls. We each need to have our own soul.

I support my child's sense of wonder and discovery.

"If I have learned anything it is that life forms no logical patterns. It is haphazard and full of beauties, which I try to catch as they fly by, for who knows whether any of them will ever return?"

—MARGOT FONTEYN
Margot Fonteyn (1975)

Being Authentic

WE ALL HAVE THIS FEAR, as mothers, of ruining our children; we fear that who we are won't be good enough; that we're "soiled humanity." But we are all soiled, and we are all blessed. We bring our whole selves to motherhood. If we hide parts of ourselves that we feel are unacceptable, we confuse our children. They sense we're hiding something, and they are left to make their own sense of it. All too often the sense they make is that they are somehow not valuable enough to share the truth with. We don't need to tell them more information than is appropriate. But we shouldn't imagine that by "not talking" we are protecting them from less-than-perfect sides of us. We tell them to tell the whole truth, but we tell them half a truth. Today I will resolve to practice what I preach. I will observe what I am hiding.

I will be genuine with my children.

"Most of all the other beautiful things in life come in twos and threes, by dozens and hundreds. Plenty of roses, stars, sunsets, rainbows, brothers and sisters, aunts and cousins, comrades and friends—but only one mother in the whole world."

—KATE DOUGLAS WIGGIN, in Charles L. Wallis, ed., *The Treasure Chest* (1965)

Guardians of Life

OUR RITUAL IS BIOLOGICAL, built into us. Nature has intended us to bring forth and nurture life. When I was first pregnant, my husband and I went to Lamaze classes to learn how to breathe, not breathe, pant, lean forward, and a host of other things that we promptly forgot when it came to the real thing. Luckily, I had helped my dog give birth six weeks before and observed how still and calm she lay, how much she let my presence support her, and still how she gave birth all on her own. She was an excellent model and I felt that, if she could offer life this channel through which to manifest on earth, then so could I. But still, in a way, nothing could have prepared me for the pain or the joy I was about to feel. My children seemed to draw love out of me from my head to my toes, from my soul. The testimony of this love for them ranged from the renewed patience I had for the tedium of daily tasks to claiming my place in the long line of humanity. They were tiny teachers of real love.

I learn to love a day at a time.

"Love is the vital essence that pervades and permeates, from the center to the circumference, the graduating circles of all thought and action. Love is the talisman of human weal and woe—the open sesame of every soul."

—ELIZABETH CADY STANTON
(1860)

Pushing Away

I WILL LET YOU ESTABLISH your own identity. Your wish to be different from me is natural and healthy. If I humiliate you for this wish, I send you away with shame. You will feel guilty as if something is wrong with you for wanting to be yourself—for wanting to push me away. Pushing me away is a normal and natural impulse in your process of growing up. I will let you push me away without shaming you—I will love you from any place I am.

You can be who you are in my presence and with my blessing.

"What we have once enjoyed we can never lose. All that we love deeply becomes a part of us."

—HELEN KELLER
We Bereaved (1929)

You Are Glorious

I AM TOUCHED by your growth as a person. Touched, moved, and exhilarated. Proud. You move me. I am watching you become more of who you are. I am part of your journey. You are your journey. My love for you allows me to see the face of God. I learned to see through loving you. It was you who gave me the courage to face all of who I am. It was you who taught me the meaning of love. I have been your parent, but you have been my teacher. Your tender touch, your love for me, your acceptance of me just as I am opened the door to life itself. I am humbled by your presence in my life and grateful beyond words for your love. Watching you become who you are—embracing your life with energy, courage, and spirit—is magnificent. It's a privilege to be your mother.

Go, kid, go—go for it—whatever it is.

"She tended to be impatient with that sort of intellectual who, for all his brilliance, has never been able to arrive at the simple conclusion that to be reasonably happy you have to be reasonably good."

—CAROLYN KIZER
A Slight Mechanical Failure (1972)

Inner Strength

I HAVE THE INNER STRENGTH to allow you to be your own person. When you do not need me as much as you did as a toddler, it can hurt. You have made me feel so important and needed. You have given me a life's purpose and a sense of place on this earth—a place in the scheme of things. But I cannot make it your responsibility to provide my life with meaning all on your own. I have to do that for myself and let you find your meaning.

I am strong enough to let you live.

"Your life is the one place you have to spend yourself fully—wild, generous, *drastic*—in an unrationed profligacy of self. . . . And in that split second when you understand you finally are about to die—to uncreate the world, no time to do it over, no more chances—that instant when you realize your conscious existence is truly flaring nova, won't you want to have used up all—*all*—the splendor that you are?"

—ROBIN MORGAN
The Anatomy of Freedom (1982)

I Witness You Building a Self

I WILL SUPPORT YOU in your slow and steady building of a self. On the one hand, you are not the person you will be. On the other hand, who you are today will be part of who you will be tomorrow. How can I maintain appropriate goals for you and, at the same time, allow you to grow toward them slowly, making mistakes, and having bumps along the way? I will take the appropriate action to help you build a good life today and let go of the results. I will be patient and wise rather than give way to momentary fears and impulses. I will not act out on my fears and anxieties. I have so many small fears and anxieties that they can keep me walking around in a fog. I miss the day as it is and am more likely to foul things up with you, me, or us. My fears make me anxious, result-oriented, and critical. Then I want quick results, perfection in your behavior so I can stop feeling nervous. But this is a trap. The more anxious I get, the more anxious you get, and the more things don't work well because we're both stressed out. Good things emerge from a relaxed, centered state of mind. Growing up takes its own time.

We have all the time in the world and building a self will take that.

"I long to accomplish a great and noble task, but it is my chief duty to accomplish humble tasks as though they were great and noble. The world is moved along, not only by the mighty shoves of its heroes, but also by the aggregate of tiny pushes of each honest worker."

—HELEN KELLER
The Treasure Chest (1983)

Home

YOU ARE SO EXCITED. I never knew having growing children could be this much fun. I love to see you go after your life. I feel so good supporting you, helping you to launch yourself into more of you. I remember how scary it was to take on the world and to try to go after my life. I am here to be your cheerleading section—to tell you you can do it and to provide you with a place where you will always be special, always be a success—our home. Take this home into your heart wherever you go; it's yours. We made it together and whenever we are together home is there too. We remind each other of who we are deep down. We hold a very special space safe for each other. We are a family.

We carry our home in our hearts.

"I cannot forget my mother. Though not as sturdy as others, she is my bridge. When I needed to get across, she steadied herself just long enough for me to run across safely."

—RENITA WEEMS
"Hush Mama's Gotta Go Bye-Bye,"
in Patricia Bell-Scott et al., *Double Stitch* (1991)

Maintaining a Healthy Distance

I NEED TO EDUCATE myself on standing back. Adolescent and teenage years are turbulent, full of ups and downs, strong feelings, constant tiny identity crises, hopes, and fears. When I over-identify with each of your changes, I get lost in you and lose much of me. I become thrown off-balance inside and have trouble in being a parent—I lose my objective position and my ability to be a rational, helpful support. Your wish to separate and become your own person does not mean that I have in some way failed in my job as mother. Rather, it means I have succeeded. You need to have a self that feels like your own in order to feel excited about your life. There is plenty of room for you to be you and me to be me.

I support your wish to be you.

"We all carry the houses of our Youth inside, and our Parents, too, grown small enough to fit within our Hearts."

—ERICA JONG
Fanny: Being the True History of the Adventures of
Fanny Hackabout-Jones (1980)

Rushing It

I CANNOT SEEM TO FORGIVE you for being who you are. You're confusing. You don't behave just as I wish you would. You dress in such an odd way, and your room is always messy. It's an effort to keep you in line. You eat junk food, and you walk around looking sort of lost. I take it personally. I want you to make this stage of your life easier for me. I want you to act in a way that is less unnerving. Seeing these years as a necessary "growing-up" time is hard for me. I want you to just grow up—I want this period to be over so I can see whether or not it worked. How will you turn out? Will you be responsible enough to create a good life? Will you get it together? Will you ever start acting like an adult? Will you ever want to act like an adult? I want to learn to have patience—to give you time to grow—to become—to experiment and change.

Steady my heart, things will work out.

"If you aren't your own agent, you are someone else's."

—ALICE MOLLOY
"In Other Words" (1975)

"Trivial things and important things wound into and against one another, all warring for her attention. Changing the goldfish water wasn't vital, but it couldn't wait; teaching the children their Bible was vital, but it could wait. Listening to them, growing with them, that was vital; but the bills had to be paid now, the dinner was burning right now."

—JOANNE GREENBERG
"Children of Joy"
Rites of Passage (1972)

Creative Visualization

EACH DAY I WILL VISUALIZE your happy life and future. I will hold in my mind's eye the image of you doing what you love, thinking and feeling independent and productive. There is much I can do as a mother in the silent places of life. I will visualize you whole and happily engaged in a constructive, fulfilling life. Not only might this benefit you in some unseen way, but also at the very least it keeps my thoughts moving in a positive direction. When anxiety grips me, rather than have it leak out and make us both more anxious, I will turn my thoughts toward a more positive direction. In a way, this is a great transitional activity for me during that period when I am getting used to your becoming more independent. It's a way of mothering you from a distance. I can think of you. I hold your image—strong, happy, self-actualized.

I see you full, strong, whole, and happy.

"Any of us can dream, but seeking vision is always done
not only to heal and fulfill one's own potential, but also
to learn to use that potential to serve all our relations: the
two-leggeds, the four-leggeds, the wingeds, those that
crawl upon the Earth and the Mother Earth herself."

—BROOKE MEDICINE EAGLE, in Joan Halifax,
Shamanic Voices (1979)

Playing My Role

I WILL PLAY MY ROLE of being your mother, but I will remember that it is not the only role available to me in my life. I still need a self if we are to be alive in our relationship. If I lose myself to the role, eventually I will be relating to you one step removed from my real nature. Though I am committed to you completely, I can still step out of the role of your mother and into other roles throughout the course of my day. I need this role relief or I will become fatigued and jaded on the subject of motherhood and resent you for taking up all the space inside of me. The more I allow myself to play a variety of roles in which I experience nurturing, competence, and satisfaction, the less I will demand that you supply me with a total identity. When I forget myself and become a role, I lose the best of me—my authenticity, my uniqueness—and all I bring to you is a hollow role with no one inside it. I lose my ability to connect with you in an authentic, alive way. I remember that I can play more roles in the world than mom and still put motherhood as a top priority.

I will appreciate the roles available to me throughout my day.

"Biology is the least of what makes someone a mother."

—OPRAH WINFREY
in *Woman's Day* (1988)

"The simple idea that everyone needs a reasonable amount of challenging work in his or her life, and also a personal life, complete with noncompetitive leisure, has never really taken hold."

—JUDITH MARTIN
Common Courtesy (1985)

Modeling

WHO WE ARE speaks louder than what we say. Modeling is one of the deepest forms of learning. The way to teach our children who to be is by being it ourselves. If I want honest children, I cannot lie in word or deed. If I want kind children, I have to treat them with kindness. If I want my children to understand me, I need to understand them. If I want them to show me respect, I will show them respect. I cannot ask my children to be for me what I am not willing to be for them. Otherwise, the integrity of our intimacy will be compromised. My children not only read me like a book, I am their encyclopedia, their reference volume, their first source of knowledge.

I understand my impact on my children.

"Parents have become so convinced that educators know what is best for their children that they forget that they themselves are really the experts."

—MARIAN WRIGHT EDELMAN, in Margie Cassady's
"A Sense of Place,"
in *Psychology Today* (1975)

"An ounce of mother is worth a pound of clergy."

—SPANISH PROVERB

Passing on Pain

WHATEVER I STORE in my shadow side, the side that follows me everywhere but that I do not see, gets felt and absorbed by my children. They stand in my shadow because they stand at my side. My shadow contains the parts of me that I have relegated to silence. Though I do not see into those parts, they follow me nonetheless. Where I am they are. Where I stand, they are present. How can my children not experience this part of me? When my words say one thing and the atmosphere around me says another, I confuse them. They see one thing and feel another. They hear the words that make their way past my filters, and they sense what remains hidden. I kid myself when I think that my kids don't see the real me. When I won't own the truth, I ask them to live the same lie I am living—to collude with me in my own self-deception.

I am willing to see my shadow.

"... it was a skyblue day in December sixty-nine ... it was the kind of time in the life of a family when something happens to nudge its hidden morality from its resting place and make it bubble to the surface and float for a while. In clear view. For everyone to see."

—ARUNDHATI ROY
The God of Small Things (2000)

Purposeful Ignoring

I WILL BE EASY TO IGNORE. I will be easy to find so that my children can ignore me with purpose and ceremony. They will know where I am and can walk by me like a cat moving past a potential predator on soft paws, keeping it in line of vision in order to avert a possible attack. Ignoring me is one of their ways of telling me that they are becoming separate people. My children need to locate me so that they can ignore me, so that they can measure their individuation in terms of visible, emotional, and psychological distance from where they started (me). If I disappear, they lose their bearings; they can't measure their distance *from* me *into* the world.

I will stand fast while my kids ignore me.

"What parent ever thought the child has arrived at maturity?"
—MRS. MARY CLAVERS
A New Home (1839)

The Right Distance

IT CAN BE DIFFICULT to find the right distance and closeness to our children. And the right distance is constantly changing. What is vital at one stage may be detrimental at another. We need to be flexible and secure enough within ourselves to allow the ratio of distance and closeness between us and our children to make necessary developmental shifts. In order to do this we need to have a self. Growing up or living with addiction and dysfunction can distort our sense of self in insidious ways. We need to reach out and get the help we need to restore a healthy sense of self so that we can pass it on to our children. Dysfunction may have taught us to fuse with family members so that we wouldn't feel too alone or the opposite, to cut them off and withdraw into our own world disconnected from them. Somewhere in between is the more comfortable place to live. Connected but not fused, separate but not cut off. Establishing this balance is one way of breaking a dysfunctional pattern. The wholeness, satisfaction, and pleasure that we experience within ourselves are passed on moment by moment to our children.

I will be open to shifting my sights.

"Life is a tragic mystery. We are pierced and driven by laws we only half understand, we find that the lesson we learn again and again is that of accepting heroic helplessness."

—FLORIDA SCOTT-MAXWELL
The Measure of My Days (1968)

Choppy Waters

I STILL HAVE SO MANY important roles to fill. I need to usher my children into adulthood—to be the tree that they come to for shelter, the brook that helps to quench their thirst. They need me now more than ever and I will not let my pain at their small rejections of me blind me to how important it is that I play my role well at this time. So often I have observed mothers and fathers deal with the pain of separating children by pushing their children away. Because they can't go into the pain, they act out. They sell themselves a bill of goods—"My kids don't need me anymore. They hardly want to be with me. They ignore me so that must mean I'm no longer important to them." This is shortsighted thinking at best and tit for tat at worst. If I take personally my children's normal and natural wish to knock me off the pedestal that they once put me on, I might retaliate and try to knock them off their young legs. Do I really want to do that to them?

I will allow my teens to meet their developmental need for rejecting me.

"All is pattern, all life, but we can't always see the pattern when we're a part of it."

—BELVA PLAIN
Crescent City (1984)

A Sense of Place

YOU GIVE ME A SENSE of place in this world. I belong somewhere unquestionably. I belong to you. The world supports my
doing what I like to do best, looking after you. Loving you
comes so naturally and taking care of you feels so good. It just
feels right to fulfill your needs each day. It fulfills mine, too, I
guess. It lets me be both young again and a grown and mature
woman. What I give to you I give to me too. I suppose it appears
selfless, but in truth we are both being nourished as I take care of
you. You give me a sense of belonging to someone in a vital and
important way. I feel so important to your life, your well-being,
your very survival, and that feeling allows me to feel important
too. I feel useful and vital each and every day. Can I feel useful
and vital if you're not in the home?

I miss that sense of importance.

"When I had my daughter, I learned what the sound of one
hand clapping is—it's a woman holding an infant in one
arm and a pen in the other."

—KATE BRAVERMAN, in Judith Pierce Rosenberg's
"Creative Tension,"
in *Ms.* (1994)

Being Enough

AM I UP TO THIS? Some days being a mother calls all of my faults and weaknesses into question. I lose my confidence. I want so badly to do a good job, to make no mistakes, to protect my children from harm in each and every way, to protect them from my own inadequacies. I worry. I fret. Am I doing enough? Am I doing too much? Am I enough? Motherhood feels like the most gratifying and most challenging thing I've ever done. I've never experienced greater self-confidence or greater self-doubt. I shiver inside. With joy, with love, with fear, and with gratitude. Each day I pray for my children's well-being and to have what it takes to do this job well. My children deserve the best.

God be with me on this journey of motherhood.

"Can't nothin' make your life work if you aren't the architect."

—TERRY MCMILLAN
Disappearing Acts (1989)

"To live fully, outwardly and inwardly, not to ignore external reality for the sake of inner life, or the reverse—that's quite a task."

—ETTY HILLESUM (1941)
An Interrupted Life (1983)

The Martyr
The Empty Nest

The world stands out on either side
No wider than the heart is wide;
Above the world is stretched the sky—
No higher than the soul is high.
The heart can push the sea and land
Farther away on either hand;
The soul can split the sky in two;
And let the face of God shine through.
But East and West will pinch the heart
That can not keep them pushed apart;
And he whose soul is flat the sky
Will cave in on him by and by.

—EDNA ST. VINCENT MILLAY
from "Renaissance" (1917)

The Martyr

I AM THE MARTYR. I love for the sake of the other and surrender my self-centered desires for the good of my children. I find beauty and meaning in personal sacrifice. I recognize that true happiness lies in giving and find freedom of a deeper kind when I release my self from my own self-centeredness. I am the Martyr. I am willing to go through the pain of releasing my children from the obligation to **pay** me back for what I give. I have found my joy and purpose in the giving. I understand that it is in hanging on to my children that I will lose them. If I let them go, they can follow the path through the world that leads them toward themselves, and I will be in their hearts. I am their mother. I remain a safe harbor from which they can sail and to which they can return whenever they need to. I love for love's sake, and I give with an open hand.

I understand that I love and will let go.

"Somehow, the real moment of parting always precedes the physical act of separation."

—PRINCESS MARTHA BIBESCO
Catherine-Paris (1928)

The Empty Nest

AFTER WE HAVE UPSIZED our cars, our houses, our yards, and our hearts, they leave. The day we thought would never come rushes up and bites us on the leg. These babies who needed us more than life itself do what they were born to do—move into their own lives. Unfortunately, need goes two ways. All the time they were needing us we were secretly needing them just as much—needing them to feel whole, needing them to provide our lives with the same stability and purpose that we were so busy giving them, needing them to feel like we belong. We are each carrying the unsolved questions. Who are we without our children near—who are they out in the world living independent lives? This is a moment of great challenge and importance to any family. The first thing to understand is the nest may be empty but the *family isn't over. Don't downsize just yet.* Our role as connected parent is critical to our children's comfortable passage into the turbulent seas of the world, and their role as connected child is critical to our comfortable passage into and acceptance of our next stage of living. We need each other just as much; that need will just play out a little differently. Letting the need and connection still be there but recognizing that it has been changed in its dynamics and demands is the developmental task of this stage of "familying."

"There are homes you run from and homes you run to."

—LAURA CUNNINGHAM
Sleeping Arrangements (1989)

My Pumpkins

I MISS MY LITTLE BOY, my little girl. I miss what I bonded with at some time long ago that felt so good. My little family, my bunny rabbits, my silly goofballs, my angels. There was something divine about having children, something that was better than anything else. I fear nothing could ever feel that amazing again. Being a mother has been the most profoundly gratifying experience of my life. I remember the spontaneous laughter, the giggling, the liveliness, the feeling that life was this wild adventure. Entering the world of childhood or, I should say, reentering it with you, put me back in touch with the child in me and gave me back a hidden portion of myself. It was so delicious to reenter the world of childhood with you—what a grand adventure—what a total blast. I loved it. I loved/love being your mother—at times being a genie in your magical world of childhood.

I miss my bunny rabbits.

"Life is change: growth is optional."

—KAREN KAISER CLARK
(1994)

"The most important thing she'd learned over the years was that there was no way to be a perfect mother and a million ways to be a good one."

—JILL CHURCHILL
Grime and Punishment (1989)

Mixed Emotion

I ANTICIPATE THE MOMENT of our separation with a mixture of dread and exhilaration. I feel dread because one of the most wonderful stages of my life seems to be coming to a close. My steps feel heavy, my stomach feels queasy, and I want to cry. It feels like a long walk toward saying good-bye. I feel exhilarated because we have come so far. All of these years of devotion, ups, downs, conquered fears, and fervent hopes have come to fruition. I'm exhilarated because we are actually here, at this juncture of our lives—whole and intact—with love in our hearts and commitments well fulfilled. You are a person well begun—independent with your own internal resources waiting to be drawn upon—and I have grown in ways I could never have imagined. Together we entered the mystery of life. I now know what it means to stand in awe. My soul has grown.

You will be fine. I will be fine.

"Thou, straggler into loving arms,
  Young climber up of knees,
  When I forget thy thousand ways,
  Then life and all shall cease."

—MARY LAMB
"Parental Recollections"
Poetry for Children (1809)

ᴄᴍissing You

I MISS YOU. I miss the idea that you are around. I miss buying the things you like to have to eat and preparing little treats. I miss that certain, unspoken something that is in the air when you're near. I miss knowing you will eventually emerge out of your room and rustle through the refrigerator. I miss doing for you—it has become such a lifelong habit, and I enjoy it. I miss the commotion. I miss my schedule being constantly thrown off. I miss planning my life around you. I want you to burst through the door with a trail of babbling, laughing friends. I miss you and your pals eating the food I make for you. I miss your surprises and your youthful excitement about life. You were a gas to have around. You gave the house a party atmosphere and I didn't even have to throw a party. I don't like all this quiet and order—nobody jostles the atmosphere now or turns anything upside down. I can't tell you to turn down your music because it's not playing. If I make a cake, it just sits there. You've been a pleasure to do things for—even when you don't seem to appreciate it, you let me know you do. You break that teenage code and say thank you. You let me know it matters.

I miss your goofy energy.

"To live is so startling, it leaves but little room for other occupations."

—EMILY DICKINSON (1871), in Mabel Loomis Todd, ed., *Letters of Emily Dickinson,* Vol. 2 (1894)

Filling a Hole

I AM HAVING TO LEARN to live in my relationship all over again. For so many years you have been the main focus of attention for your father and me. We have had the task and privilege of raising you to occupy us and give us a mutual concern. Your welfare in a thousand daily ways has been the subject of our conversations and our preoccupation. Who are we when you're not here? We have been task-oriented for two decades. We built a home together to surround and support you. We structured our relationship to include you. We have lived in the plural and thought as a group. How do we define ourselves and our relationship without you in the middle of it? There is an empty space between us that you used to fill, a hole where you used to be. Is our home still a home when you're not here? Is our relationship still a relationship when it's not designed around you?

There is an empty space where you used to be.

"To the true servant of God every place is the right place and every time is the right time."

—St. CATHERINE of SIENA (1378), in Vida D. Scudder, ed.,
St. Catherine of Siena as Seen in Her Letters (1905)

*D*eparture

GIVE ME STRENGTH for these many separations. Everything we have done until this point was to get you here—clean, strong, independent, and ready to move out into more of your own life. But I feel faint. I feel queasy. I feel a little ill. I feel like I am dropping part of my insides off somewhere else. Will you be all right? Will you cope well? Will you have what you need to meet this new challenge? Each time you take on a new phase of separation, I feel anxious. I feel the bond connecting us stretch, and it can pull hard at my insides. But I will handle my end of it and let you handle yours. This is how your confidence gets built, by mastering growing challenges one at a time and incorporating a gradually expanding sense of your own individuality. I will support you through each and every one of these separations. I will let you go and hold you all at the same time, but I will hold you with a free and open hand and a free and open heart.

Be well, be happy, be strong.

"A mother is not a person to lean on but a person to make leaning unnecessary."

—DOROTHY CANFIELD FISHER
Her Son's Wife (1926)

Unmoored

I FEEL STRANGELY UNMOORED. I feel vulnerable. I am used to drawing my sense of serenity and joy from a well that was within my own home. I loved the secure feeling of knowing that you were in our home—filling it out with your youthful energy—filling me out through the challenging and gratifying role of being your mother. I walked through the world carrying you with me, knowing that at the close of every day we would return to the same sustaining cocoon away from the world and toward this wonderful, nurturing gestalt-of-an-experience called family. When you're not in the home, I find it disturbing at some deep level. My bearings are off. My balance is threatened. The world feels slightly tipped on its axis, the picture is out of focus, my sights are off-kilter. Having you in the home grounded me at the same time I was grounding you. You gave me this sense of belonging somewhere, of being needed in an immediate kind of way. It was profoundly gratifying and richly rewarding. But nothing lasts forever, and I want to be a gracious loser. I don't want to dishonor what has been so good by insisting that I have it always and by complaining if it isn't there. Anyway—it's not gone—it has just shifted, and, if I don't accept the shift and learn to flow with it, I will not be psychologically or emotionally available to adjust to this new stage in our relationship. I don't want to sabotage what still can be.

I can adjust.

"Time manages the most painful partings for us. One has only to set the date, buy the ticket, and let the earth, sun, and moon make their passages through the sky, until inexorable time carries us with it to the moment of parting."

—JILL KER CONWAY
The Road from Coorain (1989)

Regrouping

Is THIS A HOME if children aren't in it? Is this a family if we aren't all under one roof? If I can't lay my eyes or hand on you, are we still connected? Who are you now, and who am I, and who are we? I don't want to risk losing you because I cannot accommodate change. I don't want to push you away because I'm afraid of needing you. I don't want to assert fierce independence to pay you back for growing up and leaving. I want to be balanced about this whole thing. To see it as a transition and not an end. I think of you all the time. You are in the front, middle, and back of my mind—my casual thought and my constant preoccupation. I suppose this is natural. After all, I have raised you since birth and even though we have come to this juncture through time—even though we have already become more separate—you've never been far from my thoughts. My life and energy have still been powerfully centered around you. How can this habit change overnight?

I will stay open to you.

"i am not you anymore
i am my own collection of
gifts and errors."

—SAUNDRA SHARP
Double Stitch (1991)

Contradiction

THE MERE FACT that "empty nest" is a named syndrome speaks to the communal nature of this experience. Nest—home—one and the same. It's the conflicting feelings that make my stomach queasy and my brain numb. I feel the joy of accomplishing the task of raising a healthy, hearty child who can successfully move on with life in a productive manner, and the sorrow of longing to reach out and touch you, smell you, hold you, hear you. I am empty and full all at the same time. Sad and proud, hurting and exalting, relieved and burdened. It's hard to process feelings when they're constantly at odds inside of me. And I'm scared. I'm scared that life will never feel full and joyous again. I'm scared that you will get lost in your own life and forget me. I'm scared that I won't be able to sustain myself without you. When I cuddled you into your little bed, my heart became sleepy and peaceful right along with yours. Our souls comingled in what felt to me like a sacred place—our home. You were my link with my own heart and the divine spirit. Motherhood opened my heart to the meaning of life and love, and now I'm scared that it will close if you're not here.

I pray that my heart and spirit stay open and alive.

"Motherhood is like Albania—you can't trust the descriptions in the books, you have to go there."

—MARNI JACKSON
The Mother Zone (1992)

Reorganizing My Insides

I REMEMBER WHAT IT WAS LIKE to adjust to having you in my life. It felt like I was giving up my own life—giving up myself. But mysteriously, in doing that, I found parts of myself and of life that I had never known about before. Can there be more? An adventure as wonderful as raising you? My own fears are my worst enemy. They eat me up from inside. I feel anxious at the thought of not being able to micromanage your life to make sure it runs perfectly. Part of me wants to deny these feelings—to stiff-upper-lip it—I can surely do that. I know how. But another part of me feels that if I deny the feelings, I am denying you somehow, and that goes against all of my maternal instincts. I get anxious; I can't help it. I am your mother, and I want your life to be problem-free. I want to protect you from harm. I feel helpless to do for you at this critical stage. Standing back and letting you do for yourself while still remaining here for you where appropriate and needed is a discipline, a new position.

I will learn to mother appropriately for this new stage.

"Sorrow was like the wind. It came in gusts."

—MARJORIE KINNAN RAWLINGS
South Moon Under (1933)

The Transforming Family

CHILDREN REACH EIGHTEEN and begin to deal practically with the next stage of their own lives. They go to college, get a job, or set off for adventure. There is so much misconception about this stage of familying in America, the biggest being that this is when the family ends. It's true that an aspect of family is ending at this point, but the next phase is just beginning. Children need an anchor, a safe harbor to sail away from and back to over and over again throughout life. If they know that we remain here as a stable source of nurturance and support, they can summon the courage it takes to face life on their own. This stage of familying is like the place on a Möbius strip where the lines cross over before they move out again into a new symmetry. Bonds at this stage are more critical than ever. Staying connected becomes sweeter and more important, and consciously nurturing ways of connecting allows bonds to deepen and strengthen and grow in resilience while withdrawing love can make them turn brittle and rupture.

We let go to stay connected.

"Nobody has ever measured, even poets, how much a heart can hold."

—ZELDA FITZGERALD (1945), in Nancy Milford,
Zelda (1970)

*H*igher *P*ower

You HAVE YOUR OWN Higher Power. You have your own will and destiny. You have the power to make or break your own life. I can still play a powerful and important lifelong role of love and support, but your life is essentially in your hands and the loving hands of your Higher Power. I pray to your Higher Power to hold you and guide you along the path that is right for you, the path that is wholesome and will lead you to a life that you can feel proud of—a life that will allow you to feel happy and whole. I have confidence in your strength. You are capable of taking this next step. This is not all or nothing—life in our home or life apart. This is just the next step, and I know that you can take it. Who could be ready—we're as ready as we'll ever be. Everything you've done up until this point has prepared you for the step you are taking now. When I get into the mentality that this is forever—as if I'll never see you again—I freak myself out, and you too probably. This is just one more step in a long succession of steps.

You have your own Higher Power, and it's not me.

"We are not human beings learning to be spiritual; we are spiritual beings learning to be human."

—JACQUELYN SMALL
Awakening in Time (1991)

Our Mutual Adjustments

YOU ARE DOING A GREAT JOB of adjusting and so will I. One of the ways in which I support you at this new stage of your life is to adjust well to it myself. Adjusting well is a middle ground sort of thing. It encompasses keeping our home open and welcoming so that you can use it as your source of deep security without making it a trap that encloses you and doesn't let you out. It also includes supporting you in your separate life and fostering your autonomy and independence. It means keeping my heart open and my values straight. It's standing at the center of my conflicting feelings of loss and joy and not getting stuck in either. If I deny the loss, I may close the door on your home to protect myself from the pain of your comings and goings—to maintain control. If I get stuck in the joy, it will be a false positive and I might block out or deny any feelings of pain, creating expectations that neither of us can meet and that will set us up for failure.

I support you by my own successful adjustment.

"Nobody lives well who is not spiritually well."

—JOAN TIMMERMAN, in Theresa King, ed.,
The Spiral Path (1992)

Waking Up

WAKING UP FEELS DIFFERENT NOW. For so long I have woken up with you in my mind and heart—jumped out of bed to attend to you. There was this quiet feeling of excitement in getting you going on your day—bundling you off to your next activity. We got to be young together in a way. I got to experience the magic of childhood all over again. You gave each day a feeling of specialness—you were excited to wake up in the morning and do all the things you had planned. You knew you were growing, and that made your life and my life purposeful and adventurous. I wish I could bottle that feeling and take it out for times like these. I wish I could inhale it, pour it into a cup, and sip it—somehow get it inside again. I long to hear the door creak open and have you walk through it. I am waiting to hear you say, "Hello," and to return your greeting. I want that feeling of your being near—of knowing you're in the next room and I can find you. I miss the sound of your voice, touching you, breathing in your familiar scent, feeling your energy.

I miss that certain je ne sais quoi.

"Experience teaches us in a millennium what passion
   teaches us in an hour."

—RALPH IRON
The Story of an African Farm (1883)

*A*ccepting the *I*nevitable

I WISH I HAD HAD so many children that I could have completely avoided this period. But then I would have had no life of my own, and I wouldn't have been able to give as much to the children I had. It's all worked out so well and I'm not sure, with more kids, I could have done as good a job and still had something left over for myself and my marriage. Bargaining. Didn't psychiatrist Elisabeth Kübler-Ross talk about this step of the grief process? I feel myself madly trying to weigh all of the variables and come up with a good scenario. I guess this is a step on the road toward acceptance. This is hard—or anyway, it's not easy. I know from years of intelligent living that, if I can feel my feelings surrounding my empty nest, I will be able to "metabolize" them, integrate them, and come out onto the other side deeper, wider, and stronger. Some days I wish I could jump over them, but I know that never really works.

I am working through my feelings.

"Sorrow fully accepted brings its own gifts. For there is an alchemy in sorrow. It can be transmuted into wisdom, which, if it does not bring joy, can yet bring happiness."

—PEARL S. BUCK
The Child Who Never Grew Up (1950)

Finding the Beauty That's Here

I NEED TO SERIOUSLY ADDRESS myself to getting my life to feel full again. I need to let myself *feel* you even though you're not filling my life. I need to allow thoughts of you to bring me pleasure throughout my day. Even though you aren't in the house, you are still mine. I have to become more reflective, to find another way of holding you. When I could wrap you in my arms, it was easier to feel you—to fill up with your presence. But I can't let your lack of presence make me walk around like an empty, lifeless container. I need to fill up on what I have—to not push away that feeling of fullness because it's not just the way I want it to be. I need to learn to live again and pull meaning and life out of my day. Beauty is still here—I will find it and let it find me.

I open to that feeling of fullness.

"Everything has its wonders, even darkness and silence, and I learn, whatever state I may be in, therein to be content."

—HELEN KELLER
The Story of My Life (1902)

The Blues

I'M SAD. I suppose that is normal, but I don't like it. It's sort of like postpartum blues eighteen years later. I should remember that. Bringing you into this world and giving you a home was a huge adjustment. It felt like this—like I was losing my life. Now I feel like I'm losing my life all over again. Before it was my life outside of the home; now it's my life inside the home. Our home gave off warmth I felt. It vibrated; it was alive and in living color. The adjustment I am making now feels a lot like the adjustment I made when you were born. Both were a curious loss of self. In the beginning it was a loss of the self I had thought was all of me. Then I awakened into a new self—a mother-self, something both divine and rooted in the ground for centuries. Now I feel like I am losing the self that gave itself over to motherhood, the self that got built around loving and caring for you.

Am I losing myself?

"In every parting there is an image of death."

—GEORGE ELIOT
"The Sad Fortunes of the Reverend Amos Barton"
Scenes of Clerical Life (1857)

The Grass Isn't Greener

IT'S NOT BETTER SOMEWHERE ELSE. I will use the wisdom and sense of grounding that I have gained throughout my years of motherhood to deepen my feeling of rootedness in my life today. I will stop looking over my shoulder, wishing I were somewhere else. I will love what I have. What I have is this stage of life—there is loss in it and potential for beauty and gain. The grass isn't greener somewhere else. I can't afford to indulge in that kind of thinking. I can do some of it, it's natural, but I have to combine it with intelligent and concerted attitude adjustments. Daily I need to remind myself that change isn't a tragedy—nothing bad has happened. In fact, a lot of good has happened. I need to appreciate the life I have today, to love what is around me—to love what I have.

I will love the life I have.

"Mine is sunlight! Mine is the morning."

—ELEANOR FARJEON
"A Morning Song (for the First Day of Spring)"
The Children's Bells (1960)

₰urrender

I AM LOOKING OUTSIDE TOO MUCH. Now that you aren't near, I want other things to fill in the emptiness in your wake—my relationship, work, social life—stuff. But maybe the only real solution to this loneliness for you is a spiritual one—surrender. Surrender to the inevitable passage of time, surrender to the pain of losing you, surrender to the joy of watching you grow and meet the challenges of your life head on. Just as I have told you that this separation allows you to feel your own strength—perhaps it is time that I feel mine too. I have strength and beauty within me that I can draw on, fullness that I can fall into, nurturing softness that I can rest on. Maybe it's not answers that I need now—or the questions for that matter—maybe I just need to surrender into the experience that is here, whatever it is.

I am enough.

"Spiritual life is like a moving sidewalk. Whether you go with it or spend your whole life running against it, you're still going to be taken along."

—BERNADETTE ROBERTS
The Feminine Face of God (1991)

The Power of the Heart

MY LIFE IS MISSING its automatic fullness. It feels empty now, and I find myself resenting those still in it because they are not you. I feel off-balance—I need to learn to re-balance my life; but I fear that if I do that, I will not have a special space kept always for you. I love you. I will hold your space safe in this changing world. This separating stuff feels unnatural and natural all at once. When you move away from me, my stomach tightens, my heart carries you, and my head knows I have to let you go. Maybe it's my heart that is the balance—maybe that's where everything stays the same no matter what—you live in my heart, and I live in yours. Going to college, leaving home, and moving can't change any of that. The heart is more powerful than time, space, or distance. I will rely on our hearts to keep us connected.

I hold you in my heart.

"Life was meant to be lived and curiosity must be kept alive. One must never, for whatever reason, turn one's back on life."

—ELEANOR ROOSEVELT
The Autobiography of Eleanor Roosevelt (1961)

Training Myself

IT IS IN MEETING the challenges of my life with heart and courage that I have always grown; through feeling the truth of my reality, facing it squarely, and forging my way through it. It hurts me to walk by your empty room—to know you aren't going to fill up this house with your energy, laughter, and commotion. Today I am going to teach myself to slowly accept that feeling. I want to do this gracefully. I have so much to be thankful for that I don't want to let myself lose perspective. Somehow I will find a way to embrace this emptiness, to sit with it until it turns into something else. If I deny it, I invite a whole new set of problems. If I lose myself in it, I invite depression and despondency, and I might get stuck in it. If I feel it, I remember that I am empty for a good reason—because I have been so full.

I will sit down with this emptiness.

"If logic tells you that life is a meaningless accident, don't give up on life. Give up on logic."

—SHIRA MILGROM (1988),
in Ellen M. Umansky and Dianne Ashton, eds.,
Four Centuries of Jewish Women's Spirituality (1992)

$\mathcal{N}$ew and Old Pain

YOU GAVE ME A MOTIVATION to be the best person I could be and to create the best life I could create. You filled my heart with reasons—reasons to live, reasons to love, reasons to stretch my own boundaries. Saying yes to life was easy when I was saying it for both of us. You made simple days feel special and holidays sing with a kind of beauty that made me feel connected to everything positive and good. You made me feel that I really had a special place all my own—the one I created for and with you. Without you here to create that feeling in me I feel alone, and it makes me remember other times I felt alone and that feels scary. Missing you triggers feelings of yearning from other times of loss in my life. The feelings get mixed up together, and I can't tell what's about you and what's about previous lonely moments. I need to separate my feelings about you from the others and to use this time to review and let go of old pain that's getting triggered by new loss.

I am afraid of this feeling.

"Sometimes a person has to go back, really back—to have a sense, an understanding of all that's gone to make them—before they can go forward."

—PAULA MARSHALL
The Chosen Place, The Timeless People (1969)

"There is, I have learned, no permanent escape from the past. It may be an unrecognized law of our nature that we should be drawn back, inevitably, to the place where we have suffered most."

—ELLEN GLASGOW
The Woman Within (1954)

Our Footprints in the Sand

MY NEXT STEP HAS BEEN your next step for so many years. Our footprints in the sand have been next to each other—just a little bit apart sometimes closer sometimes farther, but always within range. How can I find your footprints when they are so far away? It's a weird, not particularly welcome, feeling. Maybe there will be new kinds of footprints—new ways of finding each other. That's the challenge now. Things are different. Different does not have to mean worse. If I assume that it does mean worse, it may well become a self-fulfilling prophecy. Different also does not have to be better in order to be good enough. Different can just be different. A new pattern. Different priorities. Changed weightings—a little more here, a little less there. If I can accept with some level of serenity that my life will feel different, maybe I can stop comparing yesterday with today and worrying about tomorrow.

I can allow my life to feel different without panicking.

"Sorrow has its reward. It never leaves us where it found us."

—MARY BAKER EDDY
Science and Health (1875)

Rushing Thoughts

MY MIND IS ONE TRACK and you are the track. How are you, what are you doing, are you happy, are you making friends and feeling comfortable? All I can think of is you. All I want to know about is you. All of my psychic energy is flowing toward you. I'm not sure whether I am this concerned about your every move or whether I've thought about you for so long that I can't change gears. You are in every room, in every thought. I am expecting you to walk through the door, and at the same time trying to tell myself to adjust to the idea that it will not happen as it did. How do I stop planning my day around you? How do I stop planning my schedule with you as a top priority? How do I plan my day as I wish when I haven't done that for so long? I feel like the inside of me is reaching out to touch you, but you aren't within my reach.

I think about you a lot.

"One is not born, but rather becomes, a woman."

—SIMONE DE BEAUVOIR
The Second Sex (1949)

Effort

THIS ADJUSTMENT is not going to happen without some effort on my part. I want it to happen easily—I want to let the pain come and not fight it. But there is a balance. I need to feel the pain, to feel the emptiness, and then to move past it into something else. I do need to decide to recover my normal state of happiness, to give myself the right to my own stability, joy, and pleasure. The right balance. Not more, not less. This is how I can walk through this passage and come out whole on the other side. Denying the pain of the loss would cause other problems. I might shut down or push you away for self-protection. Living in the pain could lead to depression and a loss of interest and energy for my life. Both are inadequate solutions. I will work through the pain. I will mobilize my life supports and coping skills and grow.

I want balance.

"I began to have an idea of my life, not as the slow shaping of achievement to fit my preconceived purposes, but as the gradual discovery and growth of a purpose which I did not know."

—JOANNA FIELD
A Life of One's Own (1934)

*F*inding *Y*our *W*ay

I HOPE THAT YOU WILL FIND your own way, step to the beat of your own drummer, listen to the music in your own soul. And from this fine attunement I hope that you will find a life pattern that is right for you: one that actualizes your special talents and challenges you; one that encourages you toward optimum productivity in the day and wraps its arms around you at night. A life that allows you to live comfortably and fully. I know that you have dreams for yourself—private dreams. They aren't mine; they are yours. I hope that you will have the good fortune to actualize your dreams. You will learn so many things. The world awaits you and soon you will walk in it on your own steam. You are strong and you are realistic. You know that what lies ahead of you is perhaps your greatest challenge to date. You are up to that challenge. I have faith in you and in your ability to stand on your own two feet. Everything we have done to this point has been meant to prepare you for just this—for walking away and into your own life. It doesn't seem possible that this is how it all works, but I know that it is the most natural thing in the world and that this pain of letting you go is not nearly as great as it would be if, for some reason, you could not go.

Go, and God be with you.

"Life is either a daring adventure or nothing. To keep our faces toward change and behave like free spirits in the presence of fate is strength undefeatable."

—HELEN KELLER
Let Us Have Faith (1940)

*C*onnected *I*nside

OH, I JUST HEARD YOUR VOICE. Aah, breathe easy . . . I could live on that a lifetime. I am still your mommy and distance cannot change that. I will hold that thought, your voice, you within my heart. That is where I will go for comfort and strength now—to the you that lives within me. Inhale. Breathe. Feel this beautiful feeling of connection. Nothing can make us go away—we are we—together forever in our souls. That is the thing with parents and children, mommies and babies. If you give yourself to it, it is yours forever. Even time and distance can never have the power to take you from me. We are each other's on the inside where it really counts. We can fill each other up from an invisible source, from the spiritual well of our heart connection, from our soul communion. The depth of this relationship lasts forever.

I love you forever.

"My mother, religious-Negro, proud of having waded through a storm, is very obviously a sturdy Black bridge that I crossed over, on."

—CAROLYN M. RODGERS
"It Is Deep (don't never forget
the bridge that you crossed over on)"
How I Got Ovah (1975)

Setting Myself Free

I AM STILL ALL OF WHO I AM even if you're not in the home. This is the me I have built with you, the us we've built together. We each have our own selves to take to our own lives. We can set each other free and still be there for each other as a primary system of support. Just as I raised you—you raised me. We built selves together. Those selves are now ours—each of ours to take into the world and create separate lives. Separate lives that still connect. It is this way because we did something right. That's why we can thrive separately as well as together. Just as I give you the right to thrive and live on your own—I will give myself that right too.

I have a right to thrive on my own.

"The real trick is to stay alive as long as you live."

—ANN LANDERS
Since You Ask Me (1961)

*P*assages

I FEEL SICK TO MY STOMACH. Letting go is physically painful. I'm not sure if I am filled with emotion or my body is getting ill. This mixture of powerful feeling and numbness is strange. I feel like there is a traffic jam inside of me—emotional gridlock. My muscles are seizing up, tightening; my throat is constricting; and my breathing is shallow. This is not easy—but then when was it? Your first day of school, going away to camp, making friends, changing schools—everything had its hard side now that I think about it. I guess we'll get over this too. This is just another passage in the long, complex, and beautiful life we will lead together. Before when I walked into the house and found it empty, I saw it as a few stolen moments of peace before the onslaught of evening activities. It was a delicious kind of emptiness. Now it's a hollow kind that I feel incapable of filling up on my own. This is the time people downsize—I can feel it—to get away from this feeling. But I don't want to downsize. This is my home, our home. I want to pass through this period until this house feels full again. I want this house that I have raised you in to wrap its arms and its beautiful memories around me, to hold me, and I want it to be here to hold you so that you can return to it for nourishment and refueling.

We have the strength to meet the challenges of this new passage.

"Security is when everything is settled, when nothing can happen to you; security is denial of life."

—GERMAINE GREER
The Female Eunuch (1971)

Joy

I NEED TO FIND a new source of joy. My source has been you for so long—my source of boundless, spontaneous, divine joy has issued from being the center of your universe—the tree you came to for shelter. The joy of watching you grow, the joy of being needed in such an important way, the joy of your playful company has carried me and filled me for years. I need to find a new way of filling up. I need to trust that life can fill me up as you have. You stretched my heart and kneaded my soul into a soft shape that rose by itself. That improved soul is still mine. I can rest in it until it rises within me and puts me in touch with that deeper pulse of living that is always there waiting for me to connect with it.

My joy is my responsibility.

"The joy of a spirit is the measure of its power."
> —NINON DE LENCLOS (1694) in Edgar H. Cohn,
> *Mademoiselle Libertine* (1970)

"O World, I cannot hold thee close enough!"
> —EDNA ST. VINCENT MILLAY
> "God's World"
> *Renaissance* (1917)

*T*ime

THIS WILL TAKE TIME. This is both an adjustment of all my daily routines for twenty-odd years as well as a major shift in my identity. This will take time. I cannot expect my life that took so many years to build with you in it to feel normal a week after you move away from it. That would be denying or erasing too much. I will be fine and you will be fine, and it will take time. For each of us there are unique challenges. For you, the challenge is to stand on your own and create a life that feels whole, nourishing, and productive from scratch. For me it is to let you go with love and to build a new stage of my life that feels nurturing and exciting.

We are both up to this task.

"Time past is not time gone, it is time accumulated with
the host resembling the character in the fairy-tale who was
joined along the route by more and more characters none
of whom could be separated from one another or from the
host, with some stuck so fast that their presence caused
physical pain."

—JANET FRAME
An Angel at My Table (1984)

Job Training

I'M LEAVING THE HOUSE now, darling. I want to write you a note and tell you when I'll be back, but you're not here. What a strange feeling. It doesn't matter if I leave you a note or not. But you are here for me. I am waiting for that feeling to be internalized within me as okay. I am waiting for the strangeness and the yearning to stop. It lessens a bit each day, but you are built into my system. I need rewiring, retooling for a new task. I am still trained for an obsolete job. I need to expand into and define my next one.

I will in time rewire my insides.

"She stayed bound to a gone moment, like a stopped clock with hands silently pointing to an hour it cannot be."

—ELIZABETH BOWEN
The House in Paris (1935)

"Living in the past is a dull and lonely business; and looking back, if persisted in, strains the neck muscles, causes you to bump into people not going your way."

—EDNA FERBER
A Kind of Magic (1963)

Technology

GOD BLESS TECHNOLOGY. The security of knowing that I can pick up the phone and contact you is heaven. What did mothers do who sent their children across oceans and waited months for a single letter? Technology makes it possible to separate and stay connected. That most important of all developmental tasks is handed to us on a silver platter—or wire as it happens. We can be leading our own lives and still be fully in touch with each other in an immediate, up-to-the-minute way. I can know what you're having for lunch. You can ask me to get a number from our bulletin board or a recipe that you want to cook for dinner. This technology that we're all so worried about alienating us is actually allowing us to stay close.

You're just a phone call away.

"Suddenly many movements are going on within me, many things are happening, there is an almost unbearable sense of sprouting, of bursting encasements, of moving kernels, expanding flesh."

—MERIDEL LE SUEUR
"Annunciation" (1927)
Salute to Spring (1940)

Nothing Is Wrong

NOTHING IS WRONG. This feeling of separateness can trigger anxiety in either of us. Then I feel as if something is wrong that I should fix or attend to. But nothing is wrong. Quite the contrary, the world is unfolding as it should. If I act on this feeling of agitation, I am trying to fix something that "ain't broke." That would be doing you a tremendous disservice. I would probably act overly concerned about your welfare, or clingy. If I did that, you would get the wrong message. You'd think that something was wrong with you when actually it is my own feeling I'm acting out on—my anxiety—my missing—my worry. Plus, you are naturally vulnerable at this moment of separation and, if I act as if something is wrong, you start to think there is—after all—I'm your mother and you are used to listening to me.

I will hold my tongue.

"A mother is never cocky or proud, because she knows the school principal may call at any minute to report that her child has just driven a motorcycle through the gymnasium."

—MARY KAY BLAKELY,
"The Pros and Cons of Motherhood"
in Gloria Kaufman and Mary Kay Blakely, eds.,
Pulling Our Own Strings (1980)

Our Prayer

I WILL USE PRAYER as a way of staying close to you. I will pray for you on a daily basis and hold you close to my heart. I will lift us toward God so that, if you are too busy putting your life together for a while, God will not forget about us. Instead of sinking into a depression with the empty time I will now have, I will really try to sink into reverie instead. Maybe there is a way that I can use the psychic space and energy that you took up in a constructive way that will benefit all of us. I believe in prayer. I believe that if I pray for you it will make a difference. This is also a kind of mothering. I lift our hearts toward a loving God.

I pray for you each and every day.

"At the moment you are most in awe of all there is about life that you don't understand, you are closer to understanding it all than at any other time."

—JANE WAGNER
The Search for Signs of Intelligent Life in the Universe (1985)

Quiet

I FEEL GUILTY. Is it okay for me to enjoy this—to get pleasure from having more time for me—more time for my relationship? Is it all right for your father to rise on the priority scale vis-à-vis you? You have necessarily come first for so many years that it has become a habit of behavior, thinking, and feeling—body, mind, and heart. But it's nice to feel like a couple again, go out on dates, play around. Nice to have enough extra energy to give to each other once more. I feel like I found my spouse in the house again and he's taking up lots of space, and I like it. The idea of planning my time around what I feel like filling my day with is starting to sound appealing. Is this okay or will some force come down from the heavens and punish me for having too much fun—for indulging in these pleasures?

I think I'm enjoying some of this.

"Though it sounds absurd, it is true to say I felt younger at
   sixty than I had felt at twenty."

—ELLEN GLASGOW
The Woman Within (1954)

"I do the things I like to do,
 And leave undone the things I don't—
 Because I'm sixty!"

—MRS. C. B. F., in Hazel Felleman, ed.,
The Best Loved Poems of the American People (1936)

Being Touched

I AM SO TOUCHED BY YOU and the tender strength you are showing at this moment. I know how hard this is. I have done it myself before. I see the way you are pulling up what you need from deep inside of you, and it moves me. You are neither running away nor frantically plunging toward. You are showing good balance—letting yourself have all of your feelings around this important juncture but not sinking into them and allowing yourself to become overwhelmed. I am impressed with your maturity.

You move me.

"If we go down into ourselves we find we possess exactly
   what we desire."

—SIMONE WEIL
Gravity and Grace (1947)

*A*lways *C*onnected

YOU ARE YOUR OWN PERSON and so am I. Letting you go no longer feels like losing you. You just grew up. You didn't disappear. We are closer now than ever in a completely new way. I see you and you see me. We're people together—people who have shared the deepest and most cherished events of each other's lives. We carry one another's history. We hold each other's hearts, wishes, dreams, and fears. We touch at so many points. You are my dearest friend. The sound of your voice makes my heart sing, and being connected to you still provides me with a sense of place in this world. You are my legacy; my place in the scheme of life. We will span time—we connect life from beginning to end. We are not going anywhere. We belong to each other.

We are always together.

"We are all in this together by ourselves."

—LILY TOMLIN

Constant Adjusting

YOU'RE COMING HOME. I was just adjusting to an empty nest and now it's about to be full again. Then you'll go and it will be empty again. Then you'll come home and fill it up. I have this weird mixture of feelings. Excitement and fear. Excitement to see you, and fear that I'll feel full and then empty. Besides, I got used to making my own plans so I'm a little put out to change them. This is strange, but I'm glad. I'm glad you're jostling things up again even if it throws me off. That's what I was missing. I pray it will be this in-and-out for the rest of our lives. And I pray that I will have the sense to accommodate it graciously, knowing how much it means to all of our lives.

Another adjustment in pattern.

"The family. We were a strange little band of characters trudging through life sharing diseases and toothpaste, coveting one another's desserts, hiding shampoo, borrowing money, locking each other out of our rooms, inflicting pain and kissing to heal it in the same instant, loving, laughing, defending, and trying to figure out the common thread that bound us all together."

—ERMA BOMBECK
Family—The Ties That Bind . . . And Gag! (1987)

You're Gone Again

I MISS YOU ALL OVER AGAIN. These conflicting feelings tug at my insides and disturb my sleep. When you were visiting, you seemed different. Big. Disinterested. I keep thinking my toddler is going to come home from college. Then you come back a big person and at some deep level I feel confused all over again. Letting you go isn't letting you go. The roots of it go so far back that when I let you go, I feel the entire experience of raising you is being pulled at, pushed on, brought up. Someone is yanking out plants that have taken root deep inside of me—pulling on my insides. Letting you go feels like it goes all the way back to babyhood. I guess that makes sense in a weird sort of way—that letting you go calls up the full experience of you.

Are you big or small inside of me?

"Over the years I have learned that motherhood is much like an austere religious order, the joining of which obligates one to relinquish all claims to personal possessions."

—NANCY STAHL
If It's Raining This Must Be the Weekend (1979)

Not So Bad

THIS IS NOT AS BAD as I thought it would be. I really thought that I would feel as if my world were falling apart. I thought that I would feel empty, old, and used up. I thought that the house would feel like a dark, vacant cavern, an echo chamber, hollow. But the day is still the day and the night is still the night. I am here when I wake up in the morning just like always—thinking my thoughts, going about my familiar routines. The day just more or less fills in. It's not that I don't think about you. I do all the time. It's just that I realize now that you didn't disappear. You've just moved into another chapter of your life and that feels right and good.

Life has its seasons with its responsibilities and remedies built in.

"I asked myself the question, 'What do you want of your life?' and I realized with a start of recognition and terror, 'Exactly what I have—but to be commensurate, to handle it better.'"

—MAY SARTON
Journal of a Solitude (1973)

cAnd the Beat Goes On

I AM GOING TO ALLOW myself the pleasure of looking forward to being a grandparent. Being a grandparent is a role that I would like to play well, so what's the harm in giving it some preparatory thought? I have always thought that parents go into parenting too unprepared, so why should I go into grandparenting with no previous investigation? Part of my preparation will be to remember what my grandparents did for me that felt good. Another part will be to remember what my parents did as grandparents that felt good to me as your parent, and what I might add. I can play a role that will benefit both my children and my grandchildren and will continue to give my life continuity, pleasure, and purpose. I recognize the vital importance of anchoring the younger generations through loving connections.

I have critical life roles still to play.

"Age puzzles me. I thought it was a quiet time. My seventies were interesting, and fairly serene, but my eighties are passionate. I grow more intense as I age."

—FLORIDA SCOTT-MAXWELL
The Measure of My Days (1968)

Renewal

IS THIS A NEW BEGINNING? Is it a sacrilege for a mother to have a new beginning after her children have grown up? Is it okay to imagine that life still holds exciting new adventures for me that aren't completely you? But wait a minute—you aren't leaving my life—it just feels like you are. But you are already here—your feet are firmly planted in the soil of our lives together. In fact, I have no power to remove them. Thank God. Any new life I have from here on will have you in it, no matter what I do, because we are sewn into the fabric of each other's lives forever.

I can have all the life that I can hold.

"I'm not to blame for an old body, but I would be to blame for an old soul. An old soul is a shameful thing."

—MARGARET DELAND
Dr. Lavendar's People (1903)

ℕo One Is ℒost

LETTING YOU GO is not losing you. Real pain, the gnawing, desperate kind, comes when people are lost to each other on the inside. Supporting your natural movement into your own life actually makes me feel closer to you, and it allows you to feel closer to me, because you're not stuck to me. You don't have to break away in a thousand tiny ways because you have broken away in one big way. You have proven to yourself and to me that you can make it on your own. What a blessing. What a moment to celebrate. What victory and triumph.

We are bound to each other in a new way.

"As a human being, you have no choice about the fact that you need a philosophy. Your only choice is whether you define your philosophy by a conscious, rational, disciplined process of thought and scrupulously logical deliberation— or let your subconscious accumulate a junk heap of unwarranted conclusions, false generalizations, undefined contradictions, undigested slogans, unidentified wishes, doubts and fears, thrown together by chance, but integrated by your subconscious into a kind of mongrel philosophy and fused into a single, solid weight: *self doubt*, like a ball and chain in the place where your mind's wings should have grown."

—AYN RAND
Philosophy: Who Needs It? (1982)

Parenting Adult Children

I AM SO IMPORTANT to my grown children. What a welcome surprise. I am the compass that marks a part of their world. My job is not over; in fact, new roles with different job descriptions are constantly presenting themselves to me. This stage of parenting requires all of the flexibility and heart that I learned from the other stages. In order to do it well, I need to be on my toes. Where do their lives leave off and mine begin? When should I come up close and when should I step back? How do I support them to the right extent without getting in the way of their will? It's clear to me now that this stage of parenting is every bit as intellectually stimulating as others and continues to challenge me to meet it in the best way I possibly can. If I do not allow myself to understand how crucial I am in the lives of my adult children, I will inevitably hurt them by making too much out of little things or getting overly sensitive to little rejections. My importance to them is to hold my place with love and wisdom.

I understand my importance to my children's lives.

"I love you so passionately, that I hide a great part of my love, not to oppress you with it."
—MARIE DE RABUTIN-CHANTAL, MARQUISE DE SÉVIGNÉ (1671)
Letters of Madame de Sévigné to Her Daughter and Her Friends, Vol. 1 (1811)

Incorporating

THIS ISN'T SO BAD AFTER ALL. There's more to life than taking care of others, I guess—other things to do that still feel fun and special. It's not any one big thing, just more time for the little things, the same old stuff in new configurations. I forgot the world had so many things to do or even at home—cooking, reading, puttering around. I think I can adjust to this. It feels pleasant and you will always be welcome, always be a part of it. There is no pulling you out. You're incorporated in the big picture, the whole heart. This actually feels like an expansion rather than a contraction. I get you, and I get me too. Wow. This is definitely looking up. I like the way I feel.

I can have it all.

"But the self does exist and so, we know in our deepest intuitions, do close relationships. The 'I' and the 'we' are a case not of either/or, but of both/and. I am uniquely me, something in myself that only I can be, and I am also my relationships with others, something larger than myself."

—DANAH ZOHAR
*The Quantum Self: Human Nature
and Consciousness Defined by the New Physics* (1991)

*Y*our *P*resence

YOU ARE WITH ME in my heart. I never really knew how powerful that was. You are far away, it's true, but for me you are completely present. The touch of you seems absolutely near. I can almost hear you and sense you close. You play in my mind—how are you doing? What's going on, is your world filling in around you, do your new surroundings feel comfortable? Are you adjusting happily? My habit of mind is to think about all of the details of your life, and it seems that thought process doesn't change so much. I can think of you if I want to and in this way bring you close to me.

You are present inside of me.

"No matter how old a mother is, she watches her middle-aged children for signs of improvement."

—FLORIDA SCOTT-MAXWELL
The Measure of My Days (1968)

The Wise Woman
Mindfulness, Mentoring, and Meditation

🍏

I walk down the street.
 There is a deep hole in the sidewalk.
 I fall in.
 I am lost . . . . I am helpless.
  It isn't my fault.
It takes forever to find a way out.

I walk down the same street.
 There is a deep hole in the sidewalk.
 I pretend I don't see it.
 I fall in again.
I can't believe I am in this same place.
  But, it isn't my fault.
It still takes a long time to get out.

I walk down the same street.
 There is a deep hole in the sidewalk.
 I *see* it is there.
 I still fall in . . . it's a habit . . . but,
  my eyes are open.
  I know where I am.
It is *my* fault.
I get out immediately.

I walk down the same street.
There is a deep hole in the sidewalk.
I walk around it.

I walk down another street.

—PORTIA NELSON
"Autobiography in Five Short Chapters"
There's a Hole in My Sidewalk

The Wise Woman

I AM THE WISE WOMAN. I spin straw into gold and find meaning in suffering. I am aware that life is short. I feel death at my shoulder each day so that I can better appreciate this thing called life. I stand back. I see with my heart and open to its superior understanding. I know that life is ceaseless change, that this too shall pass. I accept both my darkness and my light knowing that denying one or the other will render me half-blind and wholly false. This day is enough. I witness the lessons, joys, and pains that it contains without judgment or a wish to control. I witness life passing with a quiet kind of meaning, unfolding with a pattern of its own. I am the Wise Woman. I seek strength within me and comfort and support from those who have it to give. I do not demand more from life than it can offer, and life's gifts are not wasted on me. I am grateful for what I have and willing to work to earn it. I recognize that my real battles are fought within the privacy of my own soul.

I choose life.

"We can be wise from goodness and good from wisdom."
—MARIE VON EBNER-ESCHENBACH
Aphorisms (1893)

The Biology of the Wise Woman

IN MIDLIFE WE ARE being rewired, by nature, for self-reflection. The hormones that affect our moods and functions change as we enter the second half or so of our lives. Estrogen and proges- terone regulated us, kept us calm, and helped us to be wired for caretaking. These hormones foster instincts for nurturing and cohesion. Around menopause, our hormones change focus and are constantly stimulating the hypothalamus—the part of the brain that is associated with traumatic memory storage—and the pituitary gland, which is associated with meditation. This is why, in midlife, we more easily recall "unfinished business" from the past. If we are suddenly preoccupied with old hurts or are curious about exploring what makes us tick, it's because we're responding to nature's call to go within and take a deeper look at ourselves. If we find we need more time for relaxation and medi- tative activities, it's because our pituitary glands are being stimu- lated much of the time, producing hormones that lead us toward self-reflection and meditation.

During menopause, our bodies are wiring us for new roles, the roles that are contained within the archetype of the Wise Woman. If we understand this and use our rewiring well and to our advantage, we can still mean a lot to society and ourselves. We're being wired to reflect on ourselves, on the world, and on life, to interpret experience with greater depth and reflection.

The seeds of wisdom are growing inside me.
"Love alone matters."

—ST. THÉRÈSE OF LISIEUX (1897),
in Dorothy Day,
Therese (1960)

"At midlife, the hormonal milieu that was present for only a few days each month during most of your reproductive years, the milieu that was designed to spur you on to re-examine your life just a little at a time, now gets stuck in the on position for weeks or months at a time. We go from an alternating current of inner wisdom to a direct current that remains on all the time after menopause is complete. During perimenopause, our brains make the change from one way of being to the other.

"Biologically, at this stage of life you are programmed to withdraw from the outside world for a period of time and revisit your past. You need to be free of the distractions that come when you are focusing your mothering efforts solely on others. Perimenopause is a time when you are meant to mother yourself."

—CHRISTIANE NORTHRUP
The Wisdom of Menopause (2001)

Going with the Program

OUR TIME FOR OURSELVES IS NOW. This is the time to take the sculpture class, get into pottery, join a writing group, or adopt a healthy lifestyle. It's a great time to join a self-help program or find a therapist or growth group. It's a time for long walks, long lunches, and friendship. It's time to rediscover our spiritual faith. In his seminal work on lifelong development, psychoanalyst Erik Erikson refers to this stage of life as wisdom versus despair. Old issues of low self-esteem, fear, or unresolved hurts can be restimulated hormonally and undermine our sense of ourselves at midlife. Getting lost in our feelings can lead to despair. Yet this can also be our greatest opportunity to attain inner mastery and a new kind of freedom and creativity. If we are willing to face these parts of ourselves that have been on hold, to work with ourselves, to dive deep, we can grow and learn. We can reflect and try to understand the meaning we may have made of the events of our earlier lives and how we have been living by that narrow interpretation. We can make new meaning informed by the accumulated knowledge we have gained through years of life experience. By mining our inner depths and gaining new insight, we can reinterpret the beauty and purpose of living. We see the big picture and hold it for the next generation. We discover the joy of giving and sharing. We can choose this route at this stage of life rather than seeing this stage as a slow walk toward the graveyard. In fact, our greatest protection is to recognize the value to ourselves of resolving our inner worlds, and becoming more reflective and spiritual. In this way, we can become wise. Now is the time.

I attend to my inner world on a daily basis.

"For biological reasons, females of the human species are often easier to control intellectually, psychologically, and socially during their childbearing years than they are before puberty (from birth to age eleven) or after menopause. When we are creating a home or building a family, our primary concern is to maintain balance and peace. We seem to know instinctively that when raising a family it's better for all if we compromise and maintain whatever support we have, even if it's less than ideal."

—CHRISTIANE NORTHRUP
The Wisdom of Menopause (2001)

Taking on a New Phase

I TAKE ON THE NEXT PHASE OF MY LIFE. Things will be different. My focuses are shifting. Much of the energy that went toward raising my family is freed up, and I find new experiences that feed and challenge me. I will allow myself the same sense of commitment, adventure, and excitement in taking care of my own life that I had in taking care of my children. Today I refocus. I look at my day and figure out how I want to fill it. I feel both liberated and lonely, challenged and disoriented. But I adjust and in adjusting, I develop goals and plans for myself. This part of my life is for me to grow in new ways, to pay attention to parts of me that have been put on a back burner. This shift from taking care of others toward paying more attention to myself can bring up feelings of guilt and longing. These are part of this phase, part of my process.

I am shifting my focus; paying greater attention to my own life.

"Life goes on, having nowhere else to go."

—DIANE ACKERMAN
The Moon by Whale Light (1991)

Inner Space

I FEEL THE SELF that I have put on hold for so many years come pouring into me. If anyone had told me that I'd have this feeling, I'm not sure I'd have believed them. All I could see was emptiness around me, but I didn't fully understand that part of my new fullness would come from within. I was so used to sharing both my inner and my outer world with my children that I forgot how much of my own inner world was still waiting to rise up—to assert itself into the psychic storage space that hasn't been mine to use. Filling up from within feels right and good now. The self that has had to wait patiently in the wings is welcome and needed.

We're still here.

"Let there be many windows to your soul,
   ... Not the narrow pane
   Of one poor creed can catch the radiant rays
   That shine from countless sources."

—ELLA WHEELER WILCOX
"Progress"
Poems of Passion (1883)

The Alchemy of the Journey

As THE WISE WOMAN I understand that I can survive my powerful feelings that inevitably occur around how I experience the events of my life. This is, perhaps, the gift of years. This too shall pass. It isn't that pain doesn't exist for the Wise Woman. Only that I have learned, over time, to see it differently, to accept its inevitable presence in each and every life and to find my own kind of meaning in it. My own way of struggling through it. My own philosophy of life built on my ever-growing ability to see beauty in truth, and meaning in struggle. I see that the Wise Woman surrenders to the inevitable trials of life and learns to work with them with grace and understanding, feeling the fullness of circumstances but eventually letting go; recognizing that the days of life are limited and meant to be lived and cherished.

I process, integrate new truth, and move along my way.

"The substance of grief is not imaginary; it is as real as rope or the absence of air, and like both of these things, it can kill.

—BARBARA KINGSOLVER
The Poisonwood Bible (1998)

New Goals with New Energy

THIS PHASE OF MY LIFE is less automatic than other phases. Until now there has been a master builder—always with a plan, always a goal. And the goals came so easily. Build a life. Get a job. Find a mate. Raise a family. Now I've done all of that, so what's next? I'm not ready for a book of poetry and a mountain retreat. I want excitement and energy and life. I can use this new release of energy to let new things *into* my life. Who will not benefit if I look at this new stage as an exciting building step all over again? Why not? I don't have to throw in the towel just because my main tasks are accomplished. There's work to do in this world. This is the time when I can use those lessons I learned about selflessness in a new way—I can bring joy to myself by finding new ways to give to others—to make this world a better place.

I will search out opportunities to be of use.

"Existence is no more than the precarious attainment of relevance in an intensely mobile flux of past, present and future."

—SUSAN SONTAG
"Thinking Against Oneself: Reflections on Cioran"
Styles of Radical Will (1966)

Lighting My Own Lamp

I LIGHT MY OWN LAMP TODAY. I go within for my deepest experience of joy, of ecstasy in being alive. I get in touch with the deeper pulse of living—the thread that connects me with the divine experience. I recognize that in order to be lit from within I need to drop down inside of myself and be in the presence of inner light. Life itself has a purpose apart from any individual task or stage. Life itself is the experience. All of the things I have been trying to accomplish are both inner and outer goals. They are meant to bring me closer to myself, to develop me in ways that allow me to experience life more fully—to be more capable of pleasure.

I appreciate life.

"Now at last I have come to see what Life is. Nothing is ever ended, everything only begun. And the brave victories that seem so splendid are never really won."

—SARA TEASDALE

Opening to Abundance

I AM READY, WILLING, AND ABLE to open my mind and heart to the abundance that the world has to offer me. This world brings forth what I need. The sun shines; fresh spring water makes its way across rocky slopes to quench my thirst; food germinates from seeds and comes forth in prolific variety to nourish my body; and the sky, wind, and rain draw me toward their eternal mystery. This world is designed to nurture and sustain life. I am part of that life, and I receive solace and comfort knowing that the world and I are alive and vibrant.

I am open to abundance.

"When one's young ... everything is a rehearsal. To be repeated ad lib, to be put right when the curtain goes up in earnest. One day you know that the curtain was up all the time. That was the performance."

—SYBILLE BEDFORD
A Compass Error (1968)

Opening to the New

TODAY I AM OPEN to what life offers to me. The world comes to greet me like an old friend each morning. My daily habits comfort and ground me. The thought of moving into my day pleases me. Life unfolds one second at a time and today I am present to witness it. How much of my life do I let pass by unnoticed? How many of my feelings go unfelt? I notice today. I feel the quiet rhythm of my surroundings. I sense the energy and aliveness that is always present behind the thin veil of reality. Today I recognize that my time on earth is limited, and I choose to value and embrace it while I have it.

I am open to life.

"Our days glide gently and imperceptibly along, like the motion of the hour-hand, which we cannot discover. . . . We advance gradually; we are the same today as yesterday, and tomorrow as today: thus we go on, without perceiving it, which is a miracle of the Providence I adore."

—MARIE DE RABUTIN-CHANTAL, MARQUISE DE SÉVIGNÉ (1687)
Letters of Madame de Sévigné to Her Daughter and Her Friends, Vol. 7 (1811)

Embracing the Emptiness

TODAY I ALLOW MYSELF to fully embrace my emptiness. I do not run from it; I stand and face it. I let it fill me and recognize that it is only a feeling—a feeling that needn't rule me. Emptiness. What is in it? Those I love—memories, wishes, yearning, needing. Your faces, your beings are all around me in this emptiness. It is an emptiness I can do nothing about—nothing but surrender and allow it to be what it is. Emptiness. When will it transform to fill up with other things? I cannot force it. I cannot make it go away. God should come here if I can unblock this emptiness, if I can let there be a tiny hole in it where love and light can come in. Emptiness—it co-exists with fullness. That's all I can do for now.

I embrace the emptiness.

"Life does not accommodate you; it shatters you. It is meant to, and it couldn't do it better. Every seed destroys its container or else there would be no fruition."

—FLORIDA SCOTT-MAXWELL
The Measure of My Days (1968)

Disconnected Families

IN THIS TIME where heroes are hard to come by and values are slipping, I can become out of balance, with no one on whom to tether my need to idealize, no one to look up to. So many of the people who are blazing trails ahead of me act in ways that are disappointing. And family. Our real heroes—mothers, fathers, grandparents, older siblings—are not the cohesive unit they once were. In a subtle way this can make me feel that I can't lay claim to family members, that I can't incorporate them into my own sense of self. So many families aren't sure what they mean to each other today. With all of these fallen idols, confusion, alienation, and distance, resentment can build up beneath the level of my awareness. Anger builds and alienation creeps in. At this stage in my life I can try to model love and generosity. Giving is also receiving. I will actively look for ways to be of service to my family.

I will recognize that family bonds are a part of the inner world of all in my family.

"There are four minds in the bed of a divorced man who marries a divorced woman."

—THE PALESTINIAN TALMUD (HAGGADAH)

My Prime

I CAN TAKE MYSELF LIGHTLY. Each day that I look in the mirror, I see that I am losing my race against time just a little. If what is on my face is all that I value, I will also lose my self-acceptance and love just a little each day. I am not larger than nature. I am subject to a life cycle just like anything else. I will not rob myself of my own time simply because I am not "in my prime"; instead, I will redefine what I mean by prime. Prime is in my awareness of my own being. It is my ability to look to a day without anxiety or expectation, willing to see it anew and to experience it as if it had never happened before. Prime is when I can see not what I pretend is there, but what actually is there and appreciate it for what it is. It is when I can live on peaceful terms with life, not constantly looking to it for what it can give to me but wondering also what I might give to it. Prime is when I know how to value the relationships in my life and take good care of them as well as myself.

I see beauty in the life I have.

"I have the perfect face for radio."

—VIRGINIA GRAHAM, with Jean Libman Block,
There Goes What's Her Name (1963)

Everything *Is* One

I RECOGNIZE THAT everything I see, am, and sense comes from one source that I choose to call God. No separation from God is possible because this oneness or God exists in the smallest particle and the largest mountain or sky. Any separation is a denial of this fundamental truth. I align myself with the one mind that has created everything. The God-mind within me presses me toward higher thoughts and ignites my desire for higher knowledge. I cannot understand myself fully if I don't acknowledge that I am one with creation, a being emerging from the God-mind, made in the image of God. I understand that God is not in a distant heaven but here and now, close at hand, intimate and present.

I rest in awareness of my true nature.

"Spirituality is basically our relationship with reality."
— CHANDRA PATEL, in Theresa King, ed.,
The Spiral Path (1992)

Lifelong Passion

GOD, I AM WIDE OPEN. Come to me. Whatever energy you are, whatever entity you are, I am waiting for you. Fill my heart with your love and my mind with your wisdom. Speak to me in the silence of my meditations. Lead me with invisible hands. Guide me toward the next phase of spiritual and human evolution. I am ready, I am waiting, I am willing.

I am open to divine instruction.

"The dramatic action that we need to create a way of life on Earth that really works will be taken not through personal, social or political action, but through spiritual action."

—BROOKE MEDICINE EAGLE
Buffalo Woman Comes Singing (1991)

"How unnatural the imposed view, imposed by a puritanical ethos, that passionate love belongs only to the young, that people are dead from the neck down by the time they are forty, and that any deep feeling, any passion after that age, is either ludicrous or revolting!"

—MAY SARTON
Journal of a Solitude (1973)

The Grandmother

I WITNESS WITH LOVE and gratitude as the generations move forward. What a blessing and a miracle to be a part of a fingerprint into the future. This is my legacy. The quality of mothering I did is part of my contribution to society's future. My children learned more about parenting from me than anyone in the world. I am more for my grandchildren than a distant benevolent presence. I'm active, interested, and part of their day-to-day lives. We help to shape each other's future, and we are each other's present. I am so important to the lives of my grandchildren, and they are so important to me. I have gifts to give them that can come from nowhere else and vice versa. I steady their lives and give them strength and courage to meet their challenges. They give me joy and a sense of importance.

I am important to my grandchildren.

"Life is like a camel; you can make it do anything except back up."

—MARCELENE COX
in *Ladies Home Journal* (1945)

My State of Mind

I PROCESS and let go of regret. What I have not accomplished in my life need not define my experience of today. Constantly going over what never was or what's not just as I might like it will only set my mind on a downward spiral, giving in to the worst of my thinking and feeling patterns. I have the potential of today surrounding me. If I dwell on negativity, I will kill what can come to me right now. I will still my mind and allow my consciousness to rise like yeast surrounding myself with soft, yellow light inside and out. I will take responsibility for the state of my mind and do what's necessary to elevate it and maintain a positive outlook.

I am responsible for what goes through my mind.

"Life begins when a person first realizes how soon it ends."

—MARCELENE COX
in *Ladies Home Journal* (1942)

Consciousness

ALL IS ALIVE, all is a vibrating, intelligent consciousness. The world only looks as if it's made up of separate, unrelated forms, but we are all made of the same stuff. We all bring forth and are manifestations of one intelligent energy. This doesn't mean that we're all the same, only that we recognize a life form at various stages of evolution or expression in all living forms. If I want a plant to grow, I can give it space and energy to do so as I attend to it. If I want to support those I love, I can see them thriving, whole and strong in my mind's eye, trusting that that vision will carry creative, manifesting energy. I am in a co-conscious state with others. What I think and feel is felt by them and vice versa. All is alive.

I am part of an alive, vibrating universe.

"Never, my heart, is there enough of living."

—LÉONIE ADAMS
Never Enough of Living (1925)

Personal Responsibility

MY DAY IS what I make of it. I will enter my day with a plan of action. When I wake up in the morning, I will mentally organize the hours that lie before me. It is possible to squander time, for what is life but time? What is the gift of a new day but the gift of twenty-four hours? Why should I let those twenty-four hours pass unnoticed? Why should I be an unconscious person walking around in a semi-fog? It doesn't matter what I do; it matters how I do it. So many simple events of life take on new substance and meaning when I allow myself to bring my full consciousness to them. It is not what I do but how much awareness I bring to what I do that changes the quality of my life.

I'll do the work necessary to have a life.

"Growth itself contains the germ of happiness."

—PEARL S. BUCK
To My Daughters, With Love (1967)

Relationships

IT IS STRANGE HOW life gets shallow and deep all at once. To me relationships seem to be part of what motivates me to deepen myself. The power of love. The intensity of a bonded commitment. At the end of the day, these steel chords hold my boat steady on the changing seas of life—through the day-to-day monotony and majesty. Relationships. These are the markings along my journey, the retaining walls bordering my road. They hold me in their center as I travel from one place to another. It is they for whom I have reached down into my soul to become more than I thought I could be. It is my relationships. The faces that I carry in my heart. The ethereal bodies of those I have loved and who love me against whom I have measured my height and weight, my growth physically, psychologically, and spiritually.

I understand the value of relationships.

"What we have most to fear is failure of the heart."

—SONIA JOHNSON
Going Out of Our Minds (1987)

Personal Dreams

I CAN DREAM AGAIN. It's all right to want a life of my own and to reach toward it fully with all of the excitement and energy that I took to raising children. It's all right to want something for me. In a way it's the same as it always was because whatever I have in my own life will naturally spill over into my children's, if I want it to—or even if I don't. Water flows downward toward the sea, and the generations follow the same natural pattern. My life still belongs to those I've loved. We are as inseparable as the rocks and the earth and the sea. Nature meant us to be together in a very profound way.

I can entertain my own hopes and dreams without losing you.

"It's time for us old women to rip to shreds the veil of invisibility that has encased us. We have to fight the societal stereotype that keeps us on the periphery, outside the mainstream. We have experience to offer, judgment, wisdom, balance and charm."

—MIRIAM REIBOLD
News item (1991)

The Big Picture

I HAVE A PERSPECTIVE on life that allows me to understand how to assign correct value to each and every experience life has to offer. I see the big picture. I don't get lost in what surrounds me at any given moment, though I am well able to appreciate and live in the here and now. I don't mistake the forest for the trees. These are the things I value. The relationships that sustain me throughout my life have my value. The quality of small interactions throughout my day creates good feelings within and around me. My ability to enjoy simple pleasures—a walk through nature, a good meal, the laughter of others, quiet reverie—gives my life beauty. My belief and faith in God and the mystery of life lend meaning and perspective to events both big and small. My passion for the world and its cares and needs provides me with a sense of purpose and place in this world.

I see my life and the world in proper perspective.

"Spirit is the real and eternal; matter is the unreal and temporal."

—MARY BAKER EDDY
Science and Health (1875)

"She had accomplished what according to builders is only possible to wood and stone of the very finest grain; she had *weathered,* as they call it, with beauty."

—ETHEL SMITH (1920), on the Empress Eugénie at age 95,
in Christopher St. John,
Ethel Smith (1959)

cAppreciating Life

I HAVE THE GIFT OF LIFE. I am here. I am alive, with all of my senses, and able to experience the magic of this incredible world. Whatever this day has in store for me—I am open to receive. I will act on my day and allow my day to act on me. I am open. I will take steps that I know will make my day feel good, productive, and pleasurable, and then I will let the rest happen. Each day presents me with gifts and surprises if I know how to unwrap the present—if I remember how to be astonished, pleased, or awed.

Life itself is the gift.

"Love all the people you can. The sufferings from love are not to be compared to the sorrows of loneliness."

—SUSAN HALE (1868), in Caroline P. Atkinson, ed.,
Letters of Susan Hale (1918)

"The crucial task of age is balance, a veritable tightrope of balance; keeping just well enough, just brave enough, just gay and interested and starkly honest enough to remain a sentient human being."

—FLORIDA SCOTT-MAXWELL
The Measure of My Days (1968)

Breaks

I AM DREAMING. Dreaming of a lovely day; dreaming of what might happen down the line that could be wonderful; resting my mind. My mind doesn't want to think today. My mind is full of a thousand threads—threads going anywhere—nowhere in particular. I feel like cozying up today and doing little things that feel good: drink tea, watch a movie, read a book, putter. Rather than shape my day today, I think I'll just go with the flow and let the day shape me. I'll take a walk, chat with people I encounter, do pleasant things. My mind wants a rest today—it doesn't want to think much. That animal part of me is taking over; the part of me that wants to curl up like a house cat and watch the world go by.

I'm taking a vacation in my own home.

"How lovely to take a nap and then rest afterwards."

—SPANISH PROVERB

ﾉﾟharing Joy

I SHARE MY JOY, my laughter, my zest for life with my children, my spouse, and my grandchildren. This world is alive and beautiful, and I'm not keeping my love for it a secret. Infusing our simple, shared activities with mutual pleasure is how spirit lives in this world. Spirit lives in the moment. I won't block it. I will allow it to be; an expression of that being is our ability to take pleasure in the simple things of life. To feel joy. Good energy. Alive. The gentle moments that we pass, that we infuse with this pleasure taking, are a secret to happiness. Happiness is not a goal. It's not a permanent state. It's a turn of mind, a way of seeing and allowing. Letting it go—not holding onto it for fear of its never coming back—is the only way it persists. Being willing to feel it—rather than block it for fear of its feeling too good, for fear of losing it—is the only way to keep it.

We nourish each other.

"The most important thing to share with our children is
    our joy."

HARRIET LERNER (2000),
at Fall Conference, Ben Franklin Institute,
Scottsdale, Arizona

I Will Survive

I FEEL DETERMINED TO SURVIVE and thrive in this stage of life, determined to reinvent my life so that it feels as terrific at this stage as it has for the past two decades. I need to marshal my inner forces and re-center myself. I need to find my rhythm. I postponed so much of my own life, put aside so much of my own self to let the needs of others come first. Now it is my turn to tune in and find out what works for me—what brings me pleasure and satisfaction. My ability to see life from a spiritual perspective is a gift. It allows life to vibrate with meaning and purpose. It illuminates a deeper perspective on ordinary events. Each day I take the best attitude that I can muster toward my own life. Because I know I will one day lose my life, I am able to appreciate it as a gift.

I am grateful for this new day.

"If you wish to live, you must first attend your own funeral."
—KATHERINE MANSFIELD, in Antony Alpers,
Katherine Mansfield (1954)

The Gift of Time

THERE IS MORE ROOM for serenity in my day if I can let it in now. More room for reflection and calm—time to enter more fully into the activities at hand if I dare. I can allow a new sense of peace and ease to enter my routines. I can have time for my partner and my friends and for pursuing those activities I have put aside for "later." I find my attitude shifting. It is full of potential for other types of experiences. It's scary. My identity for so long has been fixed that I fear I might drift off into space somewhere unknown if I allow this shift to take place. I fear perhaps that I will lose what I've had if I loosen my psychological grip on my past that I treasure. Regrets and all. I wish to use this time in my life to make peace with myself and my relationships and to find ways of being useful to my community. The acceptance, calm, and wisdom I embody, I can pass along in my own small, but meaningful, way.

I feel a subtle shift beginning.

"God loves you and He knows all the secrets of your heart. . . . You've allowed the past to come between you and God. Turn the past over to God. He's strong enough to take it. And give Him your future too. . . . He'll make you strong enough to live it."

—An angel speaking to a jaded Vietnam veteran
Touched by an Angel, CBS-TV (2000)

The Table Prepared

I SEE THE TABLE PREPARED. The riches of this life are revealed to me and I understand, at my very core, that life is a banquet at which I am an invited guest. I say please and thank you, recognizing that it is my place to take what I need and what I like, enjoy it, and leave the rest for others to enjoy. I leave my place clean and tidy, a little better than the way I found it. The world is here for me to taste and savor, not to destroy. If I cut a tree, I plant two. I leave something behind for others. Our world is here for me and for others. We are meant to enjoy the things of this world, to respect them, and to honor the forces that created them.

I relish the world that surrounds me.

"Atrophy of feeling creates criminals."

—ANAÍS NIN
The Diary of Anaís Nin, Vol. 3 (1969)

"There shall be Eternal summer in the grateful heart."

—CELIA THAXTER
"A Grateful Heart"
Poems (1872)

Light My Way

DAILY I REST in the presence of your light and pray for guidance
and discernment. My love for you is ever expanding. I place my
hand in yours. Show me. Show me the way. Reveal your plan.
Steady me on my path toward you. Illuminate my darkness so
that your light does not devastate me. Give me the strength to
admit fault, to step away from my own self-centeredness and
ego-bound thinking and feeling. Release me from my lower self
into my higher self. Show me your purpose so that I can align
myself with what is right and good and wholesome. Help me
to see holiness in all that surrounds me. Teach me to see beneath
the surface—to penetrate illusion.

*I surrender my life and will to the loving care of my Higher
Power.*

"I am Thine and Thou art mine, Lord. Use me as Thine
instrument."

—SANSKRIT PRAYER

Count Me In

COUNT ME IN. Whatever are my talents, my usefulness; wherever you see me fitting into your grand scheme . . . place me there. I am willing to open my heart to your guidance. I am built to be part of this moment of transformation. I see a better world in my mind's eye and I know that others see it too. Connect me with those people who wish to quietly usher in a new world. Together we can push through the eye of the needle—together we can help it happen. I see a better world ahead of us, a world that is less selfish and more giving. A world that understands the beauty and importance of the human spirit. A world that loves and respects life.

I am open to the mystery of being alive. We are transforming together.

"We seem to be trapped by a civilization that has accelerated many physical aspects of evolution but has forgotten that other vital part of man—his mind and his psyche."

—SYBIL LEEK
ESP—The Magic Within You (1971)

*C*o-*C*reation

I LIVE IN A WORLD OF POSSIBILITIES. I live in a world in which my imagination walks ahead of me. What I can see in my mind's eye can manifest. As I rest in the quiet of my mind and allow the alive and vibrant universe to flow through and around me, I recognize that we are one with the creative mind, a product of one source. I take responsibility for my world along with all creative energies. I do my part to manifest a beautiful world. First, I have to see it, feel it, experience it as real. Then I open a door within me through which my vision can manifest in God's time. I am limited only by what I am willing to accept as possible. Life is a creative process in which I am the co-creator. God and I work together to make this world a better place to be.

I co-create a beautiful world.

"We have a lot to do. . . . People don't understand this. They think we're sitting around in rocking chairs, which isn't at all true. Why we don't even own a rocking chair."

—SADIE DELANY, age 103, on her 101-year-old sister and herself, in Sarah and A. Elizabeth Delany, with Amy Hill Hearth
Having Our Say (1993)

Life Is Not a Dress Rehearsal

I OPEN TO NEW PERSPECTIVES, to fresh starts. I need not play second fiddle to my own habits—I am in charge, not my established pattern. I am able to meditate on a situation and to see it in a variety of lights. I turn the prism in my mind round and round until it has shown me new color and multiple reflections. Simply by breathing deeply, relaxing and allowing a new perspective to enter my consciousness, I can experience a shift in perspective. I will allow a cool breeze to blow my old thinking patterns away and allow new ones to enter.

My life is happening now.

"It seems to me you can be awfully happy in this life if you stand aside and watch and mind your own business, and let other people do as they like about damaging themselves and one another. You go on kidding yourself that you're impartial and tolerant and all that, then all of a sudden you realize you're dead, and you've never been alive at all."

—MARY STEWART
This Rough Magic (1964)

A Quiet Prayer

I SAY A QUIET PRAYER for those I love. I know that my prayers have power. The prayer that I hold in my heart for another person is held in both our hearts. It is helped by invisible hands, blown by the breath of angels toward the soul of another. This love is what I have to give, not a sentiment but an energy, not a thought but a state of awe and wonder. Love leads me toward what is right and good in this life. What I cannot do, the thousands of tasks I'll never accomplish, and knowledge that I will never attain are unimportant compared to the power of love. When I can love, the rest falls into place. This love that I feel teaches and guides me. It is this experience of love that is the single-most important part of my life. Through love, all else will come; all things are possible.

Thank you for the ability to love.

"One cannot be honest even at the end of one's life, for no one is wholly alone. We are bound to those we love, or to those who love us, and to those who need us to be brave, or content, or even happy enough to allow them not to worry about us. So we must refrain from giving pain, as our last gift to our fellows."

—FLORIDA SCOTT-MAXWELL
The Measure of My Days (1968)

Thought Process

I LET MY MIND GO WHERE IT WILL. I will take time today to allow my thoughts to unravel and my mind to relax. Rather than seek to control my thought processes, I will observe them. The nature of my mind is to produce endless associations. I will observe these associations—to investigate thoughts. I am not my thoughts. I am not this endless array of associations. I am something secure, unchanging—the inner witness that watches and observes. When I witness my thought process and my emotions as they move through me, with no thought of controlling or getting lost in them, a few things happen. I synthesize the events of my day and understand how I feel about them. I make connections with other times in my life or other parts of me and I process internally. In this way, I make meaning and continue to grow a little each day. I am able, through this, to have the large view, the perspective of the Wise Woman.

I will give myself time to watch my thought process.

"I have enjoyed greatly the second blooming that comes when you finish the life of the emotions and of personal relations; and suddenly find—at the age of fifty, say—that a whole new life has opened before you, filled with things you can think about, study, or read about. . . . It is as if a fresh sap of ideas and thoughts was rising in you."

—AGATHA CHRISTIE
An Autobiography (1977)

Eternity

IT'S A BEAUTIFUL WORLD and I want to be a part of it. Life is constantly renewing itself. Leaves that were once bright green turn a gorgeous gold and red and brown, then fall away. But they don't disappear—they go into the soil where they become fertilizer for new growth. The life I live will not disappear either. It will materialize through and become metabolized into the lives of all whom I have touched. It will live in the hearts of all whom I have loved and who have loved me. My life means something today and for generations to come. My actions have deep and lasting resonance throughout time and lives. I am responsible to those I do not yet know.

I carry and make a part of history.

"We are adhering to life now with our last muscle—the heart."

—DJUNA BARNES
Nightwood (1937)

Self-Forgiveness

IT IS TIME. Time to understand what it means to "remember and forgive." If I have to rewrite wrongs I feel I've done so they somehow don't matter as much, I will be rewriting my own and other people's history; walking away with a piece of their heart. That will never set either them or me free. On the other hand, if I cling to regret because I cannot, somehow, metabolize the pain and move on, my heart will never be truly open in the here and now. I will be unavailable for a free and open relationship with those I've hurt. All I can do is work through my end so that more precious time does not get lost living in the land of the unforgiven. I can begin the work. It is the work of the Wise Woman to start anyway. The Wise Woman sees that without true forgiveness there is no true moving on, only moving forward.

Forgiveness will begin with me.

"Mother, you can still hold on but forgive, forgive and give, for as long as we both shall live I forgive you. . . . The teeth at your bones are your own, the hunger is yours, the forgiveness is yours. . . . Listen. Slide the weight from your shoulders and move forward. You are afraid you might forget, but you never will. You will forgive and remember. Think of the vine that curls from the small square plot that was once my heart. That is the only marker you need. Move on. Walk forward into the light."

—Barbara Kingsolver
The Poisonwood Bible (1998)

Staying in the Game

I DON'T NEED TO BE BEST ANYMORE, or first, or perfect. I find that I am less driven to do that which will make me succeed and more apt to do that which will make me happy. I don't rely on who I think I should be as much as on who I am, and who I am doesn't need to be better than someone else in order to be good enough. I just want to stay in the game, just be a player. I am happy I am here. I don't need to be perfect or even close to it. What's perfection anyway but an idea of the ideal separate from the experience of reality? Ideas are not what ground me; experience is. When I open myself up to all that's available in the moment, I find all that I need in order to sustain myself and be happy.

I am aware of the deep spirituality of the moment.

"Often people attempt to live their lives backwards; they try to have more things, or more money, in order to do more of what they want, so they will be happier. The way it actually works is the reverse. You must first be who you really are, then do what you need to do in order to have what you want."

—MARGARET YOUNG

A Deeper Reality Calls

TODAY I RECOGNIZE THE BEAUTY that surrounds me all the time. I take a deeper look. Other times in my life have been filled with rushing to get here and there. I wonder sometimes, now, just where I was going so fast. Life cannot be savored if I am not in a calm enough state to take it in, to let what is around me penetrate my skin. The same scene can affect me in very different ways depending on my state of rest, of inner quietness, of openness to what life is offering me. Today I will let my life affect me because I have the time. And the wisdom to understand that life is what happens between the lines. What I am looking for is already here. It's as if a thin veil divides me from seeing a deeper, fuller reality. Today I will wait peacefully and allow that veil to lift. What could be more pressing or important than to appreciate life?

I use my time in a new way.

"If old age in the shape of waning strength says to me often, 'Thou shalt not!' so do my years smile upon me and say to me, 'Thou needst not.'"

—MARY HEATON VORSE
Autobiography of an Elderly Woman (1911)

Wave-Particle Theory

THE RELATIONSHIPS THAT I ENGAGE IN are alive in the universe that surrounds me. They vibrate. They interweave. They change and flux. What is in my mind and heart is present in the energy of the relationship. If I fill this space with resentment and judgment, that is what will exist in the relationship. If I fill it with love, acceptance, and forgiveness, that is what will be there. If I force myself to think "good" thoughts but continue to feel negative emotions, ambivalence and dissonance will naturally be felt. Relationships are part and parcel of an alive universe just as I am and as those I know are. There is no dead space, vacuums maybe, but everything is alive. What am I putting into the energy fields of my relationships?

I take responsibility for the state of my relationships.

"Intimate relationship, the type of relationship that gets inside the self, that influences and even defines its being from within, is the *sine qua non* of the quantum self. Viewed quantum mechanically, I am my relationships—my relationships to the subselves within my own self and my relationships to others, my living relationships to my own past through quantum memory and to my future through my possibilities. Without relationship I am nothing."

—DANAH ZOHAR
The Quantum Self:
Human Nature and Consciousness
Defined by the New Physics

My Grandchildren

MY GRANDCHILDREN LIGHT UP MY LIFE. It's happening all over again, the magic, life renewing itself before my eyes. What a wonder. These little people are utterly thrilling to know. I have new little beings to assist in their peoplehood, new little ones to relish and admire. I can be so useful to my children at this stage by taking some of the pressure off their parents, by sharing their joy. We are an even bigger family. What blessings; what a feeling. We're expanding rather than contracting. I want to be a good grandmother to my grandchildren, hold the same sacred space for them that I held for my children. My children need me to love their children, not raise them, not control them, but love them. I feel my world expanding in the sweetest way.

Life continues to bring forth; my cup runneth over.

"I loved their home. Everything smelled older, worn but safe; the food aroma had baked itself into the furniture."

—SUSAN STRASBERG
Bittersweet (1980)

"Grandma was a kind of first-aid station, or a Red Cross nurse, who took up where the battle ended, accepting us and our little sobbing sins, gathering the whole of us into her lap, restoring us to health and confidence by her amazing faith in life and in a mortal's strength to meet it."

—LILLIAN SMITH, in Tillie Olsen,
Mother to Daughter, Daughter to Mother (1984)

The Greatest Gift

MY HIGHER SELF IS SELFLESS not because it's a goody-two-shoes self, long suffering, smarter, or better. It's selfless because it has *transcended, tapped into,* or *risen into* a higher or deeper or more centered place. It's selfless because it isn't self-bound. I glimpse it, dip in and out, pass through and back again. I do not hold onto it, which is about as effective as holding onto air, but I experience it, sometimes through grace, meditation, deep relationship, just being. I spend more time here as life goes on. I have inner peace, a sense of well-being, an awareness of the unity and oneness of life. I fill my well of wellness and draw on it throughout the day. I share it with those I come in contact with and that is a gift. It is contagious; it grows through conscious awareness. It turns day-to-day living into a path toward enlightenment, and women into spiritual seekers. I will rest in conscious awareness for a while today.

I cultivate a transcendent state of mind.

"Spirit and body differ not essentially, but gradually."

—ANNE VICOUNTESS CONWAY
Ancient and Modern Philosophy (1692)

"That it will never come again is what makes life so sweet."

—EMILY DICKINSON, in Mabel Loomis Todd
and Millicent Todd Bingham, eds.,
Bolts of Melody (1945)

Life Review

LET'S REVIEW OUR LIVES to learn, measure growth, and consolidate gains. Try this exercise. Slowly walk around the photographs you have in frames or hanging on a wall, or leaf through photo albums. Let yourself be drawn to an image of yourself from some time of your life that speaks to you. When you have your photograph, hold it in your hands and look at it carefully. How do you sense what you felt in this picture? What do you feel you would like to be saying? What do you feel you would like to do? First reverse roles with yourself in the photograph and write a journal entry as the person in the picture, saying everything you feel you would have said then but were not able to. When you are fully finished with that, reverse roles back to yourself today and share some wisdom with the "you" in the photograph. What would your present-day self like to tell yourself then that you had no way of knowing when you were younger? What do you wish you knew then that you know now? Why do you think this photograph is of particular meaning to you?

I reflect on the physical, psychological, emotional, and spiritual events of my life.

"Imperial Self beyond self that I call my soul,
  Climb up into the crow's-nest.
  Look out over the changing ocean of my life
  And shout down to me whither to change my course."

—SARAH N. CLEGHORN
"The Lookout"
Portraits and Progress (1917)

Letters and Memoirs

I AM CARRIER OF MY FAMILY HISTORY. The story of my life sets the groundwork for other stories and I know the lives of those I have raised as no other person could. I will write these things down. I'll write letters to those I love telling them who I am, what is important to me, and how I see life. I'll share my accumulated wisdom with them. And let them know my wishes and dreams for them. I'll share and write also about the important, life-altering experiences I've had and what they taught me about life. I'll record with love the simple pleasures, comic moments, and memorable times that we've shared together, letting them know what moved me, what meant something and why. I'll add pictures, poems, and mementos that help tell the story or have special meaning. I'll make a little book that can be cherished for generations to come. Our stories are worth so much. I want to record and share them with those I love and who love me. This is a gift to myself as a way of reviewing my own life and our life together and to my family as an expression of love.

I will write my own, simple memoir stories and mental snapshots as a gift to myself and my family.

"Writers live twice."

—NATALIE GOLDBERG
Writing Down the Bones (1986)

"I wear the key of memory, and can open every door in the house of my life."

—AMELIA E. BARR
All the Days of My Life (1913)

Thanksgiving

I RECOGNIZE THE IMPORTANCE of gratitude in my life and today and every day I count my blessings. I see the glass half full. I look at the bright side, while acknowledging the dark side. I give thanks for being alive. Life is a gift that I have been given. I co-create with God. God's presence in my heart is what gives my life its center and all blessings issue from this source. I see God at work in this world in all of the situations and relationships of my life. I count each blessing and hold it close to my heart. I am aware of the treasures that are mine. I will not use life's problems as proof that I have a right to lose my faith; rather, I will possess a deep and profound faith. This is my thanks. No force on earth will move me from this place. If I stumble, I will get up; when I falter, I will reach out; when I am lonely, I will endure until a better time.

I give thanks today for all of the blessings in my life.

"It needs a great nature to bear the weight of a great gratitude."
—OUIDA, in Sydney F. Morris,
Wisdom, Wit and Pathos (1884)

Today

I LIVE IN THE PRESENT, grateful to be alive and in this radiant world for one more day. Living in the present brings its own perspective. What is not worth getting preoccupied about falls away, while what is truly meaningful and important rises up and into focus. I appreciate and live life, grow, and share my heart and soul with those around me. If I miss today, I will not get it back. I allow the moment to work its beauty inside of me, and it fertilizes tomorrow's garden. Today is what I know I have. All of life is here, woven into the atoms of the world that surrounds me. I am with this day; I am with all of life.

I am part of an alive universe.

"Yesterday is history,
Tomorrow is a mystery, and
Today is a gift.
That's why they call it the present."

—UNKNOWN

Life and Death

PERHAPS WE NEVER REALLY UNDERSTAND LIFE until we understand death. Death is something we try to block out of consciousness, to protect our children from. But death can be our friend and our teacher. Not only an end, it can be seen as a friend who takes us by the hand and leads us toward a life of spirit, a life unburdened by cares of this world. Life is a gift, a privilege that can be taken away at any time. None of us know the hour of our death; whatever we can control in our lives, whatever wealth, success, or fame we might create, we cannot conquer this. But what we can do is to live while we are alive. To recognize life as a journey of the spirit and to embrace it with all that we can be, to live it and love it and value it. To open our minds and hearts to the true treasures of this world, to love and be loved without reservation. What will we leave behind in the hearts of those who have loved and needed us? Peace or pain? How have we recognized not only our aliveness but that of others as well? How have we loved? If we do not understand this fundamental truth, that life is a gift, then death will indeed appear as the Grim Reaper, the end of something, a squelched dream. But if we are willing to live knowing that death will come for us, knowing that this is our chance to live, our responsibility to take our lives into our own hands and make something of them, then death can arrive as a friend. Because the only thing that can really be taken away from us is the thing we've never had. And the only life that is really tragic is the life that wasn't lived. All great teachings arrive finally at this point, that the life of spirit is here and now, that the flesh is mortal and subject to disease and death but that our spirits can be lifted and nourished each day.

I am willing to work for my life.

"You never realize love until you realize death."

—Katherine Butler Hathaway (1928)
The Journals and Letters of the Little Locksmith (1946)

"Stretch out your hand!—let no human soul wait for a
  benediction."

—Marie Corelli
The Master Christian (1990)

Soul Dip

WE CAN CULTIVATE INNER QUIET and expand a reservoir of calm within us. This reservoir can be drawn upon any time we need it, whether we're stuck in traffic or feeling anxious over some life issue. Souls grow. This is one way to rest in inner quiet so that we can replenish and nourish ourselves.

Close your eyes. Sit comfortably in your chair. Breathe in and out easily and completely without a pause between inhalation and exhalation and relax. Lengthen your spine and open your chest so that your breath flows freely. Let each breath fill and expand your body. With each in-breath imagine that you are filling your being with a vibrating yellow light. With each out-breath exhale any tension and anxiety that you might be carrying. Mentally scan your body for any areas that are holding tension and ask your mind to ask your body to *relax*. Breathe out restlessness and worry. Breathe in healing light; let it move through your body on the inhalation. Now breathe out distress and worry. As thoughts come up in your mind, simply witness them. Just as if you were sitting on the banks of a river watching the river go by with no more thought of controlling the river than controlling your thoughts. Simply witness your thoughts without getting involved with them, without trying to control them—just let them be. Breathe in and out easily and completely without a pause between inhalation and exhalation and relax. Say to yourself, "I am filling my body with light and love. I am dipping into the ever-present soul energy that is within me and without me. I am energy and light floating on a wave of energy and light. I am creating tranquility and serenity. I am dipping into my own reservoir of calm to sustain and nurture myself." Gradually, whenever you feel ready, begin to move your hands and feet. Allow your consciousness to come back into the room . . . and slowly . . . open your eyes . . . refreshed and revitalized from a visit within.

I care for my soul.

"We are learning from the teaching and example of Jesus that life itself is a religion, that nothing is more Sacred than the human being, that the end of all right institutions, whether the home or the church or an educational establishment, or a government, is the development of the human soul."

—ANNA HOWARD SHAW (1917),
in Aileen S. Kraditor,
*The Ideas of the Woman
Suffrage Movement, 1890–1920* (1965)

Perspective

THERE IS NOTHING TO DO WITH MY LIFE but live it; there is nowhere to go but forward. Each day that I am given has gifts sewn into its lining, and the trick of life is to find them, to recognize them. Life is a series of gains and losses, but so many losses have hidden gains and so many gains have hidden losses. They cancel each other out. If I align myself with the one creative mind—recognizing that this world is manifested through this mind—I have a place to go that is alive and in touch with truth and deep reality. This world I live in is in a constant state of invention and reinvention. Loss and gain are a part of that process. What hurts today will heal tomorrow. The more I can align myself with spiritual truth the more radiant and miraculous my life appears to me.

I stand in awe; I respect and treasure the mystery.

"When you get in a tight place and everything goes against you till it seems as though you could not hold on a minute longer, never give up then, for that is just the time and the place the tide will turn."

—HARRIET BEECHER STOWE, in L. F. Kleinknecht, *Poor Richard's Anthology of Thoughts on Success* (1947)

Seeing

I EXPERIENCE RADIANCE FROM DEEP WITHIN. The kind of radiance that comes when I experience the fullness of my feelings, when I take stock of the beauty of life and being alive. I rest in inner gratitude and appreciation. For each good thing that happens throughout my day I say, "Thank you, God." By the end of the day, I find I have thanked God for a number of small blessings. In this way I increase my conscious contact with God and deepen my appreciation for life itself. Life is full of small blessings. It is up to me to see them. My day is filled with things to be grateful for. It is up to me to feel that gratitude.

I see the blessings that surround me.

"Why is it that people who cannot show feeling presume that is a strength and not a weakness?"

—MAY SARTON
At Seventy (1982)

"Like the one-tenth of our brain that we currently use, I think now that most if not all of us have access to about one-tenth of our possible feelings."

—SONIA JOHNSON
The Ship That Sailed into the Living Room (1991)

Index

About the Author

TIAN DAYTON, PH.D., T.E.P., is a clinical psychologist and nationally renowned speaker, expert, and consultant in psychodrama and addictions. She was a faculty member of New York University's Drama Therapy Program for eight years. She is the director of program development at the Caron Foundation and a therapist in private practice in New York City. Dr. Dayton is a fellow of the American Society for Psychodrama, Sociometry and Group Psychotherapy and a recipient of the society's Scholars Award. She is the author of eleven books, including *Heartwounds, The Soul's Companion, The Quiet Voice of Soul, Forgiving and Moving On,* and *Trauma and Addiction,* and cocreator and editorial consultant of the film *The Process.* She has been a consultant and lecturer on women's treatment for the Freedom Institute, SAMSHA/CSAT, Hazelden, and the Anonymous Foundation, and makes frequent media appearances, including Gary Null's Sunday show, the *Montel Williams Show, Ricki Lake,* the *Geraldo Rivera Show,* America's Health Network, and MSNBC. A professional, a wife, and a mother of two, Dr. Dayton has experienced all the archetypes of womanhood.

To reach Dr. Dayton for information on psychodrama training/workshops, psychotherapy, or consulting, e-mail her at tiandayton@aol.com.